"This is a clearly written book that will help parents improve both their relationships with their children, and their children's behavior. It is an insightful, practical guide that builds upon Kempler's many years of work as a psychotherapist and a parent. I highly recommend it for all parents who want to become more proactive than reactive, and are in the process of building stronger family and social relationships."

—Richard Goldwasser, M.D., Child, Adolescent and Adult Psychiatrist, Mill Valley, CA

"This book will be a powerful tool for parents of all types of children. Noah provides specific steps and strategies to tackle challenging behaviors in a clear, concise, and easy-to-read format. The content is relevant to managing parenting challenges large and small, and paves the way to deeper bonds between parent and child."

—Leigh Burkey, OTR/L, Co-founder/Director, Ready Set GO Therapy, Inc.

"Noah spells out what we need to do to engage our children in a way that fosters their emotional and cognitive intelligence. If you are a loving and concerned parent—get this book. I am certain it will become an often-used reference. If you are a professional—get this book. It will give you some great ideas on how to help parents become better at raising their children."

—Allen Berger, Ph.D., Clinical Director of the California Institute of Gestalt Experiential Therapy and author of *Love Secrets—Revealed* and other books

"This book provides a brilliant integration of evidence-based parenting strategies with a practical explanation of the role of emotions, temperament, and attachment in building positive family relationships."

—Barbara Easterlin, Ph.D., Assistant Clinical Professor, UC Berkeley Department of Psychology

"In over fifteen years of working in education I have read dozens of books written about the development and behavior of kids. This is the most accessible book that I have read on the subject. It is perfect for anyone who wants to better understand and connect with children."

—Thaddeus Reichley, Head of Lower School, Mark Day School

Better Behavior

Helping Kids Create Change and Improve Relationships

Noah Kempler, MS, MFT

Noah Kempler is a licensed Marriage and Family Therapist, an author, and parent educator, who specializes in helping kids and their parents develop the skills to get along better.

This book is for informational and educational purposes only and is not a substitute for appropriate medical or psychological consultation. The author and publisher disclaim responsibility for any adverse effects that might arise from the reader's use or application of the information provided in this book.

For information, contact:
Noah Kempler
P.O. Box 758
Tiburon, CA 94920
Email: info@betterbehaviorblog.com
www.noahkempler.com

For additional parenting materials, go to
www.betterbehaviorblog.com

Library of Congress Card Number: 2014917299

Edited by Vesela Simic; www.veselasimic.com

Cover design by Tom Joyce; www.creativewerks.com

Special thanks to Stacey Schoenstadt-Kempler for her help with proofreading and providing clinical content feedback.

This book is dedicated to my family: Stacey, Zane, Julian, and Serene.

And to yours.

May we all grow and learn together.

Contents

∞
Preface

This book is meant to be a general guide to help parents work on negative behaviors and improve their relationships with their children. It is a collection of ideas and interventions from my work as a child and family psychotherapist over the past thirteen years. In the examples provided, all names have been changed to protect the identity of my clients.

The suggestions and examples in this book are for illustrative and informational purposes only and are not meant to be a complete guide for all parent-child difficulties. Many childhood developmental and psychiatric disorders require close supervision by a mental health professional, and this book is not a substitute for that. Rather, it is a general guide to help with behavior problems. It can be used for parenting and educational purposes or as a supplement to a clinically supervised treatment plan, depending on the scope of the child's issues. Although I have had much success creating behavior change with these methods, there is no guarantee that these methods will work in every situation. Child development and family dynamics are a complex process with many variables, which can limit the success of any prescribed intervention.

∞
Introduction

I am a parent-in-progress—just like you. I'm also a child and family psychotherapist. In both arenas, I have moments of triumph and failure, as I continuously try to improve my game and do a better job. This book is part of that process; the process of getting better, doing better, and helping others do the same. This process isn't easy, but it is important—because kids are involved.

In this book, you'll notice that I switch the narrative's point of view, sometimes using *you* and other times using *we* or *us*. I do this because I am speaking to you from several perspectives: sometimes as a child-development professional, teaching you about things you may not know, and other times as one parent to another. Anyway, just as water bends and forms to take many shapes but still remains itself, it's all me, and I hope it's not too confusing to hear from both the parent and the professional all in one place.

This book was born out of two basic desires. First, I wanted—maybe a better word is *needed*—a complete and easy to apply set of ideas that would help parents effectively deal with their children's difficult behaviors. By *complete,* I mean a set of ideas that could move parents beyond just *behavioral control,* to help them understand as well the multitude of factors that create negative behaviors in kids.

For many years, I worked with families whose kids were struggling with self-control in one way or another. I sat with them, side by side in my office, through literally thousands of therapy sessions, trying to find an answer to the most basic questions: how do we understand all of the factors involved here, and what will work to get this child's behavior back on track? In desperation, and sometimes frustration, we tried to sift through the myriad of ideas already out there designed to help parents improve their kids' behaviors and relationships. There were many good ideas, many good books—and yet something was still missing.

Over time it became clear to me that the central frustration my clients and I faced came from the fact that many current parenting theories carefully focus on one aspect of parenting. As a result, they do not cover all the necessary areas that together would provide a *complete* set of ideas to help parents understand and thereby impact the whole picture. This *complete game plan* became my ultimate goal, and it's what I've spent the last decade developing in my clinical practice. What I've come up with is a consistently effective approach for creating lasting behavioral change in children, as well as better parent-child relations.

Some of the ideas presented here are not new areas of focus in parenting, though many are. I have done my best to take some general ideas about effective parenting and then add many of my own to fill in the gaps. In addition, I have tried to combine them into an *understandable whole*, which shows the interrelation and connections among areas such as *behavior management, emotional attunement, family dynamics,* and *temperament*—all of which impact a child's behavior. What has emerged from this endeavor is an organized and simple yet effective guide to parenting both the challenging and the easy-going kids. And while no set of ideas works perfectly for every kid in every situation, I have experienced time and time again, that the ideas outlined in this book do have the power to help parents help their kids develop the skills they need to understand themselves and others, to make good choices, and to work together to problem solve almost any difficult situation.

One difficulty I faced in coming up with a complete parenting strategy was figuring out how to combine the traditional parenting focus on controlling behaviors with what I had in my clinical practice come to see as an equally powerful force for change in kids—a focus on their emotional development. Also, it was important to me to have this framework move parents from a *reactive* to a *preventative* orientation with behavior problems. Eventually, I came to identify five core skills that emerged as common abilities among the kids I met who were functioning well in their family, school, and social lives. These skills were present in kids who were solid in both the behavioral and emotional realms and so became the essential ingredients for creating a balanced, prevention-oriented parenting approach.

Once I had identified the core skills, it then became essential to figure out how parents could use their influence as the leaders of the family to help kids work on these skills. Separating parenting into two main areas, which I came to call "the two arms of parenting," was my next accomplishment, and it provided the vehicle for how we can exercise our power as parents to help kids work on the five core skills.

Developing a framework and a vehicle to help kids with the five core skills has been extremely helpful in my work with parents and their kids. The benefits of this system have helped hundreds of families move from conflict and mistrust to increased respect and mutual cooperation, and they have stood the test of time. Over the years, many parents have asked me to put all this down in a book, and so now it is time. If I achieve my goal, we will walk together through the book's topics and you will learn what I have learned—a simple yet powerful way to approach parenting that helps control kids' negative behaviors, while promoting their emotional maturity and adding strength and balance to the parent-child bond.

Remember I said earlier that I had two reasons for writing this book? Well, the second had less to do with parenting strategies and more to do with me, standing in the middle of my life with three young kids of my own and looking toward their future. So, the second reason for writing this book, equally important to me, was the desire to contribute something to my kids' world, something positive that could help shift the focus in human relationships from competition and aggression to problem solving through understanding, empathy, and a cooperative spirit. This balanced approach to parenting is my contribution to *the new way*—a way of creating relationships based on collaboration, with equal respect for one another, our earth, and ourselves. This book is my contribution to creating a better world for my kids.

Who Should Read This Book?

This book is for parents, grandparents, teachers, and nannies—really anyone connected to a child—who wants to better understand why kids behave the way they do. It's also for anyone who wants to develop a deeper connection with a child—an emotional connection. It's for all the fathers who were taught to keep feelings out of relationships, who have a sense that something's missing but don't know what to call it or how make it happen with their kids.

It's also for those who know a child who is struggling with difficult behaviors. There are so many kids and parents who are trying so hard to make it work but can't seem to find a way. It's especially for them—a guide to help kids build the essential skills for managing themselves well. For the parents, this book offers a way to increase your understanding of kids' behaviors and a means to foster behavior change. It also guides you to balance your influence with empathy and authority, which together create effective and connected parenting.

The Book's Structure

A last note about the structure of this book: it contains the three essential components needed to create change, which are *explanation, application,* and *examples.* Most people reading this book are looking for help creating change in their kids' behavior. There are many sections with lists of suggestions for creating behavioral change, which you may be tempted to skip ahead to. However, I recommend that you practice patience and read the sections in the order they're presented because it's essential to start with increasing your understanding of the behaviors themselves before moving in to control them. Essentially, you need to grasp the concepts before you can apply them, so take in the information in each chapter first. Then it will make more sense when it comes time to apply the suggestions listed afterward.

Chapter 1

∞

Building Skills

This book is about helping kids do better. It's about behavior change and what we as parents can do to help create better behavior in our kids. It's also about relationships. Good behavior grows in strong, cooperative, and respectful relationships. It's up to us, the adults, to define our relationships with our kids as such. We teach them how to be constructive in their relations with their families, friends, and also themselves. Along with a few other things we'll explore together, this is what will create the behavior change we are looking for.

But first, let's take a moment to think about a very important concept: *acceptance.* There are always behaviors to work on—things that need changing or tuning up with kids. This list of "things that could go better" is never ending, and we can all fall into the trap of wanting to address every little thing that arises. This is especially true if you feel like things are already difficult. When problems arise in family life, we naturally focus more on the problems, which is helpful in most cases. However, there is also the matter of maintaining balance and not getting so focused on a current challenge that we lose the joy in our relationship with our child.

This brings us to the issue of *acceptance*, which is both an attitude and an action. Maintaining an accepting attitude or disposition with our children, even when they are challenging us, is important. Self-esteem is fostered through acceptance, so our kids need us to transmit frequent messages of tolerance for who they are and what they do, even when they make mistakes. This is especially true for kids who struggle with self-control because they already get a lot of negative feedback from others about their behavior. An accepting attitude also prevents parent burnout. Remembering that kids learn through making mistakes enables us to step back and allow the natural ups and downs of their behaviors to happen, without our getting too worked up about every little infraction. So an accepting attitude (rather than an intolerant one) goes a long way toward nurturing our kids' relationship with themselves as well as preserving our relationship with them.

Acceptance is also a choice. When challenged by difficult behavior, we are put in the position of choosing whether to try to change the behavior or to let it go and focus our energy elsewhere. Some behaviors need to be changed; others don't. And some behaviors can't be changed even though we want them to. There are always pieces of the picture that we have no control over, and so we need to accept. Temperament, developmental level, and life transitions are examples of these pieces of the picture, and though they may cause problems for us, they are better addressed with a healthy dose of acceptance than they are with resistance and pressure.

So how do we strike a balance between creating behavior change and practicing acceptance? We start by adding *acceptance* to our list of most important parenting skills. Keep it in mind as you go about helping your child grow and change, especially when your child is challenging you. With even the most difficult behaviors, pause and ask yourself, "How can I practice acceptance right now?" Stop and consciously decide to maintain an accepting attitude with your child. Then decide whether you're going to take on the job of trying to change the behavior at that moment or whether you and your child are better served by you practicing increased acceptance. And don't worry if you decide to let it go, practice acceptance, or ignore it and move on. Maybe you're just too tired to take the behavior on. Maybe you realize that this particular behavior will change on its own over time as your child matures. As long as the decision to accept or to change behavior is a conscious one, you'll be on the right track. If the difficult behavior persists, you may change your mind and decide that it needs to be worked on. At that point, you'll practice consistent, effective responses using strategies outlined in this book.

If you're not sure whether to address a specific behavior or to practice acceptance, consider these two questions. First, "In the grand scheme of things, how big of a problem is this behavior?" If the answer is something like "fairly small," then you might just decide to let it go and save your energy. The second question to ask yourself is,

"If I do address the behavior, how much of an impact am I likely to have on it?" Some behaviors change with a little effort, while others don't change no matter how hard we try. These are important questions because they can help you pick your battles and apply your energy toward the behaviors that are most likely to actually change. If you consider these questions and still have trouble deciding which behaviors need addressing, consult with a parenting group, your pediatrician, or a child counselor. They can help you decide whether it's necessary to put a lot of energy into a particular behavior.

In any case, always start with an attitude of acceptance toward your child. If you've lost the feeling of acceptance you once had because of struggles with your child, then stop and make a conscious shift to reclaim an accepting attitude toward your son or daughter. It's the first step in making things better for both of you.

Many Influences

When we interact with a child who is struggling with difficult behavior, what we notice most is *the behavior*. This makes sense because it's the behavior that we interface with and it's the behavior that is causing a problem for us. But because the behavior is the thing they see, many parents assume it's where their focus should be. This is true in part, but what is also true is that the behavior is just the tip of the iceberg. Child therapists know this, and they understand that many factors need to be understood to create lasting behavioral change for a child. Understanding these behind-the-scenes influences and how they contribute to a child's behavior is critical to the process of creating change. These factors, or influences, are not always easy to see. If parents aren't aware of them, they may not even cross their minds. However, they are important, very important—critical to our understanding of how and why a child is doing what he or she is doing. Though not always visible, the factors lurking behind the scenes influence the current picture as much as the behaviors you see in front of you.

What are these factors? These are the main areas I think about when helping parents help their kids. I consider the *developmental level*, or where a child is in their natural development. Different age ranges contain different challenges for kids, so it's important to know how their developmental level is creating the backdrop for a current situation. Another important factor is *temperament*, which is how a child's nervous system is wired to react, and has a big impact on a kid's behavior. It's also important to factor in *current life issues*—for example, how a child's social relationships are doing, how family and school life are going, and what current situations are helping or stressing the child. An additional major factor is *how the parents are doing.* Are they stressed out, overworked, in conflict, or doing okay? And what kind of *skills* do they need to work on to make family life better? Lastly, what *skills* does the child need to work on? For instance, are they good at communicating their needs and upsets? Are they good at problem solving? These are certainly important skill areas for kids.

The interplay of these factors is what creates the behavior you see, so it's very important to consider these elements first. If we can start by increasing our awareness of the behind-the-scenes influences, then we will be starting with a more complete understanding of our child's behavior. This understanding provides a solid foundation from which to move on to the next step—creating solutions. Making clear sense of a child's behaviors by looking at all of the underlying factors may seem like a complicated and daunting task, but it doesn't have to be. What I do in the pages that follow is share a clear and easy-to-follow set of ideas and strategies that will allow you to consider many of the relevant factors a child therapist considers. This gives you not only the ability to understand your child's behavior more fully but also access to many of the interventions we therapists use. This information and guidance then give you the best chance at creating lasting behavior change for your child.

Let's get started by first thinking about how we can help our children build essential skills.

Beyond "No"

We as parents—and I say "we" because I am a parent and certainly include myself—spend a lot of time teaching and reminding kids what not to do. Think about it: our kids' learning experiences are absolutely dominated by the words *don't, stop,* and *no.* Now to be fair, this focus has its benefit as it alerts our children to their negative behaviors and to situations that need attention. In some cases, with safety issues for instance, it's enough just to tell kids what they shouldn't do. But there can also be a key problem with this process:

it doesn't help our kids build the skills they need to keep from making the same mistake the next time they're in a similar situation. There's no focus on *prevention*.

Imagine for a moment being lost in a foreign city and knowing only a few words of the language there. You walk up to someone and ask with your handful of words how to get to the train station. This person looks you in the eye, points a finger toward a street, and says, "Don't go down that road." If you can imagine how you might feel in that situation, you can understand an experience our children have over and over again. Listen to yourself as you teach your children about their behaviors, and you will likely notice that your language is full of messages about what not to do. We all do this, and we need to understand how this kind of teaching can be flawed. All the *stop* messages in the world won't teach our kids what else they can do instead, what their options are. As parents we need to understand that although this approach has long been the dominant model for shaping behavior, it doesn't teach basic interpersonal and self-management skills, skills that would then eliminate the need for many of the *stop* messages in the first place.

These basic interpersonal and self-management skills are what I call *the core skills: understanding feelings, communication, flexibility, respect and problem solving.* Kids who are adept at these skills are generally cooperative and responsible and have the ability to manage themselves well. They are the kids who don't need to be told so many times to stop a behavior because they have developed other, more constructive ways to express themselves and get their needs met. In my clinical practice, I have helped many children gain strength in these skill areas and have consistently seen their behaviors improve. In the following sections, I will describe these skills and show you how to help your kids develop and practice them. You will do this by exercising what I call "the two arms of parenting" (more on that later). Let's look now at the five core skills and how they benefit our kids.

The Five Core Skills

1. Understanding Feelings. This skill involves recognizing feelings, building an emotional vocabulary, communicating feelings, and understanding the feelings of others. I should note that in this book I use the words feelings and emotions as synonyms. Researchers and academic writers often distinguish between the two—and there are some distinctions—but for the purposes of this book, I'll use them interchangeably, which I hope will keep you from getting tired of seeing the word "feelings" over and over again!

One of the recurring themes that you'll find in this book is the idea that helping kids tune into the world of feelings, or emotions, is good for them. In fact, tuning into and expressing feelings is good for everyone, so there will be equal benefit for the adults helping kids work on this skill. I will talk at length about the many benefits of expressing emotions in the sections that follow; for now, I'll summarize by saying that kids who are in touch with their feelings are more developmentally integrated, self-aware, and able to problem solve better than those who aren't. This is simply because feelings permeate all aspects of life, from family and social relationships to learning and the development of identity. Not only are feelings everywhere, they are also the driving energy behind almost all behaviors.

A child's emotional life is truly the foundation for all other functioning. If a child is not doing well emotionally, it will not just affect family life but everything else, including school and social relationships. Emotions carry a lot of energy, which means they can add unwanted energy to a child's body or zap a child's energy reserves. A child who is scared, angry, or sad will not have as much energy or focus for schoolwork, peer relationships, or behavior control. The energy that such difficult feeling states contain disrupts and distracts the child from his or her current focus. For example, a child expending a portion of energy to hold upset feelings about a difficult friendship has less energy available for other important tasks, such as critical thinking or schoolwork. A child might experience the energy of negative feelings as a tired, blue, unfocused state or as the exact opposite, a fidgety, antsy, pressured body state. In either case, the impact of the emotional energy disrupts the child's current functioning.

On the other hand, children who are in touch with their feelings and can express them and release the energy constructively will be able to maintain a regulated state and have access to all their energy reserves. In addition, these children will have a more integrated sense of self, since feelings are such an essential human experience.

Kids who are in touch with their feelings and who can also exercise their cognitive (thinking) abilities experience both the emotional and rational aspects of themselves, which gives them a deeper understanding of themselves and others. It's clear then that in order for kids to have access to their full potential, they need to be resting on a solid emotional foundation. Kids who are in touch with their feelings are also more in touch with the feelings of others and so are capable of more empathy.

Ways to build this skill. Helping kids understand feelings begins with their building an emotional vocabulary. Kids need lots of descriptive words to help identify the various emotional states they experience. You can help your child build an emotional vocabulary in several ways. The most effective way is for you to model talking about your own feelings. This teaches your child how to use feelings words and at the same time gives them permission to notice and share their feelings. Comment on your own feelings in front of your child to create an emotionally open atmosphere in your home. In addition to your own feelings, begin also to attune to the emotions your child is experiencing. Comment on feelings you observe and ask your child questions about these emotional experiences. All of this will get your child oriented to and talking about his or her feelings.

If you can get your child to start talking about feelings, great. But don't stop there. There are gradients of feelings and more subtle aspects of emotional situations to be explored and communicated as well. Once your child has mastered the basic answer to "How did that make you feel?" you can move to the next level by asking about other aspects of the feeling. Understanding the size of feelings—little, medium, big, super-gigantic—is a good place to start. Many kids benefit from using a 1 to 10 numeric scale to measure feelings. You can have them draw 1 to 10 vertically on a piece of paper, like a thermometer, and then put feeling labels next to a corresponding number. For example, it might say "calm" next to 1, "angry" next to 5, and 10 would be a word for the maddest feeling, maybe "super-enraged." Kids can then fill in the other numbers with labels for the other levels of emotion, such as "frustrated," "annoyed," "kinda mad," "getting hot," etc. Kids can also add their own pictures next to the words to give a visual representation of the feeling. A visual scale helps kids understand the gradients of emotion while also building their emotional vocabulary. If you're feeling creative, you can make such a thermometer for the wall in any scaled format you and your child might like. I have made these with kids, and they've been everything from thermometers and weight scales to speedometers and even volcanoes. You can create a visual scale for any feeling you're helping your child with, whether it's feeling *mad, scared, sad, excited,* et cetera.

Having a visual scale can also help kids learn coping mechanisms for their big feelings. For instance, they can decide at what point (maybe around level 3) they need to stop and take a break or get help for their anger. If the feeling on the scale is fairly strong, say a 7 or higher out of 10, then a good question would be "Why do you think you got such a big (mad, sad, scared, etc.) feeling?" This additional question helps kids both understand their specific triggers and connect to why those triggers have such an emotional impact on them.

Another good way to raise the bar on emotional communication is to help kids move from identifying single feelings to understanding that often multiple feelings are involved. When you ask your children how they're feeling in a certain situation and they identify one feeling, inquire about other feelings that might also be present. There are frequently multiple aspects of an emotional situation, and if you suspect that your child is only describing one of the feelings involved, ask about others. The following exchange by a father and his five-year-old son illustrates this point:

Father:	How did you feel going into Arturo's birthday party?
Son:	Great.
Father:	What do you mean, 'great'? What kind of great?
Son:	Excited!
Father:	That makes sense. You were jumping up and down before we went in.
Father:	Was that it, just excited? I think I noticed something else after we got in the house.
Son:	Oh yeah, a little scared too.
Father:	Yeah, I was wondering about that, because you hid behind me for a little while.
Father:	Did you realize that people can have two feelings at once? It's good to remember because it happens a lot.

In this scenario the father does a good job of inquiring about his son's feelings. But he doesn't stop there. He also raises the bar by using his observation of other potential feelings involved (the scared feeling) to inquire further. This helps his child expand beyond the ability to describe single feelings and move into the more complex world of multilayered emotional experiences. What a great emotional education this father is giving his child! By tuning into his son's feelings and helping him move to a more complex understanding of them, he is helping his son develop self-awareness, insight, and emotional maturity. This process can be adapted to a child of any age, with more or less complexity depending on developmental level.

Books and movies, as well as real life situations, are other good ways to notice and comment on feelings. Most books and other media have emotional themes as characters face dilemmas infused with feelings. So, as you're reading or watching, stop to discuss the feelings involved. You can also notice the feelings of others in real time. When you're out to eat with your child, play the guess-their-feelings game by looking at other people's faces and taking turns guessing what a person may be feeling. This game works really well if you and your child can find someone talking on the phone. Watch the person's expressions and guess not only the feelings but also what is being talking about. Of course, be discrete—it's not polite to stare!

Journaling about feelings is a great way for older kids, around ten years and up, to stay in touch with their emotions. As kids enter the pre-teen and teen years, they become more self-conscious and need a safe, private place to reflect on their social and emotional dilemmas. Journaling also serves as a container for the powerful emotions that ebb and flow in the ever-changing bodies of pre-teens and teens. If you have a child moving into the pre-teen years, buy them a journal and encourage them to write about the things that are important to them as well as their challenges. Writing helps us release emotions we're holding and provides perspective, both while writing and later when reading and reflecting on what was written. Respect the privacy of your child's journal. Don't read it or ask what's in it—unless you're concerned about your child's safety for some reason. Instead, ask how the process of journaling is going and if anything has been figured out through journaling that your child would like to share with you. This way the journal remains a private refuge of reflection that will also facilitate communication about emotions with you, when your child feels comfortable and ready to share.

Since feelings are in part a physical experience, helping children tune into their body states is another way to get them to notice their emotions. We want to help them identify when their body is tired, tense, depleted emotionally, or bouncing with extra energy. Frequently, kids are both depleted and bouncing. This is what I call the "tired-and-wired" state, and it is frequently a precursor of accidents or meltdowns. When kids are exhausted and frenetic, we need to help them slow down and understand that although their bodies are running in circles, they're actually overtired. Younger kids will argue that they're not tired, and this is okay. This should not be a cause for argument as much as a chance to simply point out that two very different feelings can be in the body at the same time. Stopping to notice body states helps kids learn to track their internal states, which helps them take better care of themselves. They learn to stay in touch with how their bodies are doing and what they need.

Art is also a great way for even very young kids to get in touch with and express their feelings. Kids as young as two years old can put their feelings on paper using different colors. You can ask a young child, "What color is your mad feeling?" and have the child scribble anger in whatever color he or she chooses. Then when the child shows you what's been drawn, you can ask questions about other aspects of the picture, such as "Wow! That's a lot of mad red color! What feeling is that blue in the corner?" Older kids can add more form to their art by adding more detail to their drawings or representing their emotional moments through collages, sculptures, and other creative projects.

Art is such a powerful vehicle for emotional expression because it allows kids the freedom to create their own representation of their unique experience. In addition, it works well because it allows the child to begin expressing their emotional experiences in a non-verbal way, which is often less difficult and embarrassing than doing it with words. Do keep this in mind though: the art should be a middle step; a conversation about the child's feelings is the final goal. If you ask your child to draw, collage, or make a Play-Doh sculpture about an emotional event or topic, follow up the activity with some questions about the art piece that focus on feelings and the event they represent. This way the art becomes a powerful vehicle to help kids get to the ultimate goal of putting their feelings and experiences into words. Often when I have a child draw about an upsetting event, I'll ask the child if we can write three things on the back of the paper that tell about the feelings involved. This way the child is free to express through the art, and then we use the art to practice the important skill of emotional communication through language.

Remember also that emotional art is not about how good the drawing, painting, or sculpture is; it's about giving the child an emotional outlet. So be careful not to shift your child's attention away from the process by commenting on how good, bad, realistic, detailed, or colorful a piece is. Any comment on the quality of the art can make a child self-conscious and shut down the process of emotional expression. Instead, focus on the story that the art is telling and ask questions about the feelings involved.

After you have helped your child label or identify feelings, whether through art, writing, or conversation, it's important to focus next on another aspect of emotional communication: tuning in to the cause or causes of the feelings. Kids need to know what to call feelings, but they also need to be able to identify what caused the emotional response. When you stop to notice or talk about feelings, also ask, "What gave you that feeling?" or "Why were you feeling that way?" It's only after we know what caused our feelings that we are ready to move to problem solving. It certainly doesn't make sense to try to solve a problem before you understand what caused it in the first place.

Once we have helped our kids tune into and express their feelings and connect to their cause, it's time to focus on the final emotional step—letting go. Kids need to know that feelings naturally come and go and that it helps a lot to put words to them. They also need to understand that after they have processed their feelings, they have the power to either stay connected to them or let them go. In some instances, like with positive feelings, you'll make your child aware that they can always "keep that warm feeling of our hug" with them. With negative feelings, however, we want children to know that after talking about them, they have the power to let them go and move on. This can be especially helpful for kids who have a hard time transitioning out of emotional states. For some kids, negative feelings linger even after they've expressed them through words. These kids need help deciding when it's time to move on. Just remember to ensure they've processed their feelings thoroughly before deciding to re-focus. If kids (or adults) try to repress or move on from feelings without fully processing them first, they are likely to develop negative symptoms (negative behaviors, physical illness, or emotionally numbing). Ignoring one's emotions simply doesn't work.

Even with a fair amount of encouragement, some kids tend to stay away from their feelings. These are typically the more sensitive kids who experience their emotions intensely. Most of these kids have moments when they're more or less available for opening up and talking about their feelings. It's important then for a parent to track their child's emotional access points. These are the situations or times of day when a kid is most receptive to emotional conversation. For many kids, it's the calmer, quieter moments, like just before bed; for others, it might be while shooting baskets on the basketball court.

Reluctant kids also benefit from understanding that feelings are like the wind, they come swirling in, sometimes very strong, and sometimes even creating chaos, but eventually, they die down and calm returns. An analogy like this helps kids who avoid feelings out of fear to get in touch with and allow their emotions to have their natural process.

There is also media specifically geared toward helping younger kids understand and talk about emotions. I use a feelings chart in my office with faces similar to the ones shown here. When it's time to talk about behaviors or the feelings underneath, we start the conversation by putting arrow stickers on the feelings faces. Then we work together to find names for the feelings. Finally, we help the child connect to the cause of their feelings. Using a visual cue like a feelings poster chart or other media (books, figures, games, etc.) is very helpful for young kids because it takes a rather abstract concept like feelings and makes it visual and concrete.

Sample Feelings Chart Faces

Scared   Mad   Excited   Happy   Surprised   Sad

Here are some suggestions for helping your child work on the skill of *understanding feelings:*

- Notice your child's emotional states and comment on them. This helps them pay attention to their own feelings.
- Talk about your own feelings to model emotional communication.
- Give your child the message that all feelings are okay to have, even anger.
- Ask your child how they feel about relationships, events and conflicts.
- Validate your child's feelings when they share them.
- If your child doesn't talk about his or her feelings, find out why and see what you can do to help them start sharing.
- Help your child rate the size and intensity of their feelings.
- Help your child get good at talking about the hard feelings (e.g. mad, sad, scared, worried, embarrassed).
- Help your child let go of feelings after processing them. This helps them recover from emotional events and move on. It also gives them a sense of control with their feelings.

2. Communication. The ability to communicate well is an essential skill that impacts all areas of a child's life. Children's ability to communicate effectively helps them navigate the complex world of family and social relationships. It is the central skill for working out problems, asserting ourselves, and identifying feelings—all necessary elements of maintaining healthy relationships. Beyond personal relationships, the ability to communicate well is important in kids' school experience. As the grades progress, being able to participate in class discussions and group projects becomes more and more of a requirement, and teachers often view their top students as the ones who present with solid abilities in interpersonal communication.

When I say communication, I don't mean just talking. Though talking and expressing our ideas is certainly a necessary part of communication, it isn't the whole enchilada. Communication is a complex process of organizing our ideas and being able to express them clearly, while at the same time staying tuned in to the listener. Staying attentive to the listener and doing the dance of back and forth dialogue also requires paying attention to the listener's body language (eye contact, posture, facial expressions) so that the speaker knows, for instance, when the listener is getting bored with the conversation.

For kids (and some adults too) keeping it all straight so they are using good communication skills requires some practice. Notice what parts of communication are hard for your child and then help your child work on these skills. Some kids are interrupters. They have so many ideas in their heads and the ideas are coming at such a fast rate that they have a very hard time not jumping in during the middle of someone else's sentence. These kids are also frequently not solid listeners. Kids who interrupt need to work on holding their ideas as well as using communication tools such as *excuse me,* or simply telling the listener they're worried they will lose their idea if they don't say it soon. These kids also need to experience how it feels to be on the other end of the interrupting and understand that interrupting will eventually make people not want to talk with them if they don't work on this skill.

"Kids not listening" is one of the most common complaints I hear from parents. Not listening can come from several sources, so I usually work with the parents to figure out first where it's coming from. Sometimes the child is not listening as a form of protest. They're blowing you off or ignoring you in an effort to let you know that they don't like what you're saying or that they don't want to talk at the moment. If your child is deliberately ignoring to communicate protests to you, direct communication needs to be worked on. I personally would rather have a kid tell me directly that he or she doesn't want to talk than pretend that they don't hear me. When kids can use words to let me know what is going on with them, we can work on a solution together. If they don't, it just turns into frustration.

Some kids don't listen because it's hard for them to pay attention. This is a very different situation from ignoring because the child's intention is not to not hear you. It's unfair to accuse kids of disobedience when they are actually distracted. The distracted state is an aspect of temperament and not a form of protest. Adults often accuse kids with short attention spans of trying to frustrate or ignore them, when that is not their intention at all. If this happens to a child too often, the child's self-esteem will begin to suffer and the relationship with that adult will deteriorate. Nobody likes to be falsely accused. Of course, like all kids, sometimes distractible kids also deliberately ignore. If you're uncertain about why your child isn't listening, you'll need to first get a feel for whether distractibility is playing a part. This means understanding the different aspects of your child's temperament (see Chapter 5, "The Role of Temperament") as well as talking with your child about his or her intention when communication difficulties arise.

The other thing to remember about communication skills is that they vary greatly depending on a child's developmental level and overall temperament. The older kids are, the more refined their abilities should be and the more communication you can expect from them. Kids with a very sensitive temperament often have a hard time asserting themselves and raising their voice, while those who are highly active often have a hard time slowing down and lowering their voices. Beyond temperament, we run into the areas of developmental delays, and there are many that interfere with good communication: speech articulation, hearing loss, stuttering, autistic spectrum disorders, auditory processing difficulties, and non-verbal learning disability are just a few. If you suspect that something like this might be interfering with your child's communication abilities, seek out an evaluation from a pediatrician, a qualified speech therapist, or your child's school.

Remember also that emotions have a big impact on communication—which is true for all of us. As feelings get bigger, our ability to communicate clearly and rationally decreases. We'll talk a lot about emotions and communication in other sections, but it's worth stopping to remember that when kids are upset, we need to consider the impact their feelings are having on their ability to communicate clearly.

Ways to build this skill. First, make sure all the basics are in place. Kids should have good eye contact, not interrupt, and give verbal responses (not grunts, hand-waving, or the like) when spoken to. If your child is busy doing something when you're speaking to them, be respectful of the fact that you're interrupting them, but also require an answer. Start by asking for eye contact, which greatly improves listening abilities. If you still don't get an answer, put a gentle hand on the child's shoulder or on the thing the child is paying attention to (book, toy, etc.). This gives children a physical cue to shift their attention to you and should get them to listen. If the child makes eye contact, but you get the sense that his or her mind is elsewhere, ask for a verbal response or to have what you said repeated back to you. When a child can answer you with words, then you know the information has registered in the brain circuits.

Kids who get distracted often learn to fake it. They figure out early on that if they pretend they got the information, often the grown-up will move on and leave them alone. A child might even make good eye contact and give you a pleasant smile, but that child's mind is actually elsewhere. If you watch the child's eyes, you can usually pick up on how present he or she actually is. I've had kids admit they were pretending to listen to me while they were actually imagining I was a creature in their favorite video game! Of course, pretending to listen is not a good strategy for them, so if you have a child who gets distracted, you'll have to do two things. First, check up on the child's listening skills. Ask your child to repeat what you're saying often, so you can get a feel for how much information he or she might be missing. Second, give your child permission (without judgment) to miss information. Let your child know that everyone has trouble listening sometimes and that you just want him or her to be honest when it happens. Then work out something for the child to say when he or she gets distracted, like "Sorry, I got distracted, can you repeat that?" or "Could you say it again?" Statements like this give distractible kids a way to cope with information loss, which is much more productive than their pretending they got it when they didn't. If you discover your child is faking it often, explain that it makes people not trust that he or she is listening and that it will make people not want to listen to your child's ideas too. Then praise or reward your child for practicing being direct and honest whenever he or she admits to not hearing what's being said. Also, some distractible kids do better talking while doing or holding something, though others get further distracted this way. Experiment with giving your child something to do or to fidget with while you're talking to see if it helps your child stay focused and present.

If distractibility is not the issue and instead you believe your child is ignoring you on purpose, it might represent a form of protest. Kids who intentionally ignore may also feel they don't need to answer you, which is a respect issue. It's also possible that they feel they're not allowed to have their opinion, which means there's too much authority coming from the parents. Either way, the solution starts with a conversation with the child about why the ignoring is occurring. If the child says he or she doesn't care about what you have to say, help the child care with consequences for ignoring. If, on the other hand, you learn the child wants to talk but is afraid to communicate with you for fear of getting in trouble, then you need to back off on the authority a bit. Let the child know that his or her ideas can be shared and that you'll always consider them. This sets a level of mutual respect in the parent-child dynamic that will make it easier to communicate together and will also strengthen your relationship.

Another important part of communication is being able to identify intention. So many times kids (adults too) get into trouble because their intentions are misread—for example, when a kid does something by accident and the parent yells at the child as if the child wanted to cause a problem. Adults can help kids learn to talk about their intentions by modeling this type of communication for them. Take the time to explain to your child why you're doing what you're doing. This teaches children how to speak about their own inner drives so that they're not misunderstood by others. One of the easiest ways for kids to practice this is when they make a mistake. Help them learn to explain what they were trying to do (learn more in the "Taking Responsibility" section). Kids make a lot of mistakes and learning to tell others about their intentions greatly reduces the chance that the other person will be offended by one of these many slip-ups.

Lastly, kids need lots of help practicing communication when emotions are involved. Helping them start to talk about feelings before they get too upset gives them practice with this skill and helps to head off further escalation. (There will be a lot more information on helping kids communicate in the sections to follow.)

Here are some suggestions for helping your child work on the skill of *communication:*

- Help your child work on direct communication, not using gestures, grunts or facial expressions to tell the message.
- Don't speak for your child. Help them share their own thoughts, opinions and feelings.
- Help your child practice the 3 parts of good listening: eye contact, focus on the speaker's message, give a verbal response.
- Help your child know what to do if they get distracted i.e. ask the speaker to please repeat. Let your child know that it's okay to get distracted, but they still need to get the information.
- Distinguish between distractibility and intentional ignoring. These are two very different issues.
- If your child is ignoring, find out why and work on direct communication.
- Help your child stay aware of their attitude (posture, tone, facial expressions, sarcasm, etc.). If they have a negative attitude, help them express their feelings directly and give consequences for poor attitude.
- Help your child learn to communicate his or her intention— especially when they make a mistake i.e. if they meant to cause a problem or if it was an accident or just a lapse in judgment.
- Don't allow interrupting, and don't model it by doing it with your kids!
- Teach by asking questions. Kids don't learn much from lectures, so ask questions to get them thinking and communicating.

3. Flexibility. In clinical research they call it *response flexibility*, which essentially means that in a given situation a person is able to understand and exercise different options for how they might respond.

It's the opposite of rigidly clinging to the idea that there's only one way that things have to go. Kids who struggle with flexibility get stuck a lot. When emotion is high, they become even more rigid and tend to look at the situation through a myopic or black-and-white lens, clinging to their position at any cost.

This is no fun for parents. There are so many variables in family life, so many things that don't go the way you had planned, that over time even the most inflexible parent learns to survive by loosening up and going with the flow—there's just so much that you can't control. When kids dig their heels in and refuse to budge or to consider any other options, then parents are stuck too. Some parents are able to stay calm and go with it, while some become very frustrated. It really just depends on a parent's own temperament and how much flexibility he or she can come up with, especially when stressed.

All kids start out pretty rigid. Two- and three-year-olds are famous for locking up when they have an idea about how things should go. This is developmentally appropriate because they don't yet have the brainpower or communication skills to analyze options and hold multiple outcomes. When they want something, it has to be *their way!* As a child develops, though, the skill of being able to shift perspective and consider multiple solutions becomes more important and easier for the child to do.

As kids move into the school years, the social arena is one place where flexibility is especially important. The early grades are filled with group play, and there is a constant jostling for social position. This is compounded by the fact that kids at this developmental level are also bursting with imaginative and learned ideas and are really wanting to exercise these newly developed skills. The problem in this kind of situation, as in any social situation, is that there is only airspace for one speaker at a time. This means that kids have to learn to hold their ideas, take turns, and adjust their plans, depending on how the crowd responds to their idea. "Let's be superheroes!" says one boy. "No, let's be sea monsters!" says another. "Yeah, sea monsters who dig in the ocean for secret crystals!" says yet another. These situations permeate recess and after-school playtime and require constant adjustment on every child's part. Weighing the need to flex one's mental muscles against the desire to be part of the group requires a lot of flexibility, which is an ongoing challenge in these years.

For older kids, it's less about group flexibility than it is about learning to work together. School and after-school activities often require kids to team up in pairs or small groups for assignments and projects. In this arena, kids increasingly need to work plans out interpersonally with one another, which requires yet another level of flexibility. These situations require a child to work hard to come up with his or her own ideas to start but also to see the bigger picture, which is to ultimately pair their ideas with others to create a unique outcome.

For teens and beyond, flexibility is required for managing the give and take of intimate relationships as well as for balancing work, school, and social schedules. Kids in this age range have the ability to consider multiple perspectives, so they can practice mental flexibility in more intricate ways, which helps prepare them for the complexities of adult life. Whatever the developmental period, we see that flexibility is an important skill for kids to work on because it has such a far-reaching impact, affecting their family, social, and academic life.

Kids with unusual temperaments, such as those who are low on the adaptability trait, are especially prone to struggle with flexibility. They often get stuck, particularly during transitions, because they get overwhelmed with all the information they need to process to get from here to there. Highly persistent kids are another group that often struggle with this skill. They get locked into an idea and, especially when stressed, will hold on tighter and tighter to their notion, despite the fact that their rigidity is making the situation worse for them. Kids with temperaments like these are the ones who need to practice flexibility the most. They need to learn to flex this weak muscle and get stronger at tolerating the many situations that require response flexibility.

Ways to build this skill. Forcing a stressed out child to be more flexible is the least effective way to help build this skill. In high stress or hot moments, adults lose their flexibility too, and it's hard to help someone else learn something when we're tensing up ourselves. Like all other skills, flexibility is best addressed outside of the hot moment, during a rational discussion. This is when you can point out situations and begin to introduce the idea of how flexibility can be inserted to produce a better outcome. Of course, you'll adjust the conversation to the child's age and abilities, but even three-year-olds can start to get an idea of what the opposite of *bossy* is.

When engaging in problem solving with a child of any age, flexibility is important to insert as a key to the solution. When talking with your child about a fight with a friend, the "instead of screaming at her, what else do you think you could have done?" part of the problem solving is where you help apply flexible thinking to find more productive responses (see "Joint Problem Solving" section). Sometimes it's helpful for kids to make a list with you of the other things they can do in similar situations. This helps them see how many options there actually are when they practice being flexible.

We can also help children become more aware of this skill when discussing feelings. We can talk about how much harder it is to be flexible when we're mad, sad, or even excited. Feelings and flexibility also tie in to the idea of social flexibility, because upsets between friends often produce rigid responses. In the social skills groups that my wife, Stacey, and I run, we use the concept of "the flexible friend." We introduce the idea of flexibility and how important it is not only to have a flexible body but also a flexible brain. We then take the kids through scenarios and have them role-play rigid, bossy responses and then flexible ones, making sure we stop to notice with them the feelings involved and how they impact flexibility. We wrap up the exercise with a discussion about how it feels for friends when we're flexible or not and which type of response solves problems between people best. This sort of active and interactive discussion is a very helpful way for kids to get and practice the concept of flexibility while having some fun at the same time.

What I call "if-then parenting" is another great way to help kids work on flexibility. If-then parenting is a way to help kids learn about give-and-take in relationships, such as getting the things they want in exchange for practicing respect for parental authority. It's a simple idea really. If-then parenting means that when your child asks you for something, you require a trade, or something you want in return. What you trade for isn't as important as the fact that you're requiring the trade, which allows the child to practice giving to get, flexibility, and understanding that when you (the authority) set an expectation, the child must play by your rules.

Here is an example. Let's say you have a daughter who can be strong-willed and rigid sometimes. She says to you, "Daddy, can you play Uno with me?" You think to yourself, I should use this request to help her practice flexibility and gain a sense of earning what she wants, so you respond, "Sure, just as soon as you clean up those art supplies you left out." To this, she replies, "Okay." There you have it: *if* you want to play Uno, *then* you need to do what I ask first. As I said earlier, it's less important what you trade than the fact that you are having them practice the trade itself, because the trade is what requires them to practice flexibility. However, I will say that when I use if-then, I do try to have the child trade for something that helps them become more responsible. For instance, I would be more inclined to ask a child to clean up, apologize to a sibling after a fight, discuss feelings about a situation, etc., than something like, "Sure I'll play, but you have to bring me my shoes first."

Many parents use if-then naturally with their kids, but aren't aware of all the skills they're building. If your child struggles with flexibility, entitlement, or a lack of respect for authority, then start requiring if-then exchanges. This will help your child work not only on flexibility but also on skills such as respect and cooperation. These skills will become more and more necessary as your child grows. As they get older, kids need to exchange grades for their performance in school and later productivity for payment in the job market, so help prepare them for the real world by frequently using the if-then exchange.

Earning an allowance is a classic way to start doing this. Around four- or five-years old, many kids begin to get interested in the power of money. They can learn to practice the give-and-take of the if-then exchange by doing jobs for a small allowance. Parents need to decide at what age they feel allowance might be appropriate for their child; there are many differing viewpoints about this. Allowance does create a focus on money (which I'm always a bit uncomfortable with). But the fact is that kids will either be focused on the money they can earn by being flexible and responsible, or they will be focused only on the toys and things they want you to get for them—so there's really no avoiding the world of the material. I personally would rather have my kids focused on working for things they want rather than working on me to get them the things they're longing for. At about ten years old, kids will need more money for the activities they engage in outside the home, so by this age I do recommend to most families that an allowance be exchanged for some amount of household work.

Here are some suggestions for helping your child work on the skill of *flexibility:*

- Identify if your child's temperament is low on *adaptability* or high on *persistence* (See Chapter 5). These traits make it much harder to flex.
- Talk with your child about flexibility and why it's important e.g. the benefits of being a *flexible friend.*
- Validate how hard it is to remain flexible, especially when your child is upset.
- When discussing problems, help your child think of several potential solutions. This works especially well with social difficulties.
- Set up a reward for practicing flexible thinking.
- Challenge your child to be flexible in small ways to get them feeling confident about flexing.
- Use "if-then parenting" to help your child tolerate giving to get.
- Teach your child about compromise and creating "win-win solutions."
- Preview how your child will practice flexibility during potentially difficult events i.e. birthday parties, play dates etc.
- Have your child teach siblings and friends about flexibility. Teaching cements learning. Let them be your family's flexibility expert!

4. Respect. This is a hot topic lately and is a central component of the character-building curriculums at many schools these days. This is a great social advance in light of the chronic suffering so many kids have endured from bullying in decades past. When these cutting-edge schools focus on the skill of respecting others, they are also teaching tolerance—tolerance of those who look, act, function, or identify themselves differently than the majority of kids. In addition to building tolerance, which decreases bullying, the idea of respect for other kids helps kids focus more on similarities than differences, which is a great advance from the mind-set of the past.

When kids think in terms of similarities between themselves and peers, they form a stronger group identity with the whole school community, which then creates a stronger social fabric. A stronger social fabric has fewer holes for struggling kids to fall through and be lost. Fewer lost children also mean less acting out by those who become so lost that they eventually break.

Most of these programs also teach about self-respect. This aspect of respect is equally important: it promotes self-assertion and encourages kids to think for themselves. Kids who feel worthwhile, have their own ideas, and know how to stand up for themselves are much less likely to give in to peer pressure and engage in risky behavior.

Of course, self-respect is not just an idea that kids need to learn at school; it's also parents' responsibility to help their kids build a healthy and balanced sense of their own worth. Kids need to feel valued and respected at home so that they internalize a sense that this is what relationships are about. First they learn to become good citizens in the family, and only then can they expand and become good citizens of the larger community.

Respect in family life means treating others well. This means that parents need to generally have things under control at home. It makes no sense for a parent to expect a child to go out and show respect for peers and teachers if the child is not living in an environment that models respect. We already know that kids will do what parents do, not what they say they should do. So the whole respect issue falls out the window if parents are out of control, manipulating others, or abusing their power at home. The same is true for a child who doesn't feel safe from sibling abuse. Sibling relationships will always have a certain amount of competition and conflict, but what many adults call "typical sibling rivalry" may actually leave lasting emotional scars, especially for the younger sibling. Again, things don't need to be totally harmonious all the time, but parents need to have a vigilant eye on the emotional and physical safety of all the kids in the house in order to maintain an atmosphere of mutual respect.

Last, but not least, is the most common form of addressing respect, respect for adult authority. It is very important for kids to understand that adults are in charge and that they deserve the same respect given to kids. Most of the time, if adults are respecting kids—by being fair (as much as possible), maintaining good boundaries, and making family rules clear—the adults won't have to drill kids too much about respect. Kids naturally reciprocate the respect they receive.

There are, however, kids with temperaments that are more active and persistent, kids who test the rules more and need an extra helping of the lesson on respect. These kids need consistent reminders to help them adjust their responses to authority figures. They often do well when their behaviors are tied to motivators that are important to them, such as video-game time, treats, favorite activities, and the like. I have also seen many of the kids who are wired this way (mostly boys) gain a lot from participation in the martial arts. Not only do kids martial arts programs provide an outlet for physical energy, they also focus heavily on respect for elders and peers. Some parents worry that these programs train kids to fight, but in my experience it's the opposite. The main focus is often respect and learning about self-control through stances and controlled movements, rather than encouraging kids to engage in violence.

Ways to build this skill. Respectful kids are kids who feel good about themselves. And kids who feel good about themselves are more inclined to engage in cooperative behavior, rather than testing authority. Even kids with substantial developmental challenges, such as ADHD, autism, etc., are capable of a general demeanor of cooperation and an awareness of the respect relationships need. You can help raise the overall level of respect by first helping your child feel worthwhile. This means that your child also needs to feel respected by you. The first order of business is to do away with trying to control behavior using methods that make a child feel bad or chip away at self-esteem. Criticism, blame, put-downs, and teasing are all damaging to children's esteem because they make them feel disrespected, and if children are not getting respect, they are not likely to give it to others. I am not saying don't discipline kids. In fact, discipline is another important way for kids to learn respect. What I am saying is use discipline methods that preserve self-esteem. I share lots of ideas about this kind of discipline in the following sections.

Another important way to teach respect to kids is to model respectful behavior toward others and yourself. Show your kids that all humans are valuable by not putting down or making fun of individuals or other groups of people. Be careful that the humor you use doesn't make fun of the way someone behaves or talks. This kind of provocative humor is enjoyable for some adults, who usually mean no harm. The problem is that they don't realize young kids' brains are not developed enough to understand the subtlety or context of such humor, and when these finer points are not understood, the joking appears to be another way to put someone down.

Modeling self-respect and self-care are other good ways to teach your kids about respect. You can model self-respect by not letting others treat you poorly or make you do things that don't feel right to you. Having kids see us stand up for ourselves when necessary is important because it gives them permission to do the same. Self-respect is about good boundaries, which includes not letting people treat you bad and not giving too much to others. Some people are very good at being everything for everyone, which can be a recipe for burnout. Being a giver or a rescuer of others is an easy and sometimes rewarding role to slip into, but it can quickly create imbalance in your personal life. If you're sensitive to the needs of others, become aware of how much you're giving to others. Model for your kids the ability to be generous but also to say "no" to preserve yourself.

Another aspect of self-respect is good self-care. Modeling self-care means showing your kids that you can take good care of your self physically, mentally, and emotionally. Sometimes I use the analogy with kids of being a best friend to ourselves by treating ourselves the way we would treat our dearest friend. This includes obvious aspects of taking good care of one's self through good nutrition, exercise, a good night's sleep, regular check-ups, and not using drugs or abusing alcohol. Kids certainly notice these things and will use them as a model for their own self-care. There are also the more subtle aspects of self-care that kids notice too. Things like managing stress, getting your social needs met, enjoying time alone, getting absorbed in hobbies, nurturing your spirituality, and just letting yourself have a moment to do absolutely nothing are all types of things humans need for personal balance—and it's good for kids to see their parents attend to these. Granted, there is often not a lot of time left in a parent's day for these things, but even small doses of these elements of self-care help you retain balance while modeling good self-care for your kids.

Your kids are watching you, and they will notice how you do or don't take care of yourself. They will pick up on the subtlest aspects of self-respect and self-care and will use this information to construct a map for how well they need to treat themselves. So be a best friend to yourself. Take care of the physical, mental, and emotional aspects of you. Keep your life in good balance. Your kids are watching.

Respect for others is another important part of respect kids need to learn. Personal boundaries, both physical and symbolic, convey respect for others. Personal space is one aspect of this. I use the *personal space bubble* to help kids learn about respecting others' bodies and personal space. I tell kids that the personal space bubble is an imaginary bubble that surrounds each of us all the time. It's our own personal airspace, which others need to respect and get permission before moving into. The bubble extends out as far as we can reach our hands and goes all around our body. This is a good way for kids to understand and visualize personal space as well as a way to remind kids when they've entered someone's bubble without permission. If you have a child who tends to get too close for comfort with others, help your child learn about personal space and the importance of respecting this boundary.

Another aspect of respect for others is attitude. The way kids talk to others and us reveals a lot about how much respect they hold for others. Attitude is made up of the words, the tone, and the body language a person uses to communicate. Help your kids show respect for others by teaching them to use constructive words and phrases such as "please," "thank you," and "excuse me." Complete answers rather than a one-word response or grunts are another way to show respect and should be encouraged. Help your child work not only on the words but also on the tone of a message. Feelings are allowed, so if children don't like something, they should be free to say so, but they should not be allowed to communicate displeasure with a disrespectful tone. Lastly, help your child become aware of body language, which includes posture, eye contact, and facial expression. You don't need to demand military-like attention to your every word, but if you feel like your child's posture is not respectful, stop and talk about it. Kids are often short on self-awareness and may not even know that their posture can be seen as offensive.

As important as polite, respectful communication is for kids, it's also important to adjust our expectations, depending on the circumstances. By this, I mean that some parents seem to want their kids to always exercise the same level of manners regardless of the circumstance. Kids are not manners robots, and expecting them to be perfectly polite all of the time is as out of balance as letting them run wild. Kids, just like adults, will be grumpy, upset, tired, and angry, and this will make them not want to be so polite. The difficulty is that forcing politeness when a child is not feeling it teaches a child to be false. Instead of requiring a smile and a cheery "Hello, how are you?" when a child is shy or upset, help them figure out a way to say "hello" that gets the job done without forcing them to act in a way that is too far from their true feelings. There is some benefit in learning how to grin and bear it, but remaining congruent with your real emotional state is equally important. If we teach our kids about the balance between being polite and being real, we're presenting a valuable lesson to them about how to maintain good social behavior while staying true to their own feelings.

Again, learning to respect others starts in the home, so creating clear family rules and standards is a good place to start. Warnings and fair penalties help kids learn about respect for all members of the family, which then sets the tone for respecting relationships outside of the home. Working together as a family also helps kids learn to respect and appreciate each other. Having everyone in the family participate in projects like cleaning up the garage, volunteering, or helping an elderly neighbor gets kids thinking beyond themselves while showing respect for their own living environment and other people too. As children get older, allowing them to be increasingly independent is another way to help them feel respected by you and responsible for themselves. For a four-year-old, this may mean having a play date at a friend's house, and for a thirteen-year-old, this may mean going to the movies without you. However you do it, consider letting your child take small steps toward independence, and use your judgment for how best to do it in a sensible way.

Another part of increasing independence should be increased responsibility for helping out. Kids of all ages should have chores or jobs that they do in the family. In our house, our kids understand that their biggest job is to do as well as they can in school. In addition to that, though, from about three years old on, we also have unpaid family jobs for each child, based on ability. This not only helps everyone share the workload but also teaches our kids to re-spect our home and contribute to its success. Kids who take on re-sponsibility are kids who learn to take care of themselves, their things, and their relationships—all of which lend to a greater sense of respect.

Here are some suggestions for helping your child work on the skill of *respect:*

- Respect your child. Don't use discipline that damages self-esteem (physical punishment, intimidation, shame, humilia-tion, etc.).
- Build self-esteem by acknowledging your child's positive behavior and choices.
- Model respectful communication toward all family mem-bers. Get yelling under control.
- Discuss mutual respect (at an age-appropriate level) and why it's important. Ask your child if they ever feel disre-spected and work to help solve these situations.
- Explain to your child how/when you feel disrespected by them and work together on solutions for these situations.
- Promote good boundaries in your family relationships (see Chapter 10).
- Help your child understand the concepts of self-respect and self-care.
- Help your child understand how respect is shown in com-munication i.e. attitude, posture, eye contact, tone etc.
- Help your child show respect for others by taking responsi-bility for mistakes (see Chapter 7).
- Accept and validate your child's negative feelings, but don't allow those feelings to turn into disrespectful behavior. Have clear family rules and consequences for disrespectful behavior.

5. Problem Solving. Working with kids to help develop the core skills listed so far lays the foundation for development of the final skill—problem solving. All of the core skills are important, but this one in particular aids in the learning process for kids. Gaining maturity involves making mistakes and learning from them, and problem solving is a central part of that learning. Without problem solving, a child has no power, no way out of dilemmas, no way to create new solutions. A child can be good at identifying a problem and expressing the feelings involved, but without an orientation to problem solving, the "what to do about it?" never gets answered.

Kids who are not good at problem solving tend to focus on blame instead of solutions. The tendency to blame stems from a lack of problem-solving skills, but is also the result of the fact that kids make a lot of mistakes and often get blamed themselves when things go wrong. In addition, children are trying to understand the world through cause-and-effect relationships, so they often look for the cause, or the blame, first. All of these factors can contribute to a child having difficulty moving from the blame game to the work of problem solving.

Problem solving for children often requires the assistance of an adult. Kids don't easily grasp the big picture or hold all of the details and possibilities that would lead to solutions for their dilemmas. The younger the child, the more difficult this process is, so the simpler it needs to be when presented to them. Regardless of age, all kids need the adults in their lives to help them learn this skill and put it into practice. This is not to say, however, that kids should never be left to solve their own problems. They should, and it's good for their sense of competence to try to resolve issues by themselves and experience a mix of failure and success as the outcome. However, there are also many situations where sink or swim on your own is not the best process for learning, and those are the times kids and adults need to practice what I call *joint problem solving*.

Joint problem solving simply means problem solving with others. It allows children to get help with the many difficult situations that are beyond their ability to solve. It also keeps them from getting stuck and doing nothing, or worse, doing something that might exacerbate the problem. This is especially true when strong feelings are involved, because emotional states limit children's ability to access their rational mind, which makes the act of analyzing a situation and coming up with solutions very difficult. A good example of this is with very sensitive kids. They are especially prone to emotional overload and can develop the habit of giving up when difficulties arise. This is a tricky cycle for them to slip into, because the more they give up, the more self-confidence is eroded and the more likely they are to give up the next time they face a similar challenge. This cycle of powerlessness becomes hard to break as they accumulate more and more evidence that there's no reason to try at all. Having adults move in to join with them in the problem solving process is the first step to getting these kids' confidence back on track. Slowly, as the adult works with the child to practice finding solutions to the child's dilemmas, the child's ability to make progress on the particular issues increases and confidence begins to build. As the child's ability to problem solve continues to improve, the adult's job is to hand more and more of the process over to the child, breaking the cycle of fear and avoidance and replacing it with an increased sense of personal power.

Joint problem solving also helps kids practice working on problems and creating solutions with other people—a skill they will need for the rest of their lives. It instills value on cooperation with others and helps kids understand that getting help is okay. When done with parents, joint problem solving also strengthens the bond between parent and child and, especially as kids get older, keeps them on the same team. Parents often find that kids who can problem solve issues together with them have more respect for their parents and are more likely to follow their guidance.

Joint problem solving has the additional benefit of moving a child from what I call "the complaint department" to the land of solutions. Kids can easily get used to their parents taking on the task of problem solving while they sit back and register complaint after complaint. This is not good for parents because it creates an over-reliance on them for creating solutions as well as burnout. Likewise, it's not good for children because it leaves their problem-solving muscle unexercised and weak. The goal of parents problem solving with children is to increasingly hand the task over to the children so that, as they develop, children take more and more responsibility for creating solutions on their own. This process increasingly energizes kids' inner resources and helps them build problem solving confidence in themselves over time.

Earlier I mentioned that sometimes it's best to let kids try to solve their dilemmas on their own. A good question I often get from parents is "How do I know when to move in and when to let them work it out by themselves?" That is a very good question. As with many parenting issues, it's more about a sense of discernment and balance than a one-size-fits-all answer. Children who ask their parents to solve many of their problems for them are getting plenty of practice in the skill of asking for help. So these kids need to practice working toward independence by creating solutions with their parents through joint problem solving, so that they can gain confidence in working with others to produce solutions. Finally, when they master joint problem solving, they then need to focus on learning to solve problems independently. In this process, the parent's job is to help move the child from dependence to independence by helping them master the incremental steps of getting help, working with others, and then solving problems independently.

Kids who are very high on the *persistence* temperament trait can have difficulty problem solving with others. They will often refuse help from others, even with issues that are way beyond their capacity, simply because they have such a strong desire for independence. This can leave these very persistent kids feeling stuck and frustrated. Persistent kids need to learn to ask for help and to tolerate working with others on solutions. Factors such as age and developmental level can play a big part in these situations too. Kids who are going through developmental periods that involve striving for power and independence (approximately ages two to five, and again from twelve to sixteen years) often won't let others help them solve their problems. They often choose to stay stuck rather than be dependent on others for help. The work for these kids is to balance the need for independence with the ability to solve problems with others.

So, there are several variables at play—temperament, developmental level, skill set, etc.—that guide when we should move in to help our kids problem solve and to what extent. A good process to try to establish with kids is to agree that they will try to apply solutions to their problems by themselves first and then come to you for help if they get stuck. This allows them to flex their problem-solving muscles independently but also decreases the chance that they'll end up overwhelmed and without solutions. Helping kids develop both the ability to problem solve alone and with others will give them the best chance of success when facing the many difficult situations they will encounter as they grow.

Ways to build this skill. The orientation to problem solving starts with parents. Kids need to learn about the value of working on problems with others, and they need to trust that adults are interested in working with them and not just in controlling them. Kids encounter many adults who are interested only in compliance, which is an affront to their developing sense of individuality and will. So, the first order of business is to help kids trust that adults are interested in working with them on problems. This means that parents need to ask for kids' opinions and ideas in daily life and hold them as equally valid. If you ask your child to help you think about solutions to small everyday problems, it will begin to give your child a sense that he or she has the resources within to create solutions. Start by having your child give input to non-emotional situations. Remember, when feelings are involved the brain circuits can become overloaded, making rational discussion difficult. So, practice solving the problems of mundane daily life together to give your child some confidence in this ability. A good way to do this is to think out loud in front of your child about situations that need solutions and see if they add any input. You can also ask your child directly for help or advice, which builds your child's confidence in his or her problem solving abilities, while highlighting the value of your child's input.

I often try to help my kids exercise their problem-solving muscles by thinking out loud about a problem. I might say, "Looks like the handle came off that drawer. I wonder what we should do?" This kind of invitation may not always lead to viable solutions for the problem at hand, but it's very beneficial for young developing minds because it gets them thinking about solutions. Social situations can provide lots of problem solving practice too. When you invite your child's thoughts or opinions on how to solve a social dilemma it gives your child a chance to think about interpersonal solutions. Again, the feasibility of the child's solution is less important than the fact that they are practicing problem solving with you. When your child offers a solution, ask additional questions, like "How would that fix the problem or situation?" This helps them take problem solving to the next logical step and also refine their ideas. Many solutions offered by kids are not practical or realistic and adults are often too quick to point this out. Instead of discouraging your child with your logic, encourage their problem solving attempts to keep them interested in developing this essential skill.

When observing a problem with your children, have them

focus on the solution and not the blame. Explain to them that you're less interested in whose fault it is than what can be done about it. This focus keeps kids thinking in a constructive mode and helps them practice seeing the big picture instead of only one aspect of a situation. Remember that kids of all ages are steadily moving away from being rooted in concrete thinking, where things look black and white and the grey areas are not easily seen. If you keep this in mind, you will understand why they view problems and solutions in such a polarized fashion and why it's so easy for them to focus on blame, or the cause. With this in mind, help your kids consider not just the black and the white, the right and the wrong, or the blame, but all the details and possibilities that create the total picture.

Presenting the finer details can even be done with a two-year-old. When your young child says, "Bad kitty!" you can say, "Yes, the kitty scratched you, but you scared her too." This helps the child move from seeing blame alone to observing additional details of the picture. Now you and your child are armed with the information necessary to come up with a solution: for example, "Instead of telling kitty she's bad, do you think we should just give her some space so she's not scared?" This way, you've helped your child expand beyond the black and white of blame to see relevant details and to experience joint problem solving.

With a five-, nine-, or fifteen-year-old, the process remains the same, but the number of details and the depth of perspective you add increases. The ability to see the total picture and to accurately assess all of the available information—in, say, complex social situations—isn't developed in kids until their late teens, which means adults can be helpful allies for kids, from toddlers to teens, as they develop this skill. As you work with your child to develop the skill of problem solving, keep in mind that you are there to support this learning experience. So, go slow—slower than you may be inclined to go. Also, ask your child to lead the process as much as he or she can. Teaching by asking questions is a great way to steer children toward the answer, while allowing them to feel as though they are leading the process.

The following scenario illustrates this process:

Child: Mario ruined recess. He's a jerk.

Adult:	What did he do?
Child:	He wouldn't pass the ball to me. He's not my friend.
Adult:	Seems like you're pretty mad at him.
Child:	How do you know?
Adult:	Well, you're calling him names and blaming him.
Child:	What else would I be doing?
Adult:	That's a good question. I wonder what you can do about the problem?
Child:	I don't know.
Adult:	Well, who could you talk to about what happened?
Child:	Him?
Adult:	That's a great idea. I wonder what you would say.

This scenario would continue with the adult asking questions to lead the child through the problem-solving process to solutions. The adult could steer with thoughts like, "I wonder who else you could play with?," or "Do you know how to get help from an adult on the playground if you need it?" Such questions are beneficial because they lead the child through the process of expanding his awareness by thinking about available options. What's key here is for the adult to stay in the passenger seat, initiating questions, while the child drives the solution process. That way when you arrive at the destination of a solution, the child will feel he drove you both there and gain confidence in his ability to get himself from stuck to solution.

Again, with younger kids, you will simplify the dialogue and provide more help, but the goal remains the same: to help the child develop his or her problem-solving abilities by acting as the thought-provoker or asker of questions. When adults can stay in the role of helper and not jump to providing kids with solutions, kids will increasingly be able to lead the problem-solving process and become more independent as problem solvers.

Here are some suggestions for helping your child work on the skill of *problem solving:*

- Help your child practice thinking through solutions to every day problems. Help them focus on details they might be missing.
- Talk to your child about social relationships and the dilem-

mas that naturally occur. Then use these situations to think together about solutions.

- If your child is sensitive, help him or her address problems with others—not avoid them.
- Make a plan that your child will try to solve problems without help first, but then will seek help if they get stuck.
- When sibling conflict arises, get the kids together (after they've calmed down) and have each of them think of 2 solutions to the problem at hand.
- When your child complains, ask them to contribute a solution to the situation.
- When your child blames, refocus them on what they can contribute to make the situation better.
- Show appreciation for your child's solutions even if they're not feasible. Help your child refine his or her solutions to make them more realistic.
- Do *Reviews* (see Chapter 7) after difficult events.
- Reward your child for practicing joint problem solving.

Joint Problem Solving and Behavior Issues

Joint problem solving takes a bit of a different course when we ask children to participate in the process where a behavior problem with them is the issue. This kind of problem solving is presented to kids not as an invitation but as a requirement by the adult. It also emphasizes the adult's authority, which is what makes this kind of joint problem solving different from other problem-solving conversations. Be clear with your child. Are you offering problem-solving help, or is the conversation mandatory because of a behavior problem? Later, I will introduce the Review, which is a process I use for problem solving after an incident in which a child's behavior has escalated or become the problem. For milder incidents, we can usually engage children during the difficult moment and move straight to joint problem solving. If behavior escalates and emotions get too strong, however, we have to wait until the child has calmed down and use the Review instead.

Engaging a child in problem solving during a behavior incident is a good way to try to steer the difficult moment in a constructive direction. This can be a difficult process though, because with behavior incidents, there is often tension between you and the child. The fact that the child is emotional and acting out makes it harder for the child to be agreeable to problem solving. You may be emotional too, which makes it difficult to stay levelheaded and remember the correct steps to take. Regardless, attempting to problem solve with a child who is acting out is the right thing to do because it is your best chance of a constructive outcome. If your child resists this kind of discussion, you may want to use a motivator to get your child to participate (learn more in the "Motivators" section). What follows is an outline of the basic steps of joint problem solving a behavior incident. Try to engage the child before he or she is too upset; otherwise, you'll have to wait until later and then use the Review.

The Basic Steps for Joint Problem Solving a Behavior Incident

- Have your child express his or her side of the issue, including their feelings. Validate their perspective.
- Explain your side of the problem and your concerns.
- Ask your child to think of possible solutions that take into account both of your concerns. Remind the child that you want to create a win-win solution and that flexibility is important.
- Give your child feedback on his or her solutions—for instance, whether they are feasible. Add your ideas for solutions after the child has come up with a few.
- Work to agree on a solution that honors both of your concerns and needs. If that's not possible, explore what might add fairness or help your child to feel better about the situation.
- Be clear about what the child's choices are—for example, "We can find a solution together, or I will decide alone." Also, don't rush—give your child time to move from a defensive to a cooperative position.

Here's an example of the above process. In this scenario, imagine you've said "no" to a friend coming over after school, and your child is upset.

Adult: You seem upset about my answer. Can you tell me what you're feeling and thinking?

Child: I'm mad at you because you're not letting Daphne come over and it's not fair!

Adult: I can see that you feel it's unfair, almost like I'm doing it just to make you upset.

Child: Yeah, you are.

Adult: Well, I'm not. I'm just concerned because you need to work on your project tonight. Can you think of any other solutions to this issue? I know you're good at problem solving.

Child: Yeah, I won't do my project!

Adult: Well that's one idea, but it's not a solution we can use because you'd end up in trouble at school. Your schoolwork is important. Can you think of any other solutions that consider both of our ideas? Remember, it's really important to be flexible.

Child: I guess I could have Daphne over tomorrow, but that's not what I want.

Adult: I know it isn't, but it's a great solution. Tell you what: if you can be flexible with this plan, I'll take you and Daphne out for ice cream while she's here tomorrow.

Child: I guess.

Adult: Great. You really fixed this situation in a nice way. Congratulations!

This scenario went pretty well, and such scenarios will get even easier as parent and child get used to solving problems together. However, depending on the circumstances, it could get difficult. What if your child got stuck and said, "I'm not talking to you!" or "I'm not doing any other ideas except mine!" Then you would have to move in with more authority and make the child's choices clear. You might say something like, "Look, we can work on this together, or I can just say no. But that's not what I want. I'll give you a few minutes to calm down and then decide if you want to try to problem solve. Otherwise, we're stuck, and I'll decide how this will go." Your child may still challenge you and act out, but if you apply this process consistently, eventually your child will take you up on problem solving together. Your child will come to figure out that it's the best chance of getting at least some of what he or she wants.

Using the Core Skills to Solve Any Problem

As we help our children develop the core skills, we prepare them to tackle any problem that comes their way. Children who are in touch with their thoughts, perspectives, and especially feelings about an issue have mastered the critical first step—understanding feelings. In addition, when they have the skills to communicate their experience, they will be able to dialogue with others, which is the first step in creating resolution (communication). When children have developed a respectful orientation to others (respect), they will have the desire to engage in a cooperative manner with others. And finally, if all the skills we looked at in this chapter are in place, children will be able to engage in the final step, which is working with others on solutions to problems (problem solving). The five core skills not only support one another but also can be applied together to solve almost any problem children might face.

As you help your child work on developing these skills, make sure that you praise their efforts and progress. Kids are wired to learn and will take pride in any learning experience they can master. Help your child feel competent while developing these skills by viewing your child as one of the family experts on flexibility, respect, and feelings words. Let your child be the helper to younger siblings and others who need to learn these skills. This will give your child pride in this new skill set and cement the child's mastery. This process will then create even more motivation for your child to practice the core skills and integrate them into his or her developing identity.

The Core Skills and Parents

Kids aren't the only ones who need to develop the core skills. Parents need the same set of skills to function well themselves. The fact is many of us weren't raised in households where our parents thought much about the skills they were imparting to us. This is partly because those were different times with a different orientation to parenting and partly because the knowledge base that developmental research has provided in the last few decades didn't exist then.

Regardless, the fact remains that our kids need this skill set to be successful, and we are the ones who have to teach them. If you somehow did get a handle on these skills while you were growing up in your family, great. You will now pass along these skills naturally. If, however, you are one of the many adults who recognize they didn't get adequate training in these areas, you'll have to work to develop these skills yourself. As the old saying goes, you can't teach what you don't know. The good news is that it is possible to learn all of this—I've done it myself. I've also helped many parents develop these skills and immediately begin passing them down to their kids with great results. It takes effort, but if you commit to the process, you will enjoy the results.

Take some time to think about your child's skill set. Which of the five core skills does he or she need to work on the most? Flexibility? Respect? Communication? Maybe, all of them. What about you? It's important to know which skills you can rely on so you can be prepared to address issues both small and big.

I suggest making a list of the skills on a big piece of paper and calling a family meeting. Explain to your kids that the five skills are essential for good personal functioning. For younger ones, call them superhero skills; for older kids, explain that they will make them effective and successful in their lives. Then have family members rate, from one to five, how well they have mastered each skill. Let other members comment on the accuracy of each person's self-evaluation. Sometimes we see ourselves as very flexible when others see us as rather rigid, and sometimes we are harder on ourselves than we need to be. Keep the conversation friendly, but do allow others to weigh in with their impressions. Also, encourage everyone to take in the others' perceptions of them and to try to see themselves from the outside for a moment. After everyone has rated themselves on all five skills, have each family member pick one skill to work on for the week. Brainstorm some examples of how each might do better with the targeted skill. Then let everyone know that you will have another family meeting next week and that there will be a treat for all who have put effort into the chosen skill for the week. The following week, have everyone pick another skill, and follow the same process. If you can create a fun way to get all family members thinking about these skills and practicing them, you'll be giving them a gift that will benefit them the rest of their lives.

Helping kids develop the five core skills is largely a preventative process, meaning that you're helping them develop skills that will decrease the likelihood of negative behaviors. But while this is certainly true, the fact remains that all parents have to deal with a certain amount of difficult behavior from their kids as a by-product of normal child development. To help adults deal effectively with children's problem behaviors, we need to move beyond the five core skills and take a look at some other important areas, such as temperament and the power to effect change through our parenting. As we address these additional topics, you will find that everything else presented in this book supports the development of the five core skills, for both children and parents. Let's continue in the next chapter by looking at the influence we have on our kids through our parenting.

Chapter Summary

Here is a recap of some of the highlights and tips presented in this chapter:

- Practice holding an accepting *attitude* toward your kids, especially when they bring you challenging behavior. This preserves self-esteem.

- Practice the *act* of acceptance with your kids. Let the little things go and focus on changing the behaviors that are most troublesome. This prevents parent burnout.

- Notice your child's successes as much as his or her mistakes.

- Understand that many factors contribute to a child's behavior, such as: developmental level, individual temperament, current life issues (school, social, family etc.), his or her coping skills, and your own stressors.

- Commit to doing more than just telling your child what *not* to do. Instead begin to think with them about what else they *can* do to make things more successful.

- Prevent negative behavior by helping your child build the five core skills: *understanding feelings, communication, flexibility, respect and problem solving.*

- Practice joint problem solving with your kids.

- Identify which of the core skills *you* need to work on and start developing them yourself.

- Hold a family meeting to talk about the core skills. Make a plan for each member to work on at least one skill. Track and reward progress.

- Give praise for good choices and even small improvements in behavior.

Chapter 2

∞

The Two Arms of Parenting: Exploring the Empathy Arm

Several years ago I was asked to give a talk to a group of parents at a local preschool. The topic was how to create behavior change for young kids. In preparation for the talk, I wrestled with how to create an easy way for parents to conceptualize the two main positions or stances we take when teaching our kids the many lessons of childhood. After some struggle, the idea of *the two arms of parenting* came to me. It seemed to fit well: first, because parenting is literally a hands-on job, and second, because it requires arms that are used both to hold and soothe as well as to guide and show strength.

The two arms of parenting are *empathy* and *authority*. They are the two main stances or ways we influence our kids and their behaviors. Through our presentation of these two roles, we help our kids work on all the skills necessary to create good behavior and successful coping. The empathy and authority arms have different but equally important influences; neither by itself is enough to cement what needs to be learned—for instance, mastery of the five core skills. Instead, it is the combination of the two arms that provides the complete teaching and ultimately helps a child build all of the skills necessary for good functioning.

We use the empathy arm to build connectivity with our kids and to help them work on the skills of understanding feelings, communication, and problem solving, which help them mature emotionally. These emotional skills then become the foundation that, in the long run, will allow our children to control their behavior. Emotional maturity, however, takes some time to develop, so in the meantime, parents need another way to influence that can help them deal with more immediate behavior problems—that's where the authority arm comes in.

Unlike empathy, which builds emotional and behavioral maturity over time, the authority arm is used mainly to control behaviors in difficult moments. This arm of parenting contributes a lot to kids' development of the core skills of flexibility, respect, and problem solving—all of which contribute to greater behavioral control on the child's part. With the authority arm of parenting, we set expectations, give consequences, and guide our kids through difficult behavior moments. I'll have much more to say on the authority arm and how to apply it in the next chapter.

You might have noticed that furthering the core skill of problem solving falls under both the empathy and authority arms of parenting. It is, in fact, a skill that can be exercised and encouraged during either parenting stance. For instance, problem solving is a natural product of cooperative communication, which occurs when we extend the empathy arm to our kids. But problem solving is also an aspect of a parent's disciplinary action, which falls under the authority arm of parenting. There will be some crossover with all of the core skills, but certainly the most with problem solving.

The two arms of parenting work together to provide a complete parental influence. If either influence is left out of parents' toolbox, the imbalance will lead to difficult behaviors. For instance, parents who focus only on empathy and emotional understanding often have kids who know what they are feeling but are not necessarily in control of their behavior. They are emotionally aware but may not have the skills to control their impulses and to respect others. On the other hand, exercising only the authority arm of parenting (setting limits and consequences, for example) can produce behavioral compliance but doesn't teach kids the essential skills of understanding feelings, communication, and problem solving that contribute to emotional maturity. Developing this maturity is equally important for managing social relationships and becoming self-directed.

So, we can see why a combination of empathy and authority are needed for effective parenting. Parents who develop an understanding of the two arms and put them into practice in a balanced way contribute most to their children's behavioral success. Just as mastering the five core skills is the work our children have to do, mastering the influences of empathy and authority is the work we have to do as parents. When parents understand and can use the influences of empathy and authority, they are equipped to effectively help their kids develop the five core skills, which lead to better emotional and behavioral coping. Let's start by looking at the empathy arm in this chapter. Then in Chapter 3, we'll explore the authority arm in depth.

The Empathy Arm

As I've already mentioned, the arm of empathy is really about creating a trusting connection with our kids and helping them mature emotionally. I call this arm empathy because this aspect of parenting starts with our ability to attune to our children, or to tune into the experience they're having. I list this arm first because it is the way to help kids work on three of the five core skills that are needed to function well: understanding feelings, communication, and problem solving.

Focusing on the child's experience, especially their feelings, has historically been neglected. Old-school parenting put a lot more, if not all, attention on controlling behaviors. As a result, our generation has inherited an unfortunate bias toward helping kids change by focusing solely on their behaviors. Now, there's nothing wrong with focusing on the behaviors that we don't want; it's just that the behaviors aren't going to change unless the parents and the child tune into what's going on underneath. I think of behaviors as the waves on the surface of the ocean. It can get pretty stormy at times, and we definitely want to quiet the seas—but to do so, we need to understand the currents underneath that are churning the waters and causing the waves, in other words, the emotions.

There's an old and wise saying in the field of counseling that goes like this: "Mental health rests on access to the full range of emotion." I love this saying because it simply yet powerfully underscores the importance of feelings in mental balance and health.

Emotions are a natural part of our bodies, and like our muscles and nervous system, they serve an important purpose for us humans. Essentially, they tell us how things are affecting us, what kind of impact our experiences are having on us. For instance, the emotions related to fear and aggression help us understand that in some way we are feeling threatened and that we may be in danger. Similarly, the feelings of love and security help us identify those near us who can help protect and support us. Emotions carry a lot of energy with them, which is in part why they can cause such problems for us. The energy of emotion needs to be released. I often tell parents that they have two choices: "Your kids can release their feelings through *language* or *behavior*. Take your pick." When positive emotions are released through behavior, we see positive behaviors—that's not usually a problem. But what about negative feelings? When the energy of negative feelings, such as fear, anger, or confusion, are not released through language, the energy will be converted into negative behaviors that create problems for parents as well as our kids.

Some people think that there is another option, which is for children to keep quiet, "be good," and not to share negative feelings or to protest. If this kind of message is given enough times or in a severe enough manner, kids learn to disconnect from their feelings—at least from the awareness of them. Ignoring their negative feelings in the name of compliance is very hard for kids to do, but some do indeed learn to do it because of their parents' reactions or dismissal. Kids who learn to disconnect from their feelings become withdrawn and emotionally distant. They are the ones I worry about most. They've lost connection with a vital part of themselves and no longer have a sense of who they are and what they need. Their spirits have been broken in the name of compliance. These are the kids who have been drilled about manners and good behavior with no focus on their feelings. They may have been humiliated or dismissed when they tried to protest or to express their emotional position. These kids desperately need their parents to tune into their inner lives and help them communicate their perspective. They need this help because it ultimately allows them to know who they are, which gives them the confidence and decision-making ability to manage their feelings and behaviors constructively. So the old idea that "kids should be seen and not heard" isn't enough. We now understand that kids need to access and express all of their emotional events, especially the protests, if we want to avert the outcomes of their acting out or just shutting down and becoming emotionally numb.

So, the communication of emotions needs to take place. The only decision for us is how we will we teach our kids to express their feelings. The options are expressing through behavior or language. I vote that we choose words, which can release the energy and meaning contained in our kids' experiences while giving them the voice they need to begin the problem-solving process. As we talked about in the previous section, joint problem solving is the solution to parent-child conflict, and joint problem solving starts with communication of the child's position, which, of course, is rooted in their feelings.

The act of talking about feelings also helps with an important process in brain development: integration. I won't go into it too much here (for much more information, start with Daniel Siegel's writings), but will offer instead an easy and general way to think about brain development and integration. You may know that the two halves of our brain are generally in charge of different processes. The right half is more connected to bodily sensations, such as emotions, and sees the context of situations, while the left half of the brain is more oriented to rational, logical, and language-based processes. Neuroscientists agree that integration of the two halves is an important developmental process; it leads to an increased ability to cope and to control oneself. The process of adding language (left brain) to feelings (right brain) is an integrating activity, which makes it an essential contributor to brain development and maturity.

Another developmental benefit that comes from thinking and talking about feelings is that it promotes the development of insight. Insight, or the ability to understand one's own behavior and motives, is essential for self–awareness and ultimately for self-control. Any child who can participate in a back and forth of conversation can work on building self-awareness and insight. Conversations with kids about their feelings are especially helpful for developing insight because emotions are such a central component in kids' behaviors. When adults have conversations with kids that help them understand their feelings and the reasons why they behave the way they do, they are also helping kids develop insight. And kids who have the ability to look at their feelings and behaviors have a much better chance of being able to control them.

It used to be that many people thought that because kids, especially young ones, didn't have the ability to conceptualize and talk about their feelings, that they simply weren't feeling anything at all. So the emotional lives of children were rarely considered relevant, and kids learned quickly that their options were either to endure in silence or to act out in some way. Thank goodness developmental research and understanding have grown past this simplistic and limited view of kids' experience and proven it inaccurate. Children are now understood to be complex emotional beings, connected to their feelings and experiences. If you think about it, this makes sense. Young children have to be emotionally tuned in because they must rely solely on reading and expressing through nonverbal emotional communication during the first few years of their life. Think about how your baby lets you know she's happy or that he's wet or hungry. They can't tell us with words yet, but their emotions still drive them to let us know how they're feeling—even in the middle of the night! So, even very young kids are having complex emotional experiences, similar to adults. But the big difference between them and us is that we adults have the ability to express our feelings clearly with words and ideas.

By about two years of age, kids' brains are developed enough to fully experience both the physical and mental aspects of emotional experience, but it isn't until their early twenties that the more complex cognitive aspects of development—such as judgment, rational thinking and the ability to understand and communicate abstract concepts—are done developing. What does this mean? Well, there's a big period of time in which kids are experiencing complex layers of emotion without the ability to communicate those feelings to others in cohesive and rational ways. This is the essential frustration of childhood, and adults need to understand this. Think about it, your child's need to be in charge, upset over a lost toy, or frustration about a friendship contains the same emotional sensations you experience when frustrated in the workplace, when you lose something important to you, or when you and your spouse are in conflict. The difference is that the adult mind can use elaborate words and concepts to express how an experience affects them while the child cannot. So the important lesson here is not to minimize kids' feelings just because they can't express them to us in coherent or nuanced ways. As kids grow, they do steadily develop their ability to express themselves clearly, and this ability is greatly affected by parent-child communication. The more parents help kids learn to put feelings into words and concepts, the better they get at it. As parents we have the opportunity, or maybe *duty* is a better word, to help our kids develop the ability to use words to express their emotional states clearly and effectively.

It is also important not to trivialize kids' feelings because they are about "unimportant" things. Kids reside in the moment. It's partly what makes childhood such a magical time. Not looking down the road or zooming out and seeing the big picture with all its complexity and problems is a blessing. It allows children to focus on *the now* which requires that their attention be on what they can learn in the present moment.

It's easy for us to minimize or dismiss kids' little dilemmas because *their* problems are not going to stop trading on the stock exchange or cripple the economy. But what we have to understand is this: when we view the problems of childhood as insignificant in the big scheme of things, *we* are the ones with the limitation. This is because as adults we have the ability to see both the big picture and to shift perspective and see things from a child's viewpoint. Since kids develop the capacity to move beyond their own perspective slowly, over many years, we can't expect them to do it much. So it is our responsibility as adults to hold multiple perspectives and to see that kids' dilemmas are as important to them as ours are to us. Their triumphs and upsets are a product of their childhood experiences, which are certainly different from our own but no less valid. If we dismiss the feelings and experiences of kids (or any other person), then it means we have failed to use our adult capacity to shift perspective and understand that although another's experience may be different from ours, it is valid for that person. So, put yourself in your kids' shoes and understand that in your children's world, their dilemmas are as important to them as yours are to you.

The Skill of Empathy

The empathy arm of parenting focuses a lot on emotions, specifically the identification and communication of feelings. As we help kids develop the ability to understand and talk about their feelings, we are helping them build the core skills of understanding feelings and communication. In addition, when we focus on another person's feelings, especially if we validate those feelings, we are also teaching the skill of empathy. The skill of empathy, or the ability to put oneself in the shoes of another, is certainly a key aspect of the empathy arm of parenting, but it's also a distinct skill that our kids need to learn. Whereas "the empathy arm of parenting" refers to the aspect of parenting that concerns itself with creating a strong emotional bond between parents and kids, the skill of empathy is more specifically focused on teaching our kids to truly understand the experience of others.

The interesting thing about empathy is that it can't be learned through a lecture. You can't just explain to someone else that he or she needs to understand how someone else feels. Sure, kids can get the concept when we say, "How do you think that made him feel?" but they don't actually experience another's perspective without true empathy. True empathy means stopping and really putting yourself in the position of the other. It requires a shift to the other's perspective and a real understanding of what that person is going through.

Empathy connects people on a deeper level and creates a desire for cooperation. Its importance cannot be overstated. I believe it's the empathy we teach our kids to have that will have the greatest impact on the future of the human race. Empathy will help us unite us as a world culture, decrease the need for wars and injustice, and increase the desire for cooperation and benefit for all. If we are truly tuned in to the experience of others, how can we mistreat them? Empathy is the key to better human relationships.

So, how do we teach empathy? By giving it. Since empathy is more than just a concept—it's an experience—it can only be fully learned through the practice of it. Children learn to have empathy for others when they experience it themselves. A child who has been on the receiving end of empathy will fully understand it and then be able to turn to others and give it to them. The bottom line is that the more empathy we give to our children, the more they will give it to others. This putting yourself into the shoes of another is not always easy to do; it requires practice. Although young kids have a harder time shifting perspective, no one is ever too young (or too old) to start building this essential skill. I'll talk later about ways to practice building empathy with our kids, but for now, let's stay focused on how we can teach our kids to tune into feelings.

Reading Emotion

So how can we tell what kinds of feelings our kids are having? Since feelings are expressed through language and behavior, we need pay attention to both outlets. When our kids tell us about their feelings, it's easy to know what's going on with them. We just have to learn to stop and listen. But if they're not yet good at telling us, then we have to pay attention to their actions as clues to their emotional lives. This requires us to read, as clearly as we can, the signals they give that communicate their feelings. With an upset child, for example, this may mean a piercing look at you or a sibling or a folding of the arms with a downcast expression. A very sensitive child might get quiet and withdraw. Impulsive kids will be less subtle and may express with a hit, a scream, or even a full-blown tantrum. Regardless of the way a child communicates an emotion, it's important that adults see these behaviors as attempts at communication rather than behaviors designed simply to annoy parents.

There are also times when our kids have feelings but won't show them through their words or behavior. At these times, how do we know the feelings are there? This is a bit more tricky, but not impossible to solve. Notice situations that might create strong feelings in your child. Look for clues in the context of your child's life. For instance, let's say you and your child witness something scary together—say, a fight between kids or an auto accident. If your child does not say anything or show you any behavior that suggests what feelings the event stirred, then afterward, you can directly ask. "Hey, honey, I was wondering how it felt for you to see that?" is a great opener. You might be surprised how much kids hold inside that they don't talk about. These feelings do need to be released, so it's important for adults to be focused not only on feelings they can see or hear from their kids but also on the feelings that might be hiding in the silence.

I worked with a family some time ago that had a twelve-year-old daughter who was very sensitive and quiet. When her performance started to slip in school, her teachers and parents became concerned, and they brought her in to see me. There had been no big changes in her behavior, and the parents couldn't identify any unusual changes or stressors in her current life. We started talking with this girl about how things were going for her. Because of her level of sensitivity, she was slow to warm up and didn't reveal much at first. I educated the family on the importance of tuning into feelings. After several invitations from her parents, she finally began to open up and reveal herself. It turned out that she was being bullied by a small group of girls who were making fun of her developing body. She was ahead of the curve in physical development, and this difference was a source of additional embarrassment to the already awkward and very sensitive preteen. Her parents, who were also fairly sensitive, were relieved to finally understand what had been impacting their daughter in her silent emotional world. This information helped them tune into her suffering and then work together to create a game plan to help her with these kids. With her parents and teacher on board, this girl was able to problem solve the agonizing dilemma and eventually assert herself with her peers. This brought about real change for her, and her situation and school performance began to improve significantly.

Situations like this create so much concern because these kinds of kids often suffer in silence. Since they don't make big waves with their feelings, they run the risk of slipping through the cracks. This is a good reminder to keep an eye on the quiet kids. Check in with them even if you don't see any emotional signs. Also keep in mind that the emotional signals they give might be subtle. If your child is sensitive and quiet, stay tuned in and you will decrease the chance of your child struggling with an emotional issue in isolation.

We want to help kids become friends with their feelings and to see them as a natural part of themselves. This starts with you placing value on focusing on your kids' feelings. Remember that emotions are not to be feared or shut down but respected, expressed, and integrated as an important part of any person's whole self. The expression of emotion is one of the most important core skills because it has so much to do with developing other skills. When we help our kids talk about feelings, we're covering the skills of understanding feelings and communication. We're also helping our kids become integrated and emotionally regulated, which are important developmental processes that contribute to a balanced and well-functioning child.

Narration

Expressing feelings through words is more difficult for some kids than others. Younger children and children with developmental delays often have a harder time describing their emotional states to others. The same is true for kids who are emotionally guarded or shut down. For these kids, I developed a process called narration. Because feelings lie beneath all behaviors and we know we need to get our kids talking about them, narration is a good place to start. Again, if you ask your child about his or her feelings and they are willing to share—great. But what if you ask and get nothing more than a blank stare? Or what if you hear, "I don't know"? Well, then it's time to add narration to the situation.

Narration is the process of using our ability to describe feelings and their causes to our children, to show them how to put words to their feelings and to identify the causes of various emotions. Remember that young children are feeling all the feelings we experience, but the difference is that they don't yet have the cognitive ability to conceptualize and express them. Narration is especially useful because it is a model that helps younger children learn how to put words to feelings. Narration shows kids several important things at once. Foremost, it shows your attunement to their feelings and difficulties. Kids who feel understood in their difficult moments will make better behavior choices. It also provides the child with a model for how to begin to think and talk about feelings and problems.

Narration is effective and simple. Most of the time it merely requires saying the things that often go unsaid, such as mentioning a change in the child's emotional state or behavior. Commenting on the feelings a child might be experiencing is extremely helpful because it shows them how to organize their emotional world into thoughts and words. This organization begins with parents expressing their understanding of a child's emotional state "out loud," which promotes the child's growing understanding of himself or herself. Self-understanding along with the ability to channel emotions and ideas into language provide children with the tools for effective self-expression, which is a prerequisite for self-control. Simply put, children who can understand and put their feelings and ideas into words are the children who do not need to act out to communicate.

Some of the benefits of narration include the following:

- It helps you attune to your child.
- It helps your child feel understood by you.
- It helps your child begin to understand what's underneath his or her behaviors.
- It shows your child how to put words and ideas to feelings.
- It lets children know that their ideas, actions, and feelings matter, which builds self-esteem.

Ways to Narrate

1. Validate your child's experience. "I can see that you don't want to go to bed. You look frustrated and might feel like it's not fair."

2. Wonder aloud what might be going on emotionally with your child. To a younger child, you might say something like, "Your face changed when mommy left for work. Now you look sad. Do you have a sad feeling?" To an older child, you might say something like, "I can see that you're upset about something, but you won't look at me or talk to me. I wonder what you're feeling?"

3. Narrate possible causes of upset as well as potential solutions. "I think you're talking to me that way because I said no to the sleepover. If you're upset with me, you know you can tell me about it, and then we can find a solution."

4. Help your child connect to the feelings that drive behaviors. "You just hit Zoe. Maybe you're feeling angry that she drew on your picture? Let's find another way to let her know how you feel."

5. Help your child protest through language instead of behavior. To a younger child, you might say something like, "You started running around when I said it was time to leave. Maybe that's your way of saying 'I don't want to go!' Let's see if I can help you stop and find some words for these feelings you're having." To an older child, you might say something like, "I can see you giving me angry looks across the room. How about you just tell me what you're mad about?"

You can see that narration is a way for adults to begin the process of communicating about feelings. All of the dialogue above is initiated by the adult. There is benefit for the child even if he or she doesn't participate in the conversation at all. This is because constructive adult commentary on kids' emotional moments models how to talk about feelings and also invites the child to be part of the process. If adults can start the process of communication with a genuine invitation to the child to participate, the child will often begin to add ideas to the conversation. It may take a few tries, especially with kids who tend to shut down emotionally, but when children feel an adult really wants to hear from them, they eventually participate. Narration is a good way to move beyond modeling emotional communication to catalyzing a dialogue between parents and kids about their feelings.

There are countless situations for which narration is appropriate, and each one provides the child with an opportunity for learning. For the two- or three-year-old, narration provides a model for how to talk about feelings. For the seven-year-old, it can help the child learn to connect to the causes of various feelings and then point to solutions. For an eleven-year-old who is angry and shut down, it provides words the child can't access because of emotional overwhelm. And for the sixteen-year-old, narration reinforces attunement—a reminder that the parent remains a useful ally despite the adolescent's desire to be independent.

There is no right or wrong way to narrate, so experiment and find a way to do it that feels natural for you. Also, don't feel like you have to narrate everything! My rule of thumb is the bigger the feelings involved, the more important it is to narrate for the child. Also, when narrating, try to avoid telling your child how he or she is feeling, as well as giving your child a solution for the situation. These are skills children need to develop themselves. With narration, we are simply wondering out loud about the feelings that might be present. This helps children connect to their feelings and learn about expressing themselves and solving daily problems. Use narration with your kids any time they need help putting words to their emotional states.

Validation

I'm sure you understand by now that helping kids identify and communicate their feelings is important. I also want to take a moment to talk about responding to them when they *do* share feelings. I mentioned validating in the previous sections, and it's an important idea to consider. Encouraging our kids to practice emotional communication is the first step toward changing behaviors, but it's not the only one. How we respond to emotional communication is equally important because our response either encourages or discourages our kids from continuing to share their feelings with us. Once we understand the importance of building the skill of emotional communication, then of course we'll want to support our kids in continuing to practice this skill with us. The most effective way to keep our kids talking about their inner lives is to validate their emotional statements.

What exactly is validating? It's the opposite of dismissing. Many of us grew up with parents who threw out messages of dismissal when we were having feelings. These messages would have been responses like "you're not really mad," "you're overreacting," "don't be a drama queen," or "buck up." If this was how your parents responded to your upsets, you know how frustrated and misunderstood they left you feeling. There's nothing worse than someone telling you that the feelings you have don't matter.

It takes courage to share your feelings. They are a vulnerable and fragile part of our inner lives, so it's not always easy to open up and share them. This is especially true for boys, who have long been socialized to steer away from their feelings and toward aggressive competition instead. Boys in particular need to hear the message in their families that acknowledging and communicating about feelings is okay. Parents are the most important and sometimes the only source of counterbalance to all the messages of dismissal our boys get about their feelings from the rest of the world. Boys especially need their fathers to validate their emotional experiences. This can be tricky because many of us didn't grow up with a dad who modeled this. But this doesn't mean that we don't have a responsibility to teach it. We do, and have to learn how to include this as part of our parenting focus. So, dads, show your kids, especially your boys, what it means to be emotionally present—it's one of the most valuable gifts you can give your child.

The Open Channel

Validating our kids' feelings does two essential things: it helps them feel understood by us, and it opens up the channel of emotional communication—both of which lend to better behavior. The only way we're going to get our children to be interested in the way we want them to behave and what we want them to do is if they feel understood by us first. If we want our kids to genuinely cooperate in family life—rather than cooperate only to avoid punishment—then they need to feel we care about their position. This is different from their feeling that we only care about the behavior we want from them or the task we want them to do.

What you'll find when you stop to validate your child's position is a window into their world: their ideas, experiences, hopes, and dreams. All of these areas are interconnected with our children's emotional lives and have emotional significance for them. Understanding our children's emotional lives is the deepest way to know them—as is true with any person—and it's also the best way to motivate them to cooperate with you.

Validating your child's experience also creates what I call the open channel. If you want to know what's going on in your child's life, then you'll need an open channel of communication. As our kids grow, they move further and further out into the social world, spending more time with their peers and being influenced by their peers, as well as others. Some of these influences will be positive, and some will be negative—like other kids trying to get them to make bad choices. The only way you'll know about your child's struggles and dilemmas is if he or she is communicating with you about them. What makes our kids identify us as the go-to person when they're struggling? It's going to hinge on one thing: whether they feel heard and understood by us. This is the open channel, when your child has identified you as the person to share his or her emotional events with because you listen and validate what's shared. It's important to have the channel open when your child is four and going off to preschool, and it's absolutely critical to have this channel open when your fourteen-year-old is engaging in teenage activities.

Teens face social and emotional dilemmas every day. Having an open channel of communication means you will be in the loop about these personal and moral challenges. If the channel is closed, you'll be left wondering what's going on in your child's world and hoping that somehow you'll find out if your child runs into trouble. Don't make the mistake of thinking that you can suddenly open this channel on your son's or daughter's fourteenth birthday—it doesn't work like that. If parents wait until their kids are in their teens to start having emotional discussions with them, they're going to be uncomfortable and have a hard time opening up. It's much easier to start when our children are younger so that they become used to this kind of dialogue and identify you as the person who will listen. Creating an open channel when our children are young is our insurance policy for the times in later years when our kids' moral characters will be tested by offers to engage in things like bullying, cheating, drug and alcohol use, sexual behavior and social media dilemmas. If the channel is already open, we'll know about these things and can be there to help. That said, however, it's also never too late to start opening the channel. If your child is already heading into the teen years or beyond and you're just learning this, get started opening the channel now. It's never too late to start communicating and validating.

Also take care not to pretend to listen to your child. In our modern world of constant electronic distractions, it's easy to have one eye on the phone and the other on the person talking to you. Don't let this happen with your kids. You know how you can tell when someone isn't really listening to you? Our kids can too. They can figure out quickly when we're not really present and will shut the door on sharing. Reputations are hard to change. If your child feels blown off by you more than a few times you will have a hard time gaining your child's trust again. So put down the phone, pack up the iPad, shut down the laptop, and really be there to listen. Remember, the open channel is your insurance policy.

Although we've been talking about the parent-child relationship, this dynamic of listening and validating is an important part of any relationship. For instance, it's important for couples to mutually validate each other. Next time you and your partner are having a conversation, try validating what he or she has said before you present your idea. You'll be amazed at the response. Even if you have a totally different opinion on a subject, when you can stop to show you understand your partner's position, you create closeness, mutual respect, and trust—all of which are good for couples, and are also a prerequisite for intimacy. Try it. You'll see how much better adding a little validation makes discussions of just about anything.

Validation is not about memorizing a script like "How did that make you feel?" or "That's so hard." If you use the same line over and over again, the other person will wonder if your interest is authentic. While such statements are fine ways to validate, they're not the only ways. In fact, there is no exact way you need to do it. Find your own words in each situation to let the other person know you're really trying to understand the experience being shared with you. If it's hard to think of a way to validate what another person is sharing, start by simply paraphrasing what you are hearing them say. You might start with something like, "Sounds like you..." and then describe what you think his or her experience is, such as "... feel like she's being unfair" or "...are angry about what I said earlier" or "...felt confused by what he did." Then add an empathic comment that lets the person know you understand how he or she must feel given the situation that's been described, "I can imagine you'd be upset by that." This is an authentic way to start practicing validation.

There is a big difference between communication that includes validation and communication that doesn't. Consider the following example. Imagine you are feeling down, and your friend asks, "What's wrong?" You muster up the courage to share that you're feeling upset because you were so mad at your six-year-old that you got into a screaming match and couldn't stop yourself. Your friend looks at you and says nothing. A minute later, she changes the topic, and you both move on to another subject. How would this conversation leave you feeling? You might wonder why you bothered to bring up your feelings with her in the first place. I doubt this friend would be a person who'd come to mind the next time you needed to open up and share something deeply personal. The channel would be closed. Now, imagine the same scenario, but in this one your friend replies, "Parenting is so hard" or "Oh my gosh! that happened to me a few weeks ago" or "Do you feel super guilty about it?" It's a completely different experience when the listener takes a moment to say almost anything that lets you know your message was received and understood. That's the difference validation makes.

Also, it is especially important to validate the other person before you start giving your opinion or advice. Once you switch the focus from the other person's emotional experience to your ideas about the situation, the moment of validating that person's experience passes. Sharing your opinions and advice *is* paying attention to the person, but it's not the same as validating. With validation, the focus remains on the other long enough to allow the person to express his or her feelings fully. Switching from the other person's expression to your advice is a bit like walking onto the stage of someone else's play and shining the spotlight on you. If you switch the spotlight to your ideas too soon, several negative repercussions are likely to follow. First, the other person's ability to organize and release the stress he or she has been holding is interrupted—an organization and release that is essential for relief. Second, you risk losing your supportive connection with that person because the person may feel like you're more interested in your opinion on the matter. Finally, if the person does feel overlooked, he or she is much less likely to take in the solutions you're sharing, so any good advice you have will fall on deaf ears. Nobody wants to be told how to solve a problem by someone who hasn't really listened in the first place.

Dads, guys, men—this one is for you, so listen carefully. Similar to switching the spotlight to your idea is what I call *bringing the toolbox*. Guys like to fix stuff. We're better at analyzing a problem and creating a plan of action than we are at listening. What we tend to do works great when the toilet is clogged, but not so well when your wife, partner, or kids need emotional support. To be fair, most of us weren't trained to be good conversationalists, at least not in the emotional department, so we come with a disadvantage. Still, that's no excuse for missing this critical point: sometimes the fix is not the fix! By this, I mean that it's often much more helpful to leave the toolbox (advice, solutions, action plan) in the car and instead simply tune into the other person's emotional dilemma and validate what she or he is going through. Instead of immediately trying to fix the problem, simply listen. Having somebody *be there* for us is as important as solving the problem. We are social animals, and we rely on communication with those we trust to soothe our suffering.

As dads, we need to practice the skill of validation before we offer our fix for a problem. Often, listening and validating are the fix that's needed. If you just can't stop yourself from giving advice, then at least wait until after you've listened carefully and validated the other person. Once you've done that, if you want to offer your ideas for fixing what's not working, ask to see if what you've got in your shiny red toolbox is wanted, and respect the fact that the other person might not be ready for your good advice. You might be surprised to find how much your attentive listening already helped. Try this with your partner and kids. You'll also be amazed at how much more they'll value your ideas when you've done the validation piece first.

How do we validate? There's no formula. Instead, it's a response you give to the speaker that lets him or her know that you get their experience, especially the emotional impact its had on them. Imagine your child tells you, "Sammy was so mean at school today. He teased me when I spilled my juice." Following are some statements that demonstrate both validation and a lack of validation:

- "How did that make you feel?" This is a validating response because you're focusing on your child's feelings. You would then need a follow up along the lines of "I can see why you felt [fill in the blank with what your child felt] when Sammy teased you" to complete the validation.
- "Thanks for sharing that with me." Although this statement is polite, it's not validating. You're not letting your child know that you understand what he or she experienced.
- "I remember when I got teased in school. It was pretty upsetting. How was it for you?" This is validating. Sharing your past experience in a similar situation is a great way to relate.
- "Did you tell a teacher? You should have." This is not validating. It's a fix pulled from the toolbox. It's good practical advice, but it needs to come after you've tuned into your child's emotional experience and expressed your understanding of it.
- "Being teased would make me feel mad or embarrassed. Was it that way for you?" This is validating. You put yourself in your child's situation and offered that understanding as a starting point to talk about his or her experience.

These are just a few examples for what must finally be your genuine attunement to your child's experience. Remember to stay focused on your child's experience, especially the feelings. You can also use your own experience or feelings to explore your child's (this works especially well with younger kids). Save any problem solving for later, after you've validated. Especially with older kids (and spouses), ask if your advice on fixing the problem is wanted before you jump in with your tools. Follow these guidelines, and your kids will make you the go-to person when they need someone to talk to. Then you will rest assured that you'll always be informed about their personal challenges.

Chapter Summary

Here is a recap of some of the highlights and tips presented in this chapter:

- Understand how the two arms of parenting, *empathy* and *authority*, combine to create a complete parenting stance.
- Create a strong emotional connection with your child through exercising *the empathy arm* of parenting.
- Attune to your child's emotional life by noticing and talking about his or her feelings.
- Remember that your child's emotional dilemmas deserve the same level of respect as yours, even if they are about seemingly trivial events.
- Help your kids notice and communicate about their own feelings.
- Help your kids learn the skill of empathy by receiving it from you. Show empathy for their feelings and experiences.
- Narrate your child's feelings when he or she is shut down or stuck for the right words.
- Validate the feelings and experiences of those who take the time to share with you.
- Open the channel of emotional communication with your kids. Keep the channel open.

Chapter 3

∞

The Authority Arm

With the authority arm of parenting, we move from helping a child become emotionally integrated and mature to controlling and guiding a child's behaviors. The authority arm supports the development of the core skills of flexibility, respect, and problem solving. To understand this approach, let's begin by defining this term. What is authority? In essence, it is parental power. It's the influence we have to prompt, stop, or reshape our children's behavioral responses as well as the focus we put on following rules and behaving in socially appropriate ways.

Why do we have to exercise authority over our kids and control their behaviors? This is a good question that some parents ask, particularly those with the mind-set that families should function democratically, with no one having more power than another. I want to answer this question with an example. I had a parent tell me that he was trying to have a democratic family life by guiding his kids only with love and logic. This parent and his partner believed that if their kids were treated as equals and guided only with positive feelings and a clear rationale, they would all achieve a state of family harmony. These parents ended up coming to me, however, because their experiment with family democracy was not going well. What they were experiencing was far from a harmonious family life. Their kids were disrespectful and somewhat entitled, and they often did not listen to their parents' guidance.

I began my work with them by first validating their efforts toward fairness among family members and their focus on a positive and loving orientation toward parenting. Then I explained to them that the problem with their model was that there was no clear authority in their house. I explained that because of the limitations of normal brain development, kids have yet to develop the abilities to self-reflect, control impulses, measure abstract concepts like social reciprocity, and to modulate their emotional responses to the extent individuals need for self-governance. So the facts prevented their kids from being effective as equal allies. All the positive messages in the world wouldn't produce a mastery of these developmental skills. This was hard for the parents to hear because they thought they had developed a recipe for foolproof family success, and they were very invested in this philosophy.

I had them start to define the parent unit as the seat of power in the family and begin to use more authority when guiding their kids. This created some conflict, especially at first, when the kids rallied against the fact that they did not have equal say anymore. The kids did get to participate in some family decisions, but not all, and they had to work for some of the things they used to take for granted. This shift toward more authority eventually produced a dramatic decrease in the kids' fighting, complaining, and sense of entitlement, and it finally began to produce the positive, loving tone that the parents had wanted so badly.

What happened here? It's almost paradoxical that inequality and conflict in the family would lead to more harmony. Well, it isn't an impossible riddle once we understand the limitations of kids' development and the guidance and parameters they need to be successful. Of course, the extent of guidance and the kind of guidance differs depending on a child's age, but the fact remains that authority is a part of successful parenting. Even a democracy needs leaders.

Similarly, you can't be the authority and your child's best friend. It certainly is possible, and desirable, to have emotional closeness with your child, but without the clear boundary that separates you as the authority, you will not parent effectively. Parents who take on the role of their children's best friend are most often trying to create an emotional bond and a secure, protective alliance with their children. Again, these are important ingredients in the parent-child relationship, but parents need to realize that there are other key elements parenting also requires. It's far better for parents to see themselves as a guide for their children rather than a best friend. A guide is an authority figure with the capacity for emotional closeness, and so a guide can be helpful with both their child's emotional needs and their developmental needs for direction and limits.

Comfort with Conflict

Another common block for parents when exercising their authority is the issue of conflict and conflict avoidance. Many adults grew up in families that had either too much or too little conflict, and as a result they become conflict avoidant as parents. If you came from a family that was always arguing and shouting, or worse, one in which parents were in some way out of control because of anger issues, alcoholism, or drug use, then you know how scary and out of control that feels. No one who has had to endure that kind of family life wants to relive such experiences. It is easy for parents with this kind of family history to fall into a pattern of avoiding any type of family conflict because it brings back painful memories that they would never want their kids to endure.

It is also true that some people who have had high conflict childhoods will re-create that kind of drama in their own families, even though they know how destructive it is. Why would someone re-create this all over again? It may seem confusing, but we can make sense of it. These people are programmed to experience this kind of atmosphere as normal. Also, we all have a strong draw to create a sense of normalcy in our lives, even if at times it's dysfunctional. Childhood trauma can create a sort of tug-of-war inside a parent who is pulled in the direction of re-creating what he or she knew to be normal, on the one hand, while on the other, knowing on some level that it's not healthy. Unfortunately for some kids, their parents follow the drive toward dysfunctional normalcy and make their kids endure the same family chaos they suffered as children. It is also true that these parents are often aware of the price their families pay by living in this kind of emotional chaos. However, sometimes the programming is so strong that even as adults, they can't stop reliving the old patterns and infecting their current family life. Parents who are stuck in these patterns of severe dysfunction need to get counseling to be able to break these destructive cycles.

So, we can see that parents with childhood experiences of high family conflict can be left with a tendency either to avoid conflict entirely or to misperceive extreme conflict as a normal part of family life. In both cases, parenting becomes out of balance, with the ability to appropriately hold authority jeopardized.

Not being exposed to outward conflict is another kind of childhood experience that can lead to conflict avoidance in adulthood. Many families prize the absence of conflict and create unspoken rules guiding all members not to address their conflicts with others. This may be presented as respect for elders or siblings or as an ideal of family peace and love—either way, no expressed conflict becomes a central aspect of the family's identity. Sometimes this standard is bigger than an individual family's culture and is part of a national cultural influence. Regardless, many kids grow up in families whose approach to the natural conflict that happens in relationships is not to deal with it at all. Because this type of family culture does not expose the kids to conflict outright, they do not develop the skills to effectively deal with it. The kids are often very good at avoiding conflict but have a hard time knowing what to do with the friction that naturally occurs between people in close relationships. Because expressed conflict is foreign to them, these kids can be overwhelmed by even mild instances of conflict.

Anger issues, alcohol and drug abuse, or complete denial of conflict in the home are extreme situations. Many of us didn't have childhood experiences that severe. The spectrum of family conflict contains many gradients and influences and so plays out differently in each family. What is true for everyone is that we all grew up with the influence of how our parents or caretakers dealt with conflict, and that this has a big impact on how we deal with relational friction in our current families. Parents who were raised in families that leaned toward an extreme of either too much or too little conflict often find it harder both to present clear authority and to deal with the conflict that authority naturally creates. This challenge must be overcome because establishing functional authority as a part of family leadership naturally creates a certain amount of conflict, which needs to be dealt with in an appropriate manner.

I spoke to a mom who was having a hard time setting limits with her rather willful nine-year-old son. She explained that she was trying to be a good parent by giving him freedom and the ability to express himself as he wished. Over time, this turned into him frequently challenging his mom's requests and using disrespectful language toward her. I met with the family and both the mother and her son appeared unhappy in this dynamic, and the father was out of ideas to help them. In our work together, I helped the mother look at the idea of *a good parent* differently. I started by helping her understand that a good parent is not a parent who allows the child to express all negative impulses without limits. On the contrary, a good parent is one who helps the child develop the skills to succeed. I explained to the parents that this boy would have a hard time being successful if he went out into the world thinking he could express himself and address authority in the way he was practicing at home. The fact was that this boy would end up in trouble in many circumstances if he were allowed to continue to operate under such assumptions.

This mom had experienced an abusive and violent childhood, so it was understandable that she wanted to avoid parent-child conflict. But even with her difficult history, she was able to work through her discomfort with conflict to change her definition of the good parent and begin asserting more authority with clear limits and consistent consequences for her son's negative behaviors. She developed a mantra of reminding herself that raising the bar in this way was essential for helping her son develop the skills he would need to adapt well to the structures of school, work, and mature relationships. The boy responded well to this change; many of his negative behaviors vanished over a short period of time. What a success for both mom and her son!

This case illustrates that exercising the parental power you have to set and enforce rules is an important part of parenting because it helps socialize children. I think of the job of parenting as one that's really about getting our kids ready to head out into the world and function effectively around other people. One aspect of this is certainly the ability to respect authority figures, follow rules, and make good behavior choices. Using the authority arm of parenting helps kids develop these skills; it also adds valuable structure and containment to a child's experience, which is especially important for kids who are very persistent and often test boundaries. Remember that until they're in their early twenties, kids' brains are not fully developed, so clear authority can be reassuring for them because it lets them know that someone else is in charge of the bigger picture.

Despite the fact that authority provides kids with a degree of security and structure that is helpful to them, they often rally against it! This is bound to happen because normal child development includes the desire to test, especially in the periods roughly between two- and five-years-old as well as twelve- and sixteen-years-old. This desire to test you isn't actually a desire to test but a desire to define themselves. Self-definition is essential for survival outside of the family unit, and it's why kids are so determined to practice it with us. Helping our kids work their way through these developmental periods to eventually get to a place where they feel strong and sure in themselves (because they have tested limits and defined themselves) is important. However, at the same time we want them to learn the limits of their power (not end up arrogant, demanding or entitled) and to learn to respect adults' authority. Creating this balance, between our power (authority) and theirs, is essential, and it is a product of appropriately exercising the authority arm of parenting.

The Value of Protest

Protest happens. By that, I mean that the feeling of *not* wanting something will come up for both kids and adults. It happens a lot for kids, especially in response to adult authority. Adult authority holds so much of the power in the parent-child relationship, and the lives of children are also controlled by others so much of the time. These dynamics create a natural reaction of protest in children, which needs to be managed in a constructive way. And since protest is at its core a feeling, we're back to the two choices about how the feeling will be expressed: through behavior or language.

It might seem paradoxical, but it's actually helpful to encourage kids who give us too much resistance to protest more. However, I'm not talking about having them do more of what they're already doing. I'm talking about *cooperative* protest, the kind where they put into words what they don't want while we listen and validate. Then we work together on problem solving the dilemma with a compromise that they and we can both live with. If you look at kids who are regularly behaving poorly, you will often see that the skill of constructive protest is missing. Sometimes this is because they never learned that they *could* protest, and other times it's because these kids have tried to defend their ideas at home but their parents shut them down.

The ability to protest effectively is linked to the skill of self-assertion, or the ability to stand up for oneself. In fact, protest and self-assertion require the same core skill of emotional communication. A few things make protest a little different and harder for kids than other forms of emotional communication, which is worth our stopping to think about here. Protesting is different from just sharing feelings because it requires kids to confront adults, adding a major stressor for the child. Also, when kids *do* protest to adults, they often get in trouble or at the very least get a negative reaction. This happens with adults who have the misconception that kids shouldn't protest because it's not respectful—though, for some reason, in their minds often it's fine for adults to protest. This double standard overlooks the fact that kids have feelings too, and some of their feelings don't agree with adults'. Another thing is that kids often don't get the guidance they need to develop constructive protesting skills, and so they're left to figure out for themselves how to do it. All of these factors combine to make protesting a difficult task for children. With natural feelings of opposition and self-determination ebbing and flowing and little guidance from adults, kids often default to the methods their young minds come up with, such as whining, manipulating, or holding their feelings in until they explode. Of course, such forms of protest or defiance end up reinforcing many adults' ideas that kids who protest are simply problematic and should be met with a stronger adult protest. This line of thinking is flawed, however, because responding to a child's protests by simply increasing adult authority is a recipe for becoming stuck in a cycle of escalating reactivity between parent and child.

Where does all this leave us then? We need to teach our kids how to channel their natural feelings of resistance into a constructive process that allows for opposition but remains respectful toward others. It also means that if we want our children to stick up for themselves out in the world, we can't simply shut down their attempts to protest at home. The muscle of protest they exercise with us is the same muscle they will use to stand up to the bully at school.

Either our kids will have the strength to identify situations they don't like, will know what to say about it, be permitted to state their position, and have practice doing so skillfully, or they won't. This doesn't mean that we should allow inappropriate protests such as yelling, hitting, threatening, etc. But it does mean that we're careful not to shut down the skill of protest entirely. We want to work with our kids to help them learn to protest constructively so that they can go out into the world with a good sense of what doesn't feel right and the courage to state it. Protest is also the first step toward negotiation and compromise, and so protest is a valuable part of constructive problem solving with others.

Authority in Balance

To avoid problems, the authority arm of parenting needs to be delivered in a balanced way. There is real danger in overusing the authority arm, in focusing only on our kids following rules. Depending on a child's temperament, the overuse of parental authority could result in a few different problems. If your child is fairly sensitive and you assert too much authority by over-controlling, you run the risk of creating a compliant but lost child. Sensitive kids are pleasers, and they will often submit to the agenda of others, which doesn't encourage their internal strength. These kids can end up having a hard time making choices for themselves and asserting themselves with others. This may lead them to take a passive role in friendships or set the stage for them to be the victim of bullying. These kids can also become dependent on others to guide them and feel lost when required to make their own decisions. Although it's great for parents when kids don't resist authority, having such compliant kids actually becomes a burden for them because they have to tell the child what to do all the time. Without the power that resisting authority stirs in kids, they don't develop independence; instead, they are left to be followers. So, not over-controlling sensitive children will help them learn to think and act for themselves, giving them a sense of internal strength and direction.

Children who are very persistent present a different challenge to authority. When too much authority is applied to persistent children, it creates rebellion. Their temperament is designed to operate at high levels of independence, so they respond to too much control with a counterattack that lets us know they're not getting the chance they need to be in charge. These kids will oppose any system that is too oppressive and will tantrum, hit, or adopt other oppositional stances to communicate this. Any lessons we try to impart with an overuse of authority will be lost on them because they will be too invested in opposition to learn about the lesson we want to teach them. These kids have a developmental need to be independent that is stronger than their need for approval. If pushed to choose, they will choose to retain some control over their lives, even if it negatively impacts their relationship with their parents.

I often remind parents, "Don't value the lesson over the child." We don't want our kids to feel as though we're more interested in the point we're trying to make than we are in *them*. This happens when authority is overused—often delivered in the form of a lecture or a one-way conversation. Such a teaching moment is problematic because the adult is so focused on pushing his or her idea that the child's experience is overlooked. Kids have an outstanding sense of when the lecture is about to start, and most of the time, they're already thinking about other things by the time the lecture gets underway. The information that is lost during a typical lecture is great, and so the lecture becomes a waste of time for both the child and the parent. In addition, sometimes lectures will produce such strong resentment in children over time that the parent-child relationship is damaged.

Let's look at an example. Dylan, a seven year-old boy, wants to quit baseball. His father says "no," and they are now in a fight. The father wants Dylan to learn about commitment and being a team player. The more he pushes Dylan to play, the more Dylan complains. The father thinks, "This is exactly why I need to make him do this," and feels justified. Dylan's father lectures Dylan on commitment and being a team player several times. The boy gives in and stays on the team, but they don't speak about it anymore.

Thirty years later, Dylan is in my office talking to me, and what he remembers about the event is that it was the moment he decided he hated team sports. Furthermore, it was when he lost respect for his father, and when he thinks about it all these years later, he still feels angry with his dad. In this real scenario, the father's emphatic focus on "the lesson" was lost because he did not bring enough focus to his son's experience. Not only was the lesson lost, it backfired, creating a negative association with the subject of team sports as well as resentment toward the dad. Things would have worked out much better if the father had attuned to Dylan and helped him communicate his feelings about baseball. The father could have validated Dylan's position and created an alliance of understanding. After that, the father could have helped Dylan understand his desire for his son to learn about commitment and the team experience. Then they could have moved on to the next step of working together to find a way for Dylan to practice commitment and team activity in a form that was tolerable for him. The lessons would have been learned, and a moment of relating and mutual respect would have been created instead of a memory of resentment and disconnect.

Dylan didn't tell me this, but my guess is that this was not the only occasion when he felt his Dad was overinvested in his idea and underinvested in Dylan's experience. The kind of resentment that Dylan held toward his father is usually the culmination of many missed opportunities for parent-child attunement. One or two "hard lessons" probably won't damage a parent-child relationship, but many will. So balance the lessons to be learned with a focus on your child's thoughts and feelings, and you'll be in good shape. Not only will your child absorb the lessons you want to impart but also these teaching moments will be remembered as moments of connection between the two of you. There's so much for us to teach our children, but the teaching will not be absorbed if the relationship is abandoned in the process.

Authority is essential to effective parenting, but the topic is not as simple as it seems. Overusing and underusing authority can create difficulties in the parent-child relationship, ranging from overcompliance to active rebellion on the child's part. Effective use of the arm of authority involves exercising it with balance, with an awareness of the child's feelings, and with an awareness of their developmental need for power, independence, and protest. If we can keep this in mind, we will exercise the authority arm of parenting appropriately and provide our kids with the behavioral guidance they need.

Chapter Summary

Here is a recap of some of the highlights and tips presented in this chapter:

- Understand the importance of exercising *the authority arm* of parenting.
- Define the parent unit as the seat of power in your family.
- Create clear family rules and communicate expectations for children's behavior.
- Watch out for issues that prevent you from holding clear authority e.g. your own discomfort with conflict.
- Be your child's guide, not his or her best friend.
- Understand the value of protest. Help your kids practice constructive protest that decreases acting out and contributes to cooperative negotiation.
- Respect your child's assertions and opinions, but don't tolerate them being delivered through negative behavior.
- Don't value the lesson over the child. In other words, skip the lecture and instead engage your child in conversations about why problems are occurring.
- Keep authority in balance. Understand how much is needed given the situation and the child's temperament. Too much or too little creates additional problems.

Chapter 4

∞

Maintaining Balance

How do we present enough authority to guide our children, while not creating the problems that can come from the overuse of our power? It all comes back to keeping things in balance. Adults need to maintain balanced authority in their relationships with their kids, which means maintaining a balance of power, control and decision-making. This balance comes from not only helping kids practice respecting parents' authority but also from allowing them a voice and opportunities to assert their need for independence and control.

At times, adults need kids to simply comply with their requests—no questions asked. But kids also need to experience moments of having things go their way. Still, at other times, adults and kids need to work together to create compromise solutions. In each of these scenarios empathy and authority are adjusted and presented at different levels. I developed the 60-20-20 Rule to give parents a general guide for how to maintain a balance between empathy and authority in their parenting. Many parents have found the 60-20-20 Rule helpful.

There are times when your child needs to experience total control. By this I mean that they need to have things go their way without too many adult ideas getting in the way. These are the times when you will practice pure emotional attunement (the empathy arm) and give your child the opportunity to feel like he or she can have things just the way they want. Kids hear a lot of *no's* and have to do a lot of compromising, so hearing a plain old *yes* is music to their ears.

You can give your child this type of experience by turning the reins over to them occasionally. Use situations where you're not too invested in the outcome or where you feel confident your child's judgment as *the decider* will be exercised soundly. Being in charge of decisions helps kids exercise their developmental need for control and also helps them practice responsibility. About 20 percent of the time, say yes to their ideas and let them have their way. Again, make sure the idea is safe and reasonable. If it is, then it might be a good time to let your child feel the power of being in charge. Decisions like where to go out to eat, which movie to rent, what radio station to listen to in the car, what family game to play, etc., are all small opportunities to let your child practice being in the driver's seat. If you can feed their need for power and control some of the time, your child will be better able to tolerate the other 20 percent of the time when he or she must adapt to you.

So the other 20 percent is the exact opposite. This is the portion of time when you require your child to do things your way—when *you* get to be in charge. Kids need to have a clear concept of authority and need to be able to adapt to the requirements of others, so this is an equally important skill to practice. As parents, there are times when we need to assert pure authority and either don't have the time or the desire to look too deeply into the child's experience. During these times, it's okay to take a non-negotiable stance, which includes not engaging in long explanations about why we're making the decision that we're making. These are typically situations where we feel strongly about how things need to go or are in a hurry and need our children to flex to our needs. These instances usually include the occasions when you find yourself using the old *"because I said so!"* expression. Again, as long as this type of parent-child interaction is contained to about 20 percent of the time, there's nothing wrong with setting firm limits and having our children learn to just accept that that's the way it is. In fact, it's more than okay; it's essential for kids to have this type of experience with authority because it can keep them safe too. Kids need to know that when adults set clear limits, such as not running into the street, that the adult means business and that the limit will not change. That way when the parent uses that *I-mean-it* voice, the child will stop, listen, and be kept safe. Limits like this keep kids safe and prepare them for the real world. For the rest of their days, our kids will have to practice flexing to the requirements of authority figures such as teachers, coaches, and later employers, who will set limits that aren't open to negotiation. Use the *my-way-or-the-highway* parenting stance to set clear, unmovable limits with your kids about 20 percent of the time to provide them with all the benefits yielding to authority can give them.

You'll notice that we've only covered about 40 percent of our parenting time so far. What should we be practicing with our kids the rest of the time? The other 60 percent of the time should be devoted to cooperative negotiation. These are situations where parents use both the empathy and authority arms to help kids negotiate for their needs effectively. Joint Problem Solving and the Review are two great ways to accomplish this and are explained fully in Chapters 1 and 7. The important point here is to remember that the bulk of parenting should be focused on solving problems with our children by working with them to apply flexibility and cooperation to come up with solutions that work for both parties. Having this process be the main way that you solve problems helps your child develop all of the core skills. It also infuses your relationship with a sense of respect and mutual understanding, which will help your child want to cooperate and keep a constructive attitude with you. The skill of negotiating, or working with others to get everyone's needs met, is a critical skill for our kids because it is the key ingredient in successful personal and professional relationships.

One additional thought about negotiation, which is that it's important to differentiate constructive negotiation from competition. Constructive negotiation, the kind you should be working on about 60 percent of the time, is all about mutual understanding and flexibility. It's about finding solutions together and creating a win-win; it's the opposite of competition. Some kids get used to engaging in negotiation as a competitive practice with the goal of wearing you down so you'll give in. In this case, the goal is much different from cooperative negotiation; I call this kind of behavior tactic "the legal department." Some kids will try to get you into the legal department in order to keep the conversation alive and not have to deal with your final answer. They will argue the definition of every term you use and ask irrelevant questions to keep the conversation going. This behavior isn't actually negotiation; it's manipulation and needs to be treated as such. In this kind of situation, you would treat the *negotiation* like any other negative behavior and move in with the authority arm to set a limit, state clearly that the decision is made, and let them know that the conversation is over. Kids who try to pull you into the legal department are kids who need to practice either constructive negotiation or acceptance of the parent's final answer.

There are many ways to apply the 60-20-20 Rule in family life. It's certainly good for balancing power and empathy, but you can also apply this idea to create more balance in many other situations. Think of the general rule as 20 percent of the time you take a firm stance with your child and 20 percent of the time you take a permissive stance. Then the other 60 percent of the time you engage in a process that contains dialogue about each of your positions and an agreement that the outcome will be mutually satisfying. An example of this can be found when it's time to clean up. A small portion of the time, you will just clean up the messes that your kid makes. Kids, especially younger kids, do make a lot of messes and can't possibly clean up after everything they do. Because kids' brains are occupied with the job of learning and their awareness of their surroundings is limited, it's helpful and appropriate for adults to pick up some of the pieces they miss along the way. On the other hand, we do want our kids to learn about responsibility, so another small portion of the time we will insist that they alone clean things up, and we will take a hard line on this. This will help them begin to absorb the notion that as they grow, they need to increasingly pick up after themselves. In addition, it will help them develop respect for the times when we take a firm stance on an issue with them. All of the rest of the time, which is the bulk of the time we spend with our kids, we will talk to them about the need to clean up after themselves and counsel them to put things back before they take even more toys out. We will hold the bigger picture and remind them when we see things getting really messy. And whenever they end up with a mountain of toys strewn about the whole room, which they will, we will sit with them and work on a plan to get it all put away. If they feel overwhelmed with amount there is to clean up, we can offer to team up with them and do part of the job—as long as they do their part too. We will also remind them to thank us for helping them with their mess. Finally, we will help them think about a plan for the next time that won't leave them with a situation that is too hard to fix by themselves. In this way, we are not simply doing it for them (20 percent) or taking a hard line (20 percent) but instead combining our efforts in a flexible and cooperative way to problem solve situations that get difficult (60 percent).

Using the 60-20-20 Rule to maintain balance in the parent-child relationship is helpful because it orients kids primarily to work with others to create solutions, while allowing for total freedom when appropriate and total respect when requested. Stop and think for a moment about how you solve problem situations with your child. Do you give too much? Do you overwhelm them with your absolute stance and inflexible rules? Or are you able to keep things in balance by letting some things go, taking some things on, and also spending a lot of time helping them learn how to cooperate with others to create win-win solutions? Maintaining this balance of empathy and authority, or permissiveness and power, can be hard for all parents. Many of us were parented with an overemphasis on one of the 60-20-20 areas, which can make it hard to find and maintain a position of balance. Still, it's an aspect of parenting that's worth stopping to think about because it has such a big impact not only on the skills our kids learn but also on the tone of our relationship with them. Keep the 60-20-20 Rule in mind to help you exercise appropriate amounts of permissiveness and authority with your child. It's an effective guide that can be applied to many situations to add balance to your overall parenting approach.

Your Parenting Training—Filling in the Gaps

All of this focus on balance, emotions, and helping kids manage themselves might feel a bit foreign to you. If this is the case, don't be alarmed—it's just a matter of training. Helping kids learn about and practice the skills they need to function well might come fairly naturally to you, or this could feel like you're being asked to land an airplane without ever having gone to flight school. If the latter is the case, not to worry: the fact is that many of us didn't get a lot of training in this department from our families when we were growing up, and so we can't be expected to approach this piece of parenting work with ease and confidence. Some of us even got programmed with misinformation about how to help kids learn and grow, and so we need to work to overcome those influences while adding new parenting skills. This can certainly be a lot of work. The good news is that what I'm talking about is a set of skills that anyone can learn with practice—nothing more. To apply these practices, you don't have to be a natural or have some special parenting gift or intuition; you need only patience and the desire to create change. So for those of us who didn't get the training we needed, for instance, to tune into our kids' feelings and validate them, or to keep empathy and authority in balance, we just have to keep practicing our skills so that we get better at helping our kids develop theirs.

On the emotional front, we all come from whatever family culture our parents or caregivers created for us. For some families, there was a lot of focus on how members of the family felt about things. Some lucky kids even got help with problem solving their emotional dilemmas, and so now, as adults, they have the natural ability to help their kids with these kinds of situations. On the other hand, many other parents had very little, if any, focus on feelings when they were kids as a part of their original family culture. Maybe this was because their parents were emotionally shut down themselves, or maybe it was more a product of the traditions from the culture of another country. Either way, many of us were shortchanged in this department, and so now, as adults, we have to learn to pay attention to the emotional aspect of relationships to be able to make them work. For these parents, this part of the parenting job does not feel natural or easy, and it couldn't. We can't be expected to foster emotional development in our current family life if we were never exposed to it in our family while we were growing up. Parenting just doesn't work that way; you can't be expected to teach what you didn't learn. So although the job of filling in the emotional gap is hard, it is not impossible. Just because we didn't get the training from our parents doesn't mean that we're not responsible for taking on the work. In fact, we are, and we need to do our best to learn these skills so that we can help our kids learn to be emotionally healthy.

It's possible that growing up in your family there wasn't enough focus on things like consistency, rules, boundaries and consequences. If your childhood felt like a free-for-all, then you likely inherited some gaps in your parental training in the authority area. If this is the case, then this will be a parenting area where you struggle. The struggle usually manifests itself in one of two ways: either you continue the pattern of disorganization and low structure that your parents practiced, or you swing to the opposite end and focus rigidly on rules, boundaries, and consistency. The problem with either of these styles is that they are out of balance, tilting too far toward the extreme in either direction. Parents who simply do what their parents did, even though it didn't work well, will create the same set of difficulties for their own kids. On the other hand, parents who just do the opposite of what their parents did are parenting from a reactive stance, which doesn't work well either. If you find yourself *under-* or *over-*focusing on family life being organized, respectful, or in control, then you need to think about how your parenting is being influenced by your own parents. Solving problems always starts with increased clarity on the causes or influences that are helping to create the problem. If you can keep an eye on balance and think a bit about the influences at play (such as your parents' parenting style), then you have the ability to break free from the patterns that were programmed into you during your childhood and instead choose your own balanced parenting approach. If you're struggling in this area, again, remember that it's not your fault. Just like with emotions, you can't be expected to teach something to your kids that you weren't taught. You can, however, decide to work on filling in these gaps to ensure that your kids get the right amount of structure, consistency, and guidance they need to be successful.

You may find yourself feeling emotionally overwhelmed and lost as you begin to practice new skills with your kids. New interpersonal skills can be hard to develop, and changing the way you've always done things can be a monumental task. This is especially true on the emotional front. You will likely be emotionally triggered by your children and may be surprised by how reactive you are. You may, for instance, feel on some level resentful that your kids get this kind of sensitive consideration when you didn't. These feelings are natural and can be expected. There is a child inside all of us who still wants to be seen and understood, and this inner child might very well be jealous of your kids getting this kind of emotional attunement. Allow this. Accept and honor your own emotional process, just as you're learning to do for your kids. You can't change what you did or didn't get in your childhood, but you can start doing two important things now. First, start to help your kids develop the emotional and behavioral skills they need for a solid foundation. And second, be patient with yourself. This job of filling in our parenting gaps is hard, and it takes time to get it all down. Stay in touch with your own feelings as they come up and allow them the patience and respect they deserve while you're in the process of learning all this. When it feels overwhelming, don't forget: it's just a set of skills, which you can learn and get good at with practice. I know this is true, because I've done it myself.

If you do find yourself frequently overwhelmed with your own feelings toward your kids, it is a sign that there is work for you to do in this area. If, for instance, your kids are triggering a lot of anger or frustration in you, and you are having a hard time dealing with your feelings, then you've got some work to do: either to fill in or to repair the emotional gaps your parents left you. Speaking of repair; if you have parented from a reactive, angry or otherwise mis-attuned position (we all have) in the past, sit with your child and do some repair. Explain to him or her that you are learning too and apologize for your past behavior and the less-than-optimal ways you were parenting. A little repair goes a long way to heal wounds from the past and allow both parent and child to forgive and move on.

If you read this book, practice the skills in it, and are still having a hard time controlling your reactivity or making the changes you want to make—get help. Find a good counselor or therapist with a focus on parenting, and get some support. Filling in the gaps in our parenting can be extremely hard work. It is possible though. Remember: it's just a set of skills. I often tell parents, "We all have gaps in our parenting skills. The best parents are not the ones who do everything perfect, but the ones who know where their gaps are and are willing to work on them." You are a great parent already, and the proof is that you're reading a book about how to be a better parent, which means that you're way ahead of the curve already. It also means you're self-aware, motivated, and proactive—which are all elements of a solid parenting foundation. Use your motivation to fill in some of the gaps you inherited from your parents, and you will be an even better parent.

Your Parenting Legacy

The importance of making needed changes in your parenting can't be understated because you will be changing the family culture from here on out. *You* will be the one to stop a legacy of emotional misattunement or behavioral inconsistency. Think about it: this means that your children will inherit a complete set of parenting skills, which they will download to their kids, who will automatically pass them along to future generations. You will be the tipping point in your ancestral line, where a new kind of engagement between parent and child was instituted—one that gives both children and parents the essential skills they need to get along and learn effectively from family life. You will be responsible for this change in your family's history, and it will affect many, many people down the line.

This is not just a romantic, feel-good idea. This is how human behavior works. Traditions, in this case parenting traditions, are practiced and then become engrained in family culture as the way things are done. These traditions are passed down through the generations, largely unconsciously, and are seen by family members as an extension of their identity and value system. Some traditions get discarded along the way, because they are seen by newer generations as not fitting well with contemporary culture. However, these are typically traditions that are not essential, such as what families do on vacations or birthdays. Traditions that serve important functions, however, are retained—and there is no more important function than the set of practices that define child rearing. This is why the traditions of the past have persisted so long. Core traditions are slow to change, but they do change—if the new traditions create more success for the family unit. The changes you are making with your attention to things like balanced authority and emotional attunement will create better and stronger family relationships and more behavioral success for the children. These new traditions will be kept alive in future generations because they create good parent-child relations and contribute to a positive and successful family unit. You will be the one to develop these new family traditions, and future generations will have you to thank.

Self-Care

So, we understand that the work of filling in our parenting gaps is essential, and the work can be very hard. Parenting is a hard job to begin with, without all these extra skills to think about! In fact, this job of parenting can be so taxing and confusing that it can literally wear us out. All of us experience this from time to time, and many parents find themselves fantasizing about escaping to a remote, silent oasis, free from the demands and struggles of the parenting gig. Managing other people is not an easy job, and as we talked about earlier, we all come with different skill sets, depending on the parenting we were exposed to as children. Knowing what our parenting gaps are and working to fill them in will help, but there's also the matter of sheer day-to-day survival.

We will talk about kids' temperaments later, but for now, remember that you have a temperament too. You need to know what kinds of things recharge you and help bring balance to your personal life. We are not good for our children unless we are in good shape ourselves. Some people recharge through activating. If you feel rejuvenated and restored by going out and being around action or people, then you need to work some of that into daily life. This kind of energy-hungry temperament often enjoys a good deal of physical activity, like sports or exercise, to release built-up tension and stress. If this is part of your temperament, then you need to make time to escape through activation and action. Get outside and move your body. Connect with friends and exchange ideas, or go out and do something that is fun and exciting for you. Get away from the usual routine, and add some energy to your life. You will feel better.

On the other hand, many people recharge by getting quiet. These are the more sensitive temperaments of people who become overloaded by the day-to-day hustle and bustle of family life. This kind of nervous system needs to "down regulate," or return to a state of rest and quietness. These people will be restored by being alone, reading, walking in nature, or practicing yoga or meditation. They may rejuvenate through time spent with others, but it will be with one other person, having a cup of coffee and a quiet, deep conversation, versus being at something like a sports event.

Regardless of the type of system you have, plan to schedule regular recharge time for yourself—even in small amounts. If you give yourself small, regular escapes, then you will spend much less time daydreaming about being somewhere else. Experiment with activities to see what works best for you. Do anything, but don't do nothing! Skipping self-care is one of the most common problems I see with parents, and it's easy to see why it happens. Family, work, social events, and the needs of the children don't leave parents a lot of time to think about themselves. This is especially true for the parents of young kids. However, we need to remember that skipping self-care is a recipe for parents burning out, and it can have disastrous results for the whole family. Tired, frazzled, depleted, unsatisfied, out-of-balance parents aren't good for anyone.

If you're reading this book because your child has been diagnosed with a developmental issue such as ADHD, Autism, Sensory Processing Disorder, or a learning disability, then there is another aspect of self-care that I want to mention. Before we have our kids, we all engage in fantasizing about how it's going to go. We do this out of excitement and anticipation as well as the worry that getting ready to become a parent can bring. This is natural, and despite all the descriptions others provide for us, we don't acquire a true understanding of the parenting experience until the little one arrives and we're in it for real. For everyone, this is a major adjustment that will bring up many layers of feelings. However, for parents who have a child born with developmental differences—including unusual temperament profiles (such as very sensitive, highly reactive, very active, etc.)—this adjustment can be much more difficult. If this is the case with you, then in addition to the many stressors of having a new child, you have also had to endure the additional confusion and worry about what's going on with your child. Parents of children who are developmentally challenged deal with much higher levels of anxiety, stress, and uncertainty than parents of kids who fall closer to the developmental norm.

One aspect of this unique experience is the emotional consequence of having a child show up who is in some way different than what you had expected. If this difference is minor, parents will adjust more easily, but if the difference is significant, parents can be left with feelings of resentment, disappointment, jealousy of others, or sadness. Good self-care in these situations requires that the parents allow themselves to be in touch with their feelings about the difference between how they thought it would be and how it is. This doesn't mean that the parents don't love their child unconditionally or that they're rejecting their child. On the contrary, it means that the parents love their child and themselves enough to be honest about their feelings about it all. If you're one of these parents, it may also mean that you need to be in touch with feelings of grief and sadness. Parents who have kids with developmental differences can get so caught up in trying to figure out what's going on with their child and how best to help, that they often don't stop to honor their own emotional process—which likely includes some grieving. Nobody wants a hard parenting road, but some of us get it. Slowing down to *feel* is essential because it allows parents to release the emotional stress and tension they're holding. It also then allows them to loosen their grip on past ideas about how they thought things should go and instead focus their energies on what is actually happening. Parents who can process and release the stress and emotions that accumulate have the best chance of being fully present for the current challenges that need their attention and energy.

Self-care also means self-forgiveness. Children aren't the only ones making mistakes along the road of family life. We need to have tolerance for our own misguided moments. They will happen, and either we can apply the same perspective we use with our kids—that mistakes are moments of important learning—or we can get down on ourselves, which is not useful to anyone. Our kids are depending on our ability to recover successfully from our blunders, not only to maintain stability in family life but also to model for them kindness toward one's self. So, admit your mistakes to your kids, and be nice to yourself in the process. Don't try to be the perfect parent—she doesn't exist and neither does he!

If you're the type of person who is hard on yourself when you blow it, develop some positive mantras to say to yourself during these difficult moments. Say them out loud so that your kids can hear them. You might say: "Well, that was a mistake, but I learned something important," or "Oops! that was a bad one. Better remember to be nice to myself." Your kids are watching and learning how to treat themselves by observing your example. Talk to your kids about how hard it is to let go of guilt. Ask them what they say to themselves silently when they make a mistake. Make sure they have some supportive coping statements to whisper in kindness to themselves when they don't do things right. Remind them frequently that learning requires mistakes and that part of learning from mistakes is learning not to beat ourselves up, but instead to learn what the mistake teaches and to forgive ourselves and move on.

Practice good physical and emotional self-care. Teach your kids some of the self-care practices that work well for you. This not only gives them a great orientation to good self-care but also likely gives them activities that will align with their temperaments as well as yours. If you're into yoga, teach your child some poses and breathing techniques. If you rewind through sports, show your kids some of the things you do to release built-up energy. Kids love to do what their parents do, so as you take care of your own stress relief, you can teach your kids a few of the same tricks as well. And don't forget emotional self-care too, which includes self-forgiveness. Processing and releasing our feelings through talking with others, journaling, and the like, prevents parent burnout and models good emotional self-care for our kids.

Couple Care

On a similar note, it is equally important to preserve the parents' relationship. This means creating a good boundary around the relationship you enjoy with your spouse or partner. You can do this by having regular time away with each other and having conversations about things other than the daily grind. Communication creates intimacy—or more correctly, personal communication creates intimacy. So stay close to your partner by talking about your hopes, dreams and interests, those things that are personally relevant to each of you. Don't lose track of the original relationship that started this whole family thing in the first place! If there isn't a significant other currently in the picture, then make sure you preserve the other closest relationships to you. Kids benefit from this modeling because they see that caring for others doesn't require total self-sacrifice. This modeling will help our kids manage their own relationships better and care for themselves when they become the leaders of their own families.

Too many parents come to me in a state of relationship burnout. They're doing a good job of parenting but have put the maintenance of the couple relationship on the back burner for so long that they feel more like roommates than partners. The bulk of their communication is about the family calendar and the multitude of stressors and logistics of family life. This kind of pace and focus keeps food on the table and the schedule running, but it also creates personal disconnect. Many parents report feeling closer to their kids than they do their spouse, which is a problem. Of course, it's fine to be close to your kids, but the dynamics of family life shouldn't take up so much energy that there is none left for the leadership. Anyone in business knows that a successful company needs management to be well connected—leaders who are not only connected to the needs of the employees but also connected to each other. Preserve your family's first relationship by getting away from the kids and calendar and reconnecting as a couple.

Stop and remember the thoughts and feelings you had for

your partner when you first met, and realize that those feelings have not gone with time but are buried under the busy life you've created together. Then reach back in time and pull those feelings to the present. Make room in your current life to keep those memories and feelings with you in your present moments. And make sure to communicate them! Feelings that go unspoken lose their power to connect. I've treated lots of couples who thought their relationship had withered and died because there were no signs of love left. Many were surprised to find that there was still deep love that they had simply forgotten to communicate. Turns out it was the communication in their relationship that had died, not their feelings for each other.

Reconnecting is more about time together and communication than a fancy destination, so make the time and find the place—no excuses. Also, make it face-to-face time. Watching a movie or a TV show is not the same as time spent looking into each other's eyes. As they say, the eyes are the windows to the soul, which neuroscience shows has a scientific basis: eye contact facilitates the release of bonding hormones such as oxytocin, which help to build attachment and emotional connection between people. If the parents' relationship has been neglected for a while, spend some time looking into each other's eyes and find again that person you used to crave.

Here are some tips to increase and strengthen the family leadership's bond:

- Call your partner unexpectedly to remember a fun time together.
- Leave a love note.
- Ask your partner about the best and the worst parts of his or her day.
- Plan a cheap date.
- Go through some of your photos together from the time before you became parents. Remember funny or fun times you've had.
- Hug, hold hands or put your arm around your partner. Initiate touch.
- Meet for a mid-day lunch or coffee.
- Get outdoors together—sunshine and fresh air invigorate.

Notice that these suggestions are neither complicated nor expensive but instead geared toward increasing partner connection and communication. Be creative and make your own list. You'll be surprised how the old feelings come rushing back when you simply make the space to stop for a moment and reconnect to the person you used to know.

Working Together

We each come to this job of parenting with a specific set of skills and experiences that we use to solve day-to-day problems. We call this our "parenting style," and much has been written already on the topic. Suffice it to say that parenting styles go from being very permissive to very authoritarian, with most parents falling somewhere in between. Parenting styles are also impacted by the adult's own temperament, which influences how a parent approaches teaching a child the many lessons of life. I will discuss temperament in detail in the next chapter, but since it's relevant to parenting style, I'll get started here.

For example, parents whose temperaments are fairly high in sensitivity may include a lot of structure and planning in their parenting. When it comes to making parenting decisions, they are likely to go slow and consider all of the details and possible outcomes before taking action. For a sensitive adult, a high degree of structure and planning creates predictability and lowers anxiety—something highly sensitive people are prone to experience. So, a well-planned activity is an enjoyable activity for the sensitive adult. On the other hand, parents who have a lot of energy or impulsivity in their temperament may like it much better if their plans are made on the fly. This fits with a temperament that enjoys action, energy, and the discoveries that can be made along the way when things aren't all mapped out. Too much planning throws a wet blanket on this kind of person's outing because it actually decreases the chance for an experience that feeds the need for action, novelty, and movement.

When partners have very different temperaments, working together can be challenging. What feels good for one parent might be torturous for the other. A good deal of communication and flexibility are needed from both partners when their temperaments contribute to very different parenting styles.

Another big contributor to our parenting style comes from

the influence of our own childhood. We each bring a unique set of skills and values that we inherit growing up in our families. These learned parenting traits can be a source of connection and commonality with our partners or a source of conflict. Ultimately it's good for kids to have parents who each contribute different ideas and experiences, but this can also make the job of parents working together more challenging.

Given the fact that we all have our own individual temperament as well as our own set of parenting skills that we bring to the job, it's easy to understand how parents can get stuck when trying to work together. This is especially true when dealing with difficult behaviors because they can turn up the heat on the parents' relationship. Parenting is a hard job in the first place, but if you add to the mix a kid with a developmental difference, a challenging temperament, or a difficult behavior pattern, then you've got a recipe that can at times push the parents' relationship to its brink.

Working together in a cooperative and supportive fashion is difficult when stress is high because we all revert back to more primitive, self-protective behavior when we're under the weight of extreme stress. When the heat is turned up, our focus narrows as we go into survival mode to preserve ourselves. This kind of stress response, which can occur for short, acute periods or develop into long-term chronic patterns, shifts our focus from one of teamwork to one of going it alone. Kids, career stress, financial difficulties, and other life stressors can all push us into this narrow mindset, which sidelines our ability to stay on the same team.

When under stress, parents often revert to the ideas they're most comfortable with. For instance, if a four-year-old is having an uncontrollable tantrum, and nothing seems to be helping, an otherwise united couple might start to question each other's approach for handling the stressful event. The parent whose training and temperament lean toward an empathic approach might begin to see the correct solution as the child needing more soothing, but this would be directly opposite from the parent who leans toward a disciplinary approach and sees the answer as setting firmer limits for the child. The more stress that's introduced into the moment, the more likely it is that each partner will back into his or her respective corner and commit to the route most natural for them. This is okay if the parents can remain flexible and still work together to combine their ideas and influences. However, what often happens is that as stress increases we recede into our own corner and grip our ideas about how to solve the problem tighter and tighter. As we slip into survival mode our focus narrows and we convince ourselves that *our* way is the right way, and so our partner's position seems more and more "wrong," and our view of them begins to distort. When this happens, we can begin to see our partner as part of the problem—at times, even the enemy.

This is the moment when you could turn on each other and break the bonds of united parenting. Like former teammates now pitted against each other for the championship win, you will no longer note the common ideas linking you together but instead all of the differences between you. All the differences and all the frustrations of the moment will be directed not toward solving the problem in front of you but toward the big win of your idea over theirs. This is an unfortunate moment that is not simply the domain of dysfunctional parents—it will happen to anyone when stressed enough. We have to guard against the breakdown of united parenting with lots of focus on how to stay connected and communicating, especially in the difficult moments.

United parenting means working together—even under extreme stress. Realistically, staying united is more of a goal than a place you could ever be all the time. However, it is useful to put your awareness and efforts into trying to stay united as much as possible because united parenting is stronger parenting and exponentially more effective. Raising kids is a hard job, so you want the influence you have on your children to have maximum effect. Maximum effect means maximum learning for the child, and maximum learning means maximum adapting to the standards you, the adults, have set. This is certainly true for softer moments—like when you want your kids to be in touch with their feelings and the feelings of others—but it's even more important for the tougher moments, when you need to control negative behaviors and enforce rules. To have maximum influence in those moments, you need the synergistic effect of parental teamwork to get your messages heard loud and clear.

It's a fact: kids listen more when both parents are saying it. There's just more influence when the message comes from two people instead of one. This is not to say that single parents can't be effective, because they absolutely can. However, when two parents are present, the message is more deeply absorbed when the child hears similar responses from both adults. Sometimes a child respects the authority of one parent more than the other, so united parenting can bolster the other parent's influence. Sometimes a child will break a household rule and risk rejection from one parent, but the child is much less likely to risk rejection from both parents. So a united stance creates a stronger boundary for negative behaviors. Regardless of the specific situation, the fact remains that the troops are much more likely to fall in line when the commanders are giving the same orders.

I was working with a family recently who couldn't figure out why the kids (ages six and eight) were not respecting the mom's authority. They were talking back to her and frequently disobedient with their behavior. The first thing I checked into was how united the parents were. They reported being totally supportive of each other. They also reported holding the same rules and expectations for the kids, so there wasn't any confusion there. Strangely, the father reported that the kids were fine with him. They listened well, didn't complain much, and acted as though they understood his authority clearly. The mom reported that she also held pretty firm limits and didn't tolerate disrespect from the kids, but for some reason, it didn't work the way it did with dad. They just wouldn't listen to her. This was a genuine mystery—just the kind I like!

I asked them to describe their routine after dad got home from work (mom worked some mornings). Dad reported that his usual routine was to walk into the house and begin playing with the kids. Both dad and the kids had missed each other during the day, so this was a time of great enjoyment for all of them while mom made dinner. Then I asked what happened on the days when the kids had been difficult with mom earlier, and dad said, "Well, I just do the usual, play with the kids and then go say hi to mom." It was time to bring the kids into the conversation. I asked the younger child, "What happens when you disrespect mom?" to which she replied, "Well, she gets mad, but that's about it." Then I asked the older child, "What do you think it means that daddy still plays with you even when you've been mean to mom?" to which he replied, "It means that it's not that big of a deal because we still get our daddy playtime." That was the key we needed to unlock our solution. Neither parent had suspected that the kids were defining automatic playtime with dad, even on days they had disrespected their mom, as dad allowing them to treat mom that way. But that's exactly what the kids thought.

To help, I recommended that the first thing the father do when he gets home, before playing with the kids, is briefly check in with mom to discuss relevant issues from the day, especially the kids' behavior with her. I then instructed mom and dad to address the kids together if there were any problems during the day and to communicate consequences for negative behaviors together. The parents began to do this daily, and this simple change immediately began to shift the kids' behavior toward their mom. The parents fixed a crack in their united front by having dad not only *not* play with the kids on the days they disrespected mom but also stand with her to give the kids a united message of disapproval and necessary consequences. Soon, the kids held the same level of respect for mom that they held for dad, and both parents' stress levels decreased significantly.

This illustrates a point I often make with parents: kids have *all day long* to sit around and notice the cracks in the system! They are watching you for consistency and follow through, and they will take note when there seems to be a different set of rules from each parent. It only makes sense. Because kids are always in the one-down position of power, they are compelled to look for ways to find more power. The cracks in the system are opportunities for kids to move in and exercise their influence. Complicating things further is the fact that because of the limitations in their awareness, kids often define things differently than adults. This means that your child just might assume that because you didn't give the same answer mom gave, you don't agree with her, which can then lead to behavior challenges. With the kids scanning for inconsistencies, searching for power, and potentially misreading the meaning of things, it's no wonder parents need to keep as united a front as they possibly can.

A united front is not only more effective, it's also easier for parents because there's less guesswork about applying rules to kids' behaviors. If you can agree on the basic rules of the house, then you're much less likely to undermine each other (which decreases authority and creates conflict between parents). When parenting isn't fairly united, kids take advantage of the discontinuity, especially when it's time to discipline them. There's nothing more awesome for a kid (maybe you remember) than reaching the moment of discipline and suddenly having the conversation veer off into a fight between the parents about how the rules will be enforced—as the kid quietly slips away unnoticed! If a smart kid sees this happen once, he or she will try to stir the pot from then on, in an attempt to get the parents to bicker and shift their focus from disciplining the child to disagreeing with each other.

Ultimately a united front is easier for the kids too. One set of rules is a lot less complicated than two—or even three if an authority such as a babysitter introduces another set of rules. Also, partners who can form a cohesive front are happier in their relationship because they feel more supported by each other. So, how do we keep the front united when we have different viewpoints and opinions? With communication, flexibility, an understanding of feelings, and respect too. Look familiar? These are the core skills we want our kids to develop. Turns out they're good old-fashioned relationship skills that make everybody, including parents, able to get along better too.

Here are some tips for putting the core skills into action with your partner to create a united front and maximize your parenting power:

- Create an invisible table with your partner, where each of you can put your ideas about parenting. Agree that anything you put on the table will be respected and seriously considered.
- Don't put items on the table when children are misbehaving. Wait until later when you and your partner are calm.
- Remember that a united front is more important than having your idea win.
- When your partner puts an idea on the table, paraphrase what you heard your partner say *first*, before responding with your idea. Say something like, "It sounds like you feel it's important for us to...."
- Keep in mind that there are few "right" or "wrong" ideas in parenting. Mostly there are differences in opinion.
- Model constructive negotiation in front of your child or children.
- Save heated arguments for private expression and resolution.
- Agree that either parent can call for a time-out if things get

heated and that both of you will stop and save it for later.

- Practice being more flexible than your partner.
- Use "I have the same idea as your mother (or father)" often with your child or children, especially if you think your child is working you for a different answer than the one the other parent already gave (also called splitting).
- Try to support your partner's parenting ideas in front of the kids. If you strongly disagree with your partner, bring it up when the kids aren't around.
- Criticism kills relationships. Keep it out of your parenting unit.
- Remember: if your idea wins and your partner's loses, you have won as a competitor but failed as a partner.

A united front also means respecting personal boundaries. Two-parent parenting is a 50-50 game, meaning you own 50 percent of the parenting power. This is true even in cases of divorce where all the rights have been assigned to one parent. Regardless of the circumstance, if both parents participate in the parenting, then the ideas of each should be respected, held valid, or at the very least, be considered. Respecting the opinions of your partner, even when you're sure your partner is wrong, isn't easy, but it is necessary because it creates mutual respect, which makes relationships work. Don't get me wrong: it doesn't mean that you have to agree with all of your partner's ideas, but you do need to give your partner the same consideration you want. It also means that you don't move in on your partner's parenting moment, whether to take over or correct. You wouldn't walk into your neighbor's house and start rearranging the furniture would you? Well, you shouldn't step onto your partner's turf and start messing with his or her parenting either.

So what exactly does this mean? Well, let's say you walk into the house to find your child screaming and your spouse screaming back. You start to get agitated with both of them and want to take control of the situation. Maybe you feel you know exactly what this situation needs and just how to do it. This is the point where you decide to either (1) stop and respect your partner's parenting moment (even if you think your partner is doing it wrong) or (2) step into the conflict and do what you think needs to be done to calm them both down and get things back under control. This is a dilemma because you might, for instance, know that your spouse is a hothead and presently past the point of being able to control the anger in this argument. You also might be really good at calming your child down, so you actually may be the only one in the room with the skills to get this situation back under control. But the question is, do you have the right to step into this fight? The answer is no.

Here's the analogy I use with parents. The person on the front line is the general—everyone else is backup. This means that the parent involved in the conflict with the child at the beginning gets to make the decisions about how to handle the situation. The other parent has the following choices: assist as backup or stay out of the way. Assisting as backup means that you keep in mind that this is your partner's parenting moment, and so you ask your partner before you move in with your ideas. This doesn't necessarily mean that you have to silently watch things deteriorate, but it does mean that you show respect for your partner's turf if you do want to move in to help (or take over). You might say something like "Can I help here?" or "I have an idea if you want to hear it?" If your partner says, "Sure," then you can move in as backup and either add your two cents or take over altogether if it's okay with your partner.

But if your spouse says, "No, I've got it," even if you don't agree, you have to step aside anyway and respect the boundary. This is often very hard for us to do because these are usually emotionally charged moments that make everyone want to take action. In addition, you may know more about why the child is upset or what usually makes the child calm down, and so you may actually be the one who could create the best outcome. However, there's more than outcome going on here. There is the parenting moment, but there's also the partnering moment. The partnering is as important to consider as the parenting. In fact, it's not worth solving the problem with your child if in the process you also undermine your partner. The only situation I can think of in which this boundary should be violated is if in some way the child's safety is at risk. Then, of course, you would move in on your partner's turf without hesitation.

If your partner doesn't want your input in the hot moment, does this then mean that your good ideas go into the trash? Absolutely not. It means that you respect your partner's parenting moment, and later, when things have calmed down, share your view. You might say something like this:

> "Remember when you were really mad at Madeline and I started to tell you what to do, but you told me to let you handle it? Well, I stopped myself because I wanted to respect your parenting moment. But I was really upset because I felt you weren't listening to her. What you didn't know was that she was yelling because Charlie had hit her before you came home, and she was still really mad. I wanted you to know this, but you wouldn't listen, so I backed off. What I want now is to figure out how I can let you know when I have important information to add, without undermining you when you're upset and trying to manage one of the kids. Can we figure out how to do this?"

Then you both go to work to figure out a way for you to move in to get vital information to your partner in an agreed-upon way in the midst of a difficult parenting situation. Maybe there's a certain phrase or a code word that you both agree will be used to alert the other when one of you has important information to add to an escalated parenting moment. When either of you hears the code word, you agree to stop and listen to the information the other has to add to the situation. If you can create a system like this, then you'll have a way to get your ideas heard, even in the midst of your partner's difficult parenting moments. At the same time, you'll be practicing solid partnering by showing respect for the fact that this is your partner's parenting moment you're stepping into. With this kind of respect in place, you're much less likely to undermine and create resentment in your partner. This will add greatly to your ability to create a united front and to take advantage of the many benefits of a solid partnership.

One of these advantages is being able to do "the handoff." The handoff is just what it says: handing the situation over to your partner. This is a valuable intervention if one parent is burned out by the length of the struggle, is too upset, or is simply out of ideas. The thing about the handoff is that it will only work if there's a feeling of trust and respect between partners. Otherwise, it will feel like undermining. Some people ask, "Doesn't using the handoff give the child a message that the parent on the front line can't handle the situation and needs to be bailed out?" Not if you present it right. If you move in on your partner's parenting moment without permission to direct the situation, then you *do* give the message that the parent on the front line is incompetent. Similarly, if you move in not to direct the situation but to rescue the child, then you give the message that the other parent is the villain. Either of these approaches is obviously destructive to the partnership and needs to be avoided. On the other hand, if you move in and say something to your spouse like "You've been dealing with this for a while, do you want me to take over?" then the child hears that you are working together as a team, and relief can be provided while preserving the united front.

If the parenting unit in your family has become fragmented, sit with your spouse or partner and make a plan to create a more united front. Work especially on clear communication, especially for the hot moments, that allows you both to take advantage of all the power and support that a united front can provide.

Chapter Summary

Here is a recap of some of the highlights and tips presented in this chapter:

- Keep in mind the importance of balancing your parenting influences of empathy and authority.
- Use the 60-20-20 Rule as a guide to add balance to the stances you take with your kids.
- Determine where the gaps are in your parent training. We all have them.
- Commit to filling in those gaps by practicing the skills you've not yet mastered, such as tuning into feelings or maintaining clear, consistent rules.
- Be patient and kind to yourself. Filling in the gaps is hard work.
- If you're overwhelmed—get additional help.
- Practice recharging your batteries with good self-care. Parenting is hard work and can be draining.
- Develop outlets for the feelings of stress, frustration and even grief that parenting a challenging child can create.
- Practice good couple care. Find ways to get away from the daily grind and re-connect.
- Understand how your temperament and early family experiences combine to create your parenting style.
- Develop the same understanding of your spouse or partner's parenting style.
- Appreciate what your partner's parenting style brings to the mix, and respect your differences.
- Work together to create and maintain a united parenting front.

Chapter 5

The Role of Temperament

I've referred several times already to the idea of temperament in relation to both kids and parents' behaviors. In fact, I rarely get through a conversation about kids' behaviors these days without spending some time thinking about temperament. It's just that important. Why is it so important to understand how a child's temperament fits into their behavior patterns? Because temperament, or the set of response traits you're born with, creates predispositions in all of us to behave in certain ways. If we can understand how a child (or an adult) might be wired to respond, then we have a powerful means to both predict their behavior in difficult situations and also begin to create solutions. Another way to think about it is that your temperament is essentially a map of how your particular nervous system works. If we can become familiar with our kids' individual map, then we're in much better shape to understand and then help them with their behaviors. If you look carefully at any situation where you have behavior that you don't want, you can see your child's temperament at work behind the scenes.

We all have some level of all of the basic temperament traits. These traits are in-born and with you throughout life, but they do change some over the course of development. All three-year-olds, for instance, are high on the temperament trait of impulsivity and low on the trait of focus, which is not a problem because that's normal for that age. By eight-years-old, on the other hand, a child should have a much lower level of impulsivity and higher level of focus, and if this is not the case, there might be a developmental problem. So seeing where each trait falls on the temperament scale gives us not only a greater understanding of a child but also helps us understand at what point normal development might veer off track.

Counselors who specialize in assessing temperament call our individual set of traits our temperament profile. When you have someone map out your temperament profile, they're essentially helping you figure out if you're low, medium, or high on each trait. You end up with an interesting map of the main traits that contribute to your personality. I'm not a temperament counselor, but I have found it really helpful to think about the levels of these traits when talking with parents about their kids. Noticing which traits are particularly high or low, for both the parent and child profiles, helps us figure out why family members react they way they do in certain situations.

Sensitivity, for example, is one trait that is important to understand. Very sensitive kids have a hard time with authority delivered with too much intensity. It can create a state of overload and you will see them decompensate at times by getting silly or disorganized when they're in trouble. Parents often misread this as further evidence of disrespect and come down even harder and with more energy—further sending this kind of child into a tailspin. Understanding the impact of temperament (sensitivity in this case) when disciplining this type of child can make the difference between effective behavior management and pushing the child into a full-blown meltdown.

The same situation can be understood very differently with a very *persistent* child. A temperament high in persistence often means that the child will test your authority right up to the moment of consequence. So, for this child, the same silliness at the point of discipline can be seen as continued testing, for which you should respond with a higher degree of authority. Kids of this type will not be overwhelmed by a good dose of authority—in fact, they need it to contain their persistent nature and to help them develop respect for others. These are just two examples of the many ways that temperament influences a child's behavior, and illustrates why it's so critical for parents to understand the impact of temperament when providing guidance for their kids. What follows is a general description of some of the main temperament traits and the influence they often have on kids' behaviors.

Sensitivity. According to psychologist and author Elaine Aron, highly sensitive people are only about 20 percent of the general population. This means that the majority of people are not experiencing things the way that they do, which is why this trait is particularly important to understand. Sensitive kids (and adults) are literally having different experiences than most of the people around them. Highly sensitive people are finely tuned to their environment and are processing more data through all of their senses. The brightness of fluorescent light, the sounds of traffic, and the smells of foods are all experienced more intensely by the sensitive person's acute nervous system. When the sensations are pleasant, the experience is wonderful, but when they're not, it can be torturous to endure. The gift of sensitive people is that they notice the details and nuances that others miss. This makes them exceptionally intuitive and often lends to a high level of creativity. The challenge with this trait, however, is that the intensity sensitive people experience makes them more prone to states of stress and overwhelm. Sensitive people are cautious and slow to warm because they need to take in the heightened flow of data slowly, to protect against the possibility of overload. When a sensitive child reaches overload, he or she may get disorganized, silly, withdrawn, or regress into a state of rage. Sensitive adults get overloaded too, and tend to get anxious, frazzled, and depleted when it all gets too much.

Because sensitive people are so finely tuned, they are very aware of themselves and their surroundings. This awareness creates a much higher possibility that they might become self-conscious or embarrassed. Kids who are high in this trait do much better with discipline that is calm, paced slowly, and not delivered in front of others. They are also prone to guilt and shame, so you need to make sure they are not being harder on themselves than you are on them.

If you suspect your child or you have a high level of the sensitivity trait, read the books on this subject by Elaine Aron. One additional note on sensitivity. Sensitivity, like all temperament traits, presents itself on a continuum, from low to very high. The gradients within this range are understood to be within the normal range of development. However, when we go beyond highly sensitive, we move into a realm where the nervous system's ability to effectively process all of the incoming sensory information (visual, auditory, tactile, etc.) gets overloaded, and the sensory system begins to break down. This is a fairly common developmental delay, called Sensory Processing Disorder, or SPD, which often improves as the child matures. The most common symptoms of SPD include extreme sensitivity to tags or seams in clothing, to food tastes and textures, to smells and certain sounds. SPD can also affect balance, coordination, muscle strength, and the ability to regulate one's body energy. It's important to distinguish between a child who is very sensitive and one who is struggling with sensory breakdown. Adults often mislabel SPD kids as picky, rigid, or defiant, when they are actually trying to manage their physical discomfort. If your child has symptoms of SPD that are disrupting his or her family, school or social functioning, consult your pediatrician or a qualified occupational therapist.

Intensity. Also called emotional reactivity, kids high in this trait tend to be dramatic. Their feelings come on quickly and intensely, and when they want you to know about their experience, they do it with extra energy. When a toe is stubbed or a disappointment encountered, the intense child will react as if it were the end of the world. Intense kids often get accused of over-reacting, which is an unfair label because it assumes that they have a choice not to feel so strongly. This is simply not true. The reactions of intense kids should not be seen as manipulation or the desire to create drama but instead as a product of their nervous system's wiring. It's true that some kids do intentionally manipulate through dramatic behavior, but that is chosen behavior and not primarily the result of temperament, so it's a different issue. Parents need to be careful not to misunderstand the reactions of intense kids as drama for effect. Intense kids are not so much trying to get what they want with their behavior as they are trying to release the intense flood of feelings that swiftly overtakes their bodies. These kids are wired to react quickly, and they can be set off easily. They need help containing their behavior during emotional episodes, as well as the understanding that this is how they are wired to express both their positive and negative emotional states.

Persistence. This is the pit bull—the child who gets an idea in his head or her head and just can't let go. Persistent kids are tenacious and go after what they want. If they don't get it the first time, they are committed to repeating the request or just digging in and trying harder until it pays off. When a very persistent child decides, for instance, that he or she wants to become a professional soccer player, they head out into the yard and practice and practice and then practice some more. It's hard to curb persistent kids' enthusiasm.

However, this also applies to their protests. When a persistent kid decides that she hates the movie the family is thinking about seeing, she will have a very hard time joining in and just going with the flow. In this way, highly persistent kids can be challenging to parent. They can turn potentially productive conversations into endless negotiations or power struggles and can get stuck in their singular vision of how things should go. These kids do better with firm limits, a good amount of structure, and a focus on flexibility. On a positive note, a high level of persistence is almost always part of a successful professional profile, so the very thing that works against you in family life will likely serve your highly persistent child well in a future career.

Adaptability. The temperament trait of adaptability has to do with how well a child can shift gears, going from one activity or idea to another. Kids who are low in adaptability have a harder time with change. They become rigid and get stuck when it's time to move on, especially if they're engaged in an activity they like. Their parents often identify times of transition, such as during the morning or bedtime routines, as the most stressful times they have with their slow to adapt children. Challenging transitions can create a quick mood shift in these kids, as their previously positive outlook is suddenly replaced by a rigid and negative tone. For parents, this can turn an ordinarily peaceful moment into what feels like an instant power struggle. The element of surprise is one of the biggest triggers for this type of kid. Parents quickly learn that letting their child know about upcoming changes far enough ahead of time can mean the difference between a smooth and a rocky transition. Having the child help with planning the day's schedule is also helpful. This gives them a map of upcoming events and transitions, and also gives them a sense of increased control.

The skill that kids low on adaptability need to work on, which provides more balance, is flexibility. If your child has a hard time with adaptability, make sure you talk to him or her about being more flexible. Set up a system to keep track of how often your child can practice this skill, and reward your child's efforts with access to their favorite things. When kids become rigid, it can make parents react rigidly too. This dynamic can easily spiral into a power struggle. Avoid these difficult moments by modeling flexibility as well as setting clear limits and disengaging from endless negotiation. As with any pronounced temperament trait, take time to distinguish whether the difficulty you're having moving your child through a transition is the product of an intentional power struggle or your child's low adaptability temperament.

Impulsivity. Impulsive kids have lightening-quick nervous systems and make split-second decisions when reacting to things, especially if they want something. The way they react needs to be understood because it is different from the way most people respond. I would use the following sequence to describe how most people react to situations they encounter:

impulse→ thought filter→ action/no action

In other words, our experience creates an initial impulse or drive to react to a situation. We then consider things like the outcome or the effect our reaction will have on the situation. We then make the decision whether to follow through on our response. The filter is the middle stage, where we consider the impact on others or ourselves if we do choose to follow through on our response. The filter is also what helps us slow down and inhibit our actions in the name of rationality. Impulsive kids have what I call "a reverse filter," which means that it's not that the filter is missing but that it follows another sequence and comes after the action. Impulsive kids have this response sequence:

impulse→ action→ thought filter

If you ask a very impulsive kid whether it was a good idea to push the other kid down during the game of tag, the impulsive kid will say, "No, it wasn't." This shows that impulsive kids are indeed able to engage in a rational consideration of the outcome after the event. Their dilemma is not that they lack rationality, intelligence, or empathy. The difficulty is that they can't insert a filter in between the impulse and the action. This inability to inhibit their behavior creates a lot of trouble for impulsive kids, which can have a negative impact on their self-esteem. Parents of impulsive kids need to keep an eye on their self-esteem and do what they can to keep them feeling good about themselves despite their challenges. Impulsive kids make a lot of fast mistakes, and when they consider the impact of their behavior after the fact, they often feel bad about themselves. I've heard many impulsive kids say they feel like there is an invisible monster inside of them that keeps messing things up for them. Statements like this show us that impulsive kids don't want to be problematic, that their intention is not to cause the difficulties they so often do.

Impulsive kids benefit from being allowed a chance to redo situations in which they've responded too fast. If your child is impulsive, have him or her practice do-overs of their quick mistakes. Rewind to the moment of impulse and then have him or her slow down and walk through the response again—this time with a focus on considering the outcome. If your child violated a rule, tell him or her that the consequence will be reduced or eliminated if they redo the situation with thought and self-control. Redoing situations helps impulsive kids turn unconscious responses into conscious ones, while it also preserves self-esteem by allowing a second chance at the impulsive moment.

One of the best ways to make sure a child stops and thinks is to make use of language. If the child is talking out loud—to himself, herself, or to others—then the child is thinking, and if the child is thinking, there is a much better chance he or she will also think about the impact of their actions. So make sure you are teaching your child to stop and say something quietly aloud (like "stop and think") to himself or herself or to someone else before taking action. This is these kids' best chance of interrupting the impulsive moment and retraining their brain to add the missing filter. I often teach impulsive kids the phrase "words before hands" to get them to practice routing their ideas through their thinking brain and out of their mouths, before it comes out of their body.

Focus. The ability to maintain focus—or, more correctly, the ability to filter out all of the potential distractions from our field of view—is an aspect of our temperament. Though this trait is hardwired into each of us, it is also variable from person to person and also changes with age and situational context. All kids struggle with distractibility at times. Things like fatigue, hunger, or intense feelings can make typically focused kids lose their ability to stay on track. Because the ability to focus changes with age, we also have to compare any child's ability to stay focused with the ability of other kids their age. This will give us a feel for how well a particular child is doing in this area.

I think of focus as a pendulum that can swing between the three following states:

underfocused ←→ optimal focus ←→ overfocused

Most kids stay in the optimal range most of the time. Kids who struggle with focus swing from optimal to one of the other states and spend more time there. An underfocused moment is when you tell your child to go brush his teeth and ten minutes later find him only halfway there, staring instead at a crack in the wall. An overfocused moment happens, say, when your child is doing a favorite activity and becomes so entranced with the object of her focus that you can literally repeat the same message ten times without her stopping to notice you. If your child struggles with focus, you'll likely notice that he or she spends a substantial amount of time in either the under- or overfocused state. You'll also probably hear from your child's teacher because school is one area that really tests a child's ability to maintain optimal focus.

My two sons are avid baseball players, and we've noticed that some of the most unfocused kids off the field end up being the best players during the game. Interest and energy have a big impact on kids' ability to focus, and when distractible kids are engaged in their favorite activities, their ability to focus often increases substantially. On the baseball field, these previously unfocused kids seem to shift to a state of high focus, where they can filter out the noises of the crowd, shrug off the pressure to perform, and simply slip into "the zone" of optimal play. Off the field, however, these same kids often have a hard time listening and staying on track. So the focus issue can work for or against a child, depending on the situation and interest or energy involved.

When difficulty with focus creates ongoing problems for a child, whether academically, socially, or in family life, it's a good idea to have the child evaluated by a psychologist or other developmental professional.

Activity Level. Highly active kids are great—except when you want them to sit still. Dinnertime, homework time, and long stretches of sitting in school or elsewhere are difficult for active children. Their nervous systems are hungry for stimulus, and their bodies crave action and movement. Active kids are often born leaders and stars on the sports field. Their need for action combined with their will to explore takes them to the cutting edge of experience and often makes other kids want to follow their adventurous spirits.

Active kids feel their best when they're getting the stimulus they crave, and they suffer when their energy is stifled. Kids who are highly active do everything better when they're moving, including talking about their behaviors and feelings. When they don't have outlets for their energy or there isn't enough action going on, you'll hear the famous tagline of active kids, "I'm bored." Boredom is the enemy of active, stimulus-hungry children. It is a state they try to avoid at all costs because it feels so bad for them physically. Like boredom, patience is a challenging experience for active kids. They count the seconds until the next stimulating moment, so even a short wait can feel like an eternity to them.

With boredom and the mental exhaustion it creates lurking around every corner, active kids learn to avoid these states by keeping the pace as high as they can. When the pace slows down, as it does in school or during dinnertime, their bodies fatigue from holding all their energy in, and active kids begin to vibrate with restlessness. Many don't easily feel their tiredness, because, unlike the rest of us, for them exhaustion and energy go hand in hand. The continuous fatigue that is created by managing excess energy is why most high-energy kids (and adults) report feeling a combination of tired and wired much of the time. For kids, this makes it very difficult to discern whether they are feeling fatigued or energetic, which makes it hard to figure out what their bodies actually need. This is a challenge for parents too, who are often wondering if their high-energy child needs rest and quiet or a good long run. Parents in this situation will have to experiment with what seems to help their active child best. For instance, physical activity in the morning or just after school might provide a good energy release, and quiet active time, like reading or board games, might help with winding down in the evening.

Highly active kids learn differently too. They are experiential learners, who do best with a hands-on approach. They are also testers who like to find things out for themselves, which makes sense, because hands-on learning provides their nervous systems with maximum stimulus and energy input. Schools are often too theoretical in their teaching approaches for these kids, who are expected to sit still and absorb information through the exchange of concepts. This kind of "hands-off" learning makes active kids fidgety clock-watchers. I often tell parents whose active kids are struggling in school that there wouldn't be a problem if their kid were learning while working on a ranch in Montana. Being made to sit still at a desk in a quiet room is a far cry from being five feet up on a horse with the wind in your face and all of nature to invigorate the senses. It's the bad fit (the "mis"-fit) between an active kid's nervous system and the classroom that creates the problem—not the child. The best teachers understand this and find ways to engage active kids so that they don't get bored and tune out.

When highly active kids show that they can't handle low stimulus environments and start to move, fidget, or get in trouble, it's important to see the problem for what it is—an energy issue, not a behavior issue. As is often the case with impulsive kids, adults often categorize the energetic behavior of active exploratory kids as intentional defiance. This is a mistake. Though their behavior can be disruptive, the intention of most active kids is to get their stimulus needs met, not to cause trouble for others. When they do cause trouble, adults need to stop and think to consciously separate patterns of high activity from patterns of intentional defiance, rather than confuse the two. Falsely accusing these kids of trying to create problems when they're not is damaging to the adult-child relationship and is a sure-fire way to knock an active kid's self-esteem so low that he or she does then turn into someone who wants to make trouble.

This is not to say that active kids are victims. Their temperaments do cause problems at times, and they do need to take responsibility for themselves. I recently worked with a sweet, but very fidgety eight-year-old who was getting in trouble for poking his peers and talking to them in class. First, I helped him identify that his body was wired to be superfast, and then I talked with him about both the easy and the hard parts of being wired like this. I told him that it was very important for him to know how his body worked so that he could explain it to others, especially when his body goes too fast and makes him make mistakes. Together we decided that it was probably better to let grown-ups know how easily he gets bored and how restless his body gets *before* he starts getting in trouble for it. We talked about how once teachers and other adults get an impression about a kid, it's hard to change their impression, and a reputation develops. I really wanted to expand this child's awareness of his physical system and empower him to be able to communicate to others what gets hard for him, so that he could move from being a victim to being an empowered problem solver.

We talked about solutions to his moments of boredom for each of the settings that were difficult for him, and then we made a list of the adults involved (teacher, baseball coach, cub scout leader, etc.), that he was going to educate about his superfast system. Then we came up with a list of solutions to his boredom for each setting, so that he could share ways to solve the problem when he talked to the adults. I encouraged him to start using the term "restless" instead of bored, because it more accurately described to others what happens to his body. We rehearsed changing "I need to talk to you about your class being boring" to "I need to talk to you about my restlessness in class." I pointed out that how we word things is important because you want people to know you're talking about yourself, not complaining about them being boring. With his parents help, this kid went on to talk to the adults in his life, educating them about his dilemma with restlessness and working with them on solutions for each situation. This is such a good example of a disruptive kid moving from a helpless position to one of proactive responsibility for his temperament. If this boy keeps telling the adults in his life about his temperament needs, he will be able to maintain positive relations with teachers, coaches, and most importantly himself, which will allow him to continue to view himself as a good kid.

Of course, it's not only the highly active kids who need to know about their own temperament. Just as it's important for all parents to have a basic understanding of their kids' temperament, it's important for all kids to know about themselves too. It's also a matter of personal responsibility. Kids need to take the lead in letting others know about their particular challenges before they turn into problems. Think about how helpful it would be if children knew about their own specific needs and tolerances and could communicate these to others, even in basic ways. There would be so many fewer instances of kids reaching meltdown because of their heightened sensitivity, or their difficulty with transitions, or their trouble with distractibility. There would also be fewer moments of adults watching and scratching their heads, trying to figure out what is going on with a struggling child. They would no longer be confusing temperament struggles for intentional behavior and resorting to punishment instead of problem solving. Understanding temperament gives us a lot of information about how and why kids respond the way they do, and when kids can understand their own temperament and communicate this to adults, adults are much better prepared to help with the challenges.

What would this communication look like? For a sensitive child who is not participating because of embarrassment, it might sound like, "This is really hard for me because I get embarrassed easily." This statement would let adults know that the child is not opting out because he or she is not interested, doesn't know the material, or is not a team player, but because the child is experiencing the hyper self-consciousness sensitive people are all too familiar with. For a distractible child, the communication might be, "I need to let you know that I get distracted, so if we could talk where it's quiet, that would help a lot." And for an intense and reactive child, the communication might be, "I get mad fast, so I'll need some help calming down before my volcano explodes." If kids with particularly strong temperament traits can develop simple statements about their specific struggles to share with the adults in their lives, they stand a much better chance of getting the help and understanding they need.

If your child has particularly strong traits, educate your child about his or her temperament and help your child to educate coaches, teachers, and other adults they work with. Help them practice by role playing with them how they might tell others about the things that get difficult for them—"Okay, I'll pretend I'm Ms. Nash, and you practice telling me about how you want to follow the rules but it's really hard for you to sit still." For children under five, who may have difficulty putting the necessary concepts into words, parents may have to either help them or do it for them. Either way, the point is to educate others about your child's temperament so that your child isn't misinterpreted as simply trying to cause problems when they're not.

Temperament Combinations

Many kids have one temperament trait that is particularly strong and steers their personality and needs. However, there are also lots of kids who have combinations of strong traits—some of which you wouldn't expect to go together. A high level of sensitivity often pairs up with a high level of intensity, which makes sense because sensitive kids are having very intense experiences. Likewise, very active kids are often also impulsive because they're usually moving at a pace that doesn't allow them to slow down and consider the consequences of their actions. Less typical, though, is when, for instance, sensitivity pairs up with a high level of activity and need for stimulus.

I recently met with a very sweet ten-year-old boy named Carson and his parents, who were struggling to get along at home. As I sat with the family in my office and began to talk with them about their difficulties, I immediately picked up on Carson's high level of sensitivity. He looked shy and somewhat withdrawn, and his eyes were wide, as if he were taking in everything in the finest detail. As the session progressed, however, he became less shy and instead more and more restless, to the point where his parents began to reprimand him to "sit still." I began to educate the family about temperament traits with a focus on sensitivity and activity level. Carson's parents related moments when they saw each of these traits in action in family life, but then his mom added, "It's confusing, though, because he's not like his active friends. Although he likes a lot of action, Carson also gets overwhelmed and tired fairly easily. And he is sensitive, but not like our daughter, who is very sensitive but also very mellow." "You're right, Carson is different," I told her. He's like an awesome ice cream cake— several layers of very different flavors!" Carson smiled and seemed to like the ice cream analogy, but I suspect what he also liked was that someone really understood this combination of different elements in him. This was an *aha!* moment for the parents, who said, "Of course, that explains why he gets bored and restless and needs a lot of activity but also gets shy around new people and needs a lot of downtime." As we talked and I helped Carson share with his parents how these traits affect him, he also stated that he felt like he "didn't fit in" with either the active or the shy kids because he was both. I helped his parents really tune into this unique experience and the dilemmas it produced for Carson both socially and in his family. By the end of the session, all of them looked relieved because we had really begun to understand Carson by observing through the lens of his temperament, a combination that produced a unique set of challenges for him.

This is only one of many possible unusual combinations of temperament traits that can leave both parents and their kids confused about a child's behavior and experiences. As you begin to understand the influence of temperament, think about whether your child has an unusual combination of strong traits. This will help you and your child develop insight into your child's experiences. As you explore the layers of their temperament, you just might discover that your child is an ice cream cake too!

Temperament and the Stress Response

We all respond to stress in different ways, and this is largely a product of our temperament, or how we are wired. Of course, things like coping skills also factor in, but before our skills for dealing with a situation kick in, our stress is routed through our nervous system, which sets in motion a type of response that will become typical for each of us. Looking at how each temperament trait typically responds to overload can further help us understand why we and our kids react in certain ways to the stressors of daily life. What follows are the temperament traits I listed previously along with typical stress responses. I've also included a word or two of advice for what to focus on when these traits go into overload.

Sensitive. This child is highly prone to overload and usually leans toward an anxious or withdrawn response. These kids typically shut down if things get too stressful and need time to recover. However, be forewarned: if a sensitive child gets pushed too far past his or her stress threshold, they may react with uncharacteristic aggression or disorganization (the fight-or-flight response). These kids need to know they're safe and can come out of hiding when they're overloaded. They need time to recover and a calm invitation to connect with adults who understand the depth of their upset and who can provide some soothing for their frazzled nerves.

Intense. The intense child will become dramatic when stressed. They will send up a bright and colorful fireworks show to let you know how strongly they feel. They are not beyond using words and phrases with shock value to get you to pay attention to their emotional suffering. Don't get distracted by the show; instead, pay attention to the feelings underneath to provide emotional help. The other thing you can do is slow down the "no." Intense, reactive kids don't do well with surprises or sudden disappointments. If you can deliver potentially upsetting messages slowly, with some thoughtful conversation, you allow your child time to acclimate and adapt without triggering a reaction of frustration. The reactive child also needs to learn simple coping techniques—like *stop, breathe, words out*—to help him or her slow down the quick responses they experience and manage the intense feelings with language instead of reactive behavior.

Persistent. These kids become fired up when stressed and just can't let it go. They will hunt you down to try to make you understand what their dilemma is. The persistent child will become rigidly fixated on a problem and will often try to pull adults into lengthy power struggles designed to get attention for their upset, while dissipating their stored levels of stress. Adults need to remain calm and stay off of the dance floor—which means don't accept invitations to engage in power struggles about details of the event. Instead, help the child focus on putting words to his or her upset and on practicing flexibility. Adults also need to set clear limits on the behaviors that aren't working.

Adaptable. Kids who are low on adaptability are prone to getting stuck. When stressed, they can have a variety of responses, but the common denominator is that they have a hard time with the recovery. These kids need adults to help them switch gears and find a way to get back on track. Sometimes this will be a distraction, other times it will be time alone, and sometimes it will be the adult lowering the expectation for the moment to help them find a way to recover instead. Flexibility is an important skill for these kids to work on. It should be prompted for and rewarded when they do practice flexing to get unstuck. As with very sensitive kids, kids low on adaptability do better when they know the game plan. Letting them know ahead of time what changes and transitions are coming helps them begin to plan for the change and cope better when it happens.

Impulsive. Impulsive kids lash out, whether at a person, an object, or themselves. They don't keep the state of overload inside them for very long. These kids often make mistakes when they're upset because their bodies react before their brains have a chance to consider the consequence. Impulsive kids need adults to understand that their bodies betray them under stress, and they need to be forgiven for their rapid responses. Impulsive kids also need to know that the adults in their lives understand that they usually don't mean to do what they've done. Impulsive kids also benefit when you can help them anticipate the situations that might provoke impulsive reactions so that they can plan ahead for good coping. Learn to anticipate with your impulsive child the types of situations that are triggers (for example, when energy is high or feelings are intense) and together create good coping plans in advance.

Focus. Kids low on focus tend to retreat to their world of daydreams when the outside environment becomes too much. They often become hyper-focused on an activity or imaginary play as an escape mechanism for the stressor at hand. Low focus kids can be very reactive too, because their distractibility distracts them from their feelings until they've reached such an intense level that they explode. Distracted kids need adults to help them stay connected to their feelings and stay organized by understanding the sequence of events and details that have caused them stress. These details are often lost on the distracted child, and by the time they get focused and oriented, the situation is upon them. Stressors, then, are often experienced as surprises for these kids. Helping them stay present to deal with stressful events usually helps them tolerate the events better, softening the surprise factor.

Active. Active kids get into motion when overloaded. Stress builds in their bodies and adds extra energy to an already full tank—a bit like drinking one of those tall energy drinks right after your morning coffee! Active kids will look for ways to dissipate their extra energy, and they can be destructive and prone to tantrums if they don't have another constructive outlet. Attempts to calm or contain their energy sometimes backfire because too much has already built up in their bodies. It's often best to have predetermined, nondestructive outlets for their energy, which adults can prompt the child to use first thing (for example, run around the yard, squeeze your pillow as tight as you can ten times, do jumping jacks counting backwards from twenty, etc.). After some energy has been released, the child then needs to focus on expressing his or her feelings and working with others to solve the problem that caused the stress and energy buildup.

Temperament and Social Roles

We all find social roles that are comfortable for us, roles that fit well with our temperament. Some of us are the funny ones, some of us are the organizers, and some of us are the peacemakers, for example. This is as true for kids as it is for adults. It is a naturally occurring social phenomenon. We are also not limited to just one role and have the ability to switch our social roles depending on the circumstance. Parenting provides a good example of this. At times we are the disciplinarian, at others the comforting ally, and at still other times the silly playmate. The ability to assume several different roles is healthy because it allows us to practice not just one set of social skills but many. It also allows us to be seen by others as the multidimensional beings we all are. When kids' temperaments include traits that are extremely high or low, they run the risk of being trapped in one particular role, which is socially limiting and doesn't help them practice a well-rounded set of social skills.

The highly sensitive child, for instance, can get very used to letting someone else with a more forceful personality be the leader. Some of this is okay, but everyone needs some practice leading. Parents need to make sure their sensitive kids build leadership skills even though it may create discomfort for them. The same is true for the natural leader, who naturally organizes and directs activities because of his or her energy and confidence. Natural leaders will be required to follow others at times, and so they also need to know how to be a supportive team member. Here are some guidelines for expanding kids' social roles beyond the ones they're naturally inclined to occupy given their particular temperament.

- Help a persistent child teach someone else about flexibility.
- Help a reactive child to be the planner.
- Help an impulsive child move beyond being the funny guy or girl.
- Help a highly active child to be a follower.
- Help a sensitive child lead the exploration.
- Help an unfocused child be the organizer.

- Help an intense child assist a friend or sibling to calm down.
- Help an impulsive child create rules and then help others slow down and follow them.

Help your kids try on social roles and develop skills that do not come naturally for them. Remember that working on anything that does not feel natural is hard, so don't push too hard or too fast, but do push a little. Your kids will thank you, because later in life they will be able to step into roles socially and professionally that are beyond what their temperaments are comfortable with.

Teaching is a great way to cement learning, so give your child the assignment of helping someone else build the skills they themselves need to work on. You could, for instance, have your somewhat rigid and controlling child be in charge of teaching his or her little brother how to be Mr. Flexible, or you could have your sensitive and shy child teach his or her best friend how to ask for help at a store. Use the bulleted ideas listed as a springboard to create your own assignments to help your kids become teachers. Teaching others skills that they themselves are developing will help them experience additional social roles and contribute to a well-rounded set of interpersonal skills.

Your Own Temperament

As you think about your child's temperament, stop to consider your own also. It's as important to know the kind of nervous system you have as it is to know your child's. If you stop to notice, you'll find that many of the traits you see in your kid(s) are similar to your own. This has to be true because temperament is genetic, and as they say, "the apple doesn't fall far from the tree!" Temperament similarities and differences between kids and their parents can be both helpful and difficult.

A highly sensitive parent, for instance, can tune into a highly sensitive child and have a special understanding of the child's experience—one that the other parent might not have. This can be very helpful when trying to figure out why the child is behaving a certain way. On the other hand, that sensitive parent can be absolutely overwhelmed with the job of parenting a reactive or a persistent child, who always tests and creates lots of conflict.

Similarly, an adult who is high on intensity might overwhelm a child who is low on adaptability, especially during a transition like getting ready to leave the house. Kids who are low on adaptability need a calm and structured warning system to anticipate change. A parent with a loud voice who is moving too fast may confuse or agitate this child. On the other hand, an intense parent might be just what a highly active child needs when it's time to get out of the house because they both enjoy the stimulus of higher volumes and a faster pace.

You can see, then, that there are many ways to combine these temperament traits and that each combination can contribute to more or less harmony in the parent-child relationship. I recall talking to a mom who was in tears because she was having such a difficult relationship with one of her two boys. She described her older son as "easy to parent" but could not, despite all her efforts, figure out how to parent her younger son effectively. She was experiencing a chronic state of frustration with this child because the things that she did to help or guide him rarely seemed to work; in fact, much of the time her parenting seemed to make things worse. She described feeling like he was from another planet. What worked with her other child just didn't work with him. She also told me about her sadness. This mom said she felt like a failure as a parent and horribly guilty because she could not figure out how to help her son in his moments of greatest need. This dynamic had an impact on her relationship with her older son too. Because she felt guilty about how easy it was with him, she frequently had a hard time enjoying her time with him. This sweet and very sensitive mom was really struggling. She didn't feel she had a natural ability to parent her youngest child.

I educated this mom about temperament traits. We discovered that her younger child was wired with a temperament profile almost exactly opposite to hers and that her oldest son was very similar to her. In addition, she had not had any experience managing a child with the active and persistent profile her younger son had, so she didn't have much to draw upon. We figured out that it was understandable, even predictable, that given their differences in temperament, along with her lack of experience with this type of child, that she would be lost parenting him. This understanding was a great relief to this mom, who now knew that there wasn't anything wrong with her as a parent or anything wrong with her younger son—it was just a matter of temperaments and an uneasy fit. I told her that the most important thing to remember was that it's okay not to have a perfect fit and that plenty of parents and kids out there are not a natural fit. Even so, everyone could still work to understand each other's experience and develop deep and meaningful connections. Sure, it takes work, but when it's your child, that effort is more than a worthwhile investment. This mom recommitted to developing some different ways to guide her younger son, based on his unique temperament profile. I'm confident that because she was able to see the temperament connection—and release her frustration and guilt—she'll now have the energy to work on making things better.

There are other circumstances that create temperamental differences between parents and kids. Adoption and surrogate parenting are two examples of this. This is not to say that adoptive parents may not share certain strong traits with their kids. They can. But it's certainly less likely that they will recognize their own particular temperament combination in a child who doesn't share their genetics. There are also instances when a child is born to biological parents but arrives with a temperament unlike either of them. I have worked with a handful of these families, where both parents experience their biological child as somewhat alien to them. Some of them even wonder if there was a mix-up at the hospital! This is certainly an odd experience for parents because neither of them feels naturally equipped to understand and deal with their child. In talking with these parents, often a reference to another extended family member is made, whether a grandparent, an aunt, or an uncle, to whom the child seems similarly wired. Because parents in these situations are challenged to try to understand their child's unique experience without their own natural reference point, extra effort on the parents' part is required.

If you are in this type of situation in which your child's temperament is hard for you or both parents to relate to, then you'll need to do a few things. First, get a good feel for your child's temperament profile. Go through the list of temperament traits I shared earlier to see how each fits your child's behavior patterns. There are also a number of books about temperament, which will give you even more information on your child's unique profile. You'll also need to employ a lot of empathy and communication in your parenting. Take the time to put yourself in your child's shoes to try to see the world through his or her eyes, especially when they're struggling. Ask a lot of questions about what they're feeling and why they experience things the way they do. Also, remember that it's okay. There's nothing wrong with having a child who feels very different from you—there's nothing wrong with your child or you. Don't get stuck on trying to change your child into you or trying to pretend that you get your child when you don't. Instead, work on understanding each other. Lastly, always find common ground. Even people with different temperaments have some similar experiences. Find ways to relate to your child through shared experiences and common interests. This will help you build emotional closeness, which will help you get through the more difficult moments.

To summarize, notice your child's more pronounced temperament traits and spend some time thinking about how they interface with your own, especially if they feel very different from you. If you have a child who is particularly hard to parent, it may be because of a significant temperament difference between the two of you. Although this type of relationship may feel less natural, it can still be very successful. You will just need to work on understanding these differences and come up with some effective ways to connect with and guide your child.

Overidentification

Another temperament-related issue that can happen between a parent and a child is what's called overidentification. Overidentification happens when a parent's temperament and a child's temperament are very similar. In this case, the parent loses perspective because he or she shares so many similar experiences with the child. Let me explain. If a parent sees himself or herself as very similar to the child and recognizes experiences that seem the same for both of them, the parent can begin to overestimate the similarities and assume that he or she knows exactly what the child is thinking and feeling. It might be true that this parent "gets" the child on a certain level, and it might even be true that the parent understands the child's experience much of the time. However, it is also true that the child is having his or her own unique experiences, which the parent in this scenario might miss due to over-focus on similarities with the child.

Missing the individual differences in the child's experience creates a false sense of knowing the child on the parent's part, which then leads to moments of mis-attunement between parent and child. If this happens too often, it will lead to the child feeling misunderstood by the parent or feeling confused because he or she isn't actually having the experiences the parent describes. Over time, this dynamic can be very disruptive to the parent-child relationship.

Let me give an example. I worked with a family of a thirteen-year-old boy who had all of the relevant markers for ADHD. He was suffering in school with both his schoolwork and his social relationships. When I first met his father, I immediately noticed similar traits in him (distractibility and restlessness, for example). I began to talk to the boy and his parents about these traits in the boy. The father stated that he had recognized these traits in himself also, which I thought would be helpful because it would help normalize these traits for the child. The father then began to tell me that he knew exactly what his kid's experience was because they both were so similar. He also stated that he knew what should be done, because he had had the same childhood experience. But when I asked him what he thought the solution was and heard his answer, I became very concerned about overidentification. The father went on to explain that he saw himself as a very successful adult, which he appeared to be, and that all his success came from having to "tough it out" as a kid. He explained at length the benefits of struggling with these traits as a child "without help from anyone." It eventually got him to where he was. He said that no one else understood his child and the road that lay ahead like he did.

To add perspective, I began by first appreciating this father's understanding of his child's unique challenges, as well as the successful results this father got from working so hard to overcome his own challenges. I also shared with him my concern that if he interpreted his child's experiences too much using the lens of his own experience, he ran the risk of superimposing his childhood onto his child—which would be problematic. I reminded the parents that this boy had half of his mother's genetics too. Specifically he shared her sensitivity, which gave him different experiences from his father's. Finally, I told the dad that in my experience I'd learned that certain temperament combinations do well with the "tough-it-out" approach (as he did), but others become overwhelmed and develop chronic problems as a result of the emotional stress. I stated that it was mostly for this last reason that I wanted to make sure he wasn't standing too close to his child's experience, which would prevent him from seeing all the relevant factors clearly and understanding his child's own unique experience. In the end, the father got the point. He realized that it was as important to understand the differences in his child's experience as it was to recognize the similarities to his own. We then worked on a plan that was a compromise between the father's preconceived notions about what was best for his son and additional supports that could help prevent this sensitive but distracted kid from slipping into a state of chronic stress.

We all want to know our kids. We want to know how the world looks to them and what kinds of things make them feel both good and horrible. We want to ensure that they have meaningful experiences and a happy and safe childhood. Parenting gives us the chance to secure experiences that create safety and happiness— experiences we ourselves would want. In a way, becoming a parent is a second chance at childhood. Our genetics, through our temperaments, make it possible to understand our kids on a deep level, a level beyond words. Use your intuitive understanding of your child to empathize with your child and to inform your parenting decisions. But also remember that no matter how similar your child may be, he or she is only 50 percent of your genetic pool. Your child needs to be seen as having his or her own individual unique experiences and dilemmas. The solutions to your child's dilemmas may very well require solutions beyond those you would use to solve the same problem for yourself.

Temperament vs. Intentional Behavior

I know I've said this before, but I can't emphasize enough the importance of distinguishing between difficult behavior that comes mainly from a child's temperament and the struggles that come from chosen behavior. This is an important distinction because separating temperament from intention allows us to look at behavior from a different angle, which then changes our attitudes and responses toward the child.

Let me give an example. A typically difficult time for parents and kids is the morning rush to get ready and get off to school. Let's say a parent tells the child to get up, get dressed, and get ready to leave for school. Ten minutes later the parent walks by the child's bedroom door and sees the child playing with a toy. The parent again, maybe with some agitation, reminds the child to get ready. Fifteen minutes later the parent notices the child isn't at the breakfast table with everyone else. The parent heads to the child's room again only to find the child daydreaming in his or her underwear, with one sock on. The parent now feels pressure and agitation and screams, "Why are you doing this to me? I gave you several warnings, but you're blowing me off. Now we're going to be late for school! If you're going to make it hard for me, I'll do the same for you. You've lost your TV time for two days." The child looks up, bewildered at first, but then quickly becomes angry and screams back at the parent. A big fight ensues, which makes them even later for school.

In this scenario, the parent is focused on the child's behavior, which is difficult but may or may not be intentional. What would happen in this scenario if the parent understood that the child's temperament included a low level of focus and a high level of reactivity? If the parent knew about the child's temperament, then this parent might respond in a different way, which would produce a different outcome. For instance, after the first communication, when the child still wasn't dressed, the parent might think along these lines: "I know focus is a challenge for her. This seems like a particularly hard morning. I also know she's a pretty reactive kid, so I'd better stick around and help her stay on track so that we don't get too wound up with all this pressure to get out the door on time." Then the parent might ask the other parent or an older sibling to help with breakfast while this parent stays with the child to create a game out of getting ready (because the parent knows arousing interest and energy helps kids with low focus). The game approach works, and the child's increased focus and energy help her get dressed and ready for school on time. This is a very different scenario from the first one. The parent does have to put extra energy into the child in this situation but accepts that this is the case because of the child's temperament and stage of development. And so, the parent does what must be done to help.

So what's the difference between the two scenarios? Well, besides the fact that one ends in a fight and one doesn't, it's this: seeing the child's temperament in play helps the parent in the second scenario not take the behavior personally. The child didn't wake up thinking, "I'm gonna make things hard for mom this morning!" The child simply got lost along the way to getting ready for school. It's still a lot of work for a parent to understand and respond to temperament, but if the choice is to spend extra energy helping the child or to spend extra energy fighting, it makes sense to spend the extra energy in a constructive way. The other major benefit is that the child ends up feeling understood in the relationship. If a parent were to insist that a child with low focus was "trying to drag your feet just to make it hard for me," the child would feel falsely accused. Trust in the relationship would then be eroded, and the erosion of trust would create more behavior problems.

You may be thinking, "Yes but how do you know the child wasn't dragging her feet on purpose? How do you know when the behavior is the product of temperament and not just poor choices?" The answer is that we don't ever know for sure, but if we've taught our kids to talk about their feelings, we can ask them what's going on. In addition to communicating, you can factor in what you already know about your child's temperament, based on seeing it in action in other situations. Temperaments create behavior patterns, so if the kind of struggle you're dealing with is familiar to you—such as trouble staying focused during transitions—then that's more evidence that the behavior might be coming primarily from the child's temperament. Now, in reality, it's never purely either temperament or a behavior choice but usually a combination of the two. Nevertheless, trying to keep the two separate is valuable. When you look at a difficult behavior closely, you can usually tell whether it's mostly temperament or mostly a behavior choice that is creating the challenge. The more you practice separating temperament from choices in behavior, the more you'll be able to see clearly the cause of the disruption and the more effective your response will be.

When parents are struggling to figure out whether a pattern of problem behavior is coming mainly from temperament or a behavioral choice, I often recommend that they do the following. Sit down and talk with the child about the problem—for example, maybe not getting to bed on time is the problem. Ask your child if this is being done on purpose, which gives your child a chance to be honest. Then work together on a plan to make the bedtime routine go smoother. Problem solve anything that is getting in the way, and establish an incentive for doing better with the new plan. Follow through by checking in with your child every few days to make adjustments to the plan if needed. And make sure you deliver the agreed upon rewards. Do this for two weeks, and see if the behavior improves.

If the behavior improves, then it is likely that the problem was more a product of the child's choice than temperament. However, if the behavior doesn't significantly improve, then that is evidence that there are likely temperament factors at play, which are making success difficult. It would then be more effective to identify the temperament traits contributing to the problem and to help your child with them. In this case, you'll also want to adjust your expectations for what the child can realistically manage, rather than increasing pressure by accusing your child of not trying hard enough. This experiment can be done with any problem behavior that makes you uncertain whether it's deliberate behavior or a result of temperament.

Keep in mind that taking a child's temperament into consideration does not mean you give him or her a free pass from taking responsibility. We still want our kids to make their best effort at self-control and self-management, and we will always find ways for them to do this. It's just that when we take into account what we know about their strengths and weaknesses (their temperament), we'll be able to set the bar at an appropriate level, which will create a better chance of success for them and us.

Temperament and the Craving for Electronics

Electronics dominate our world these days—phones, tablets, video games, and to a lesser extent TV—and many parents are trying to understand not only why these devices have such a strong influence on their kids but also how to keep their use in some sort of balance. This is a complex topic, full of facts and strong opinions, and it leaves many parents confused about how to define both their relationship and their kids' relationship with these modern devices. In my work with kids, I have been able to make some connections between electronics and temperament, which I'd like to share to give you a starting point for understanding how the two influence each other.

Electronics, especially video games, are a source of high stimulus and reward. They are also structured and predictable, which gives kids a sense of power and control. For most kids, this is very attractive, and they enjoy the challenge and reward of playing video games. For certain kids, however, this attraction is much stronger because of their temperament. For highly active, stimulus-hungry kids, for instance, electronics are not just a source of stimulation but the ultimate stimulus. These kids quickly develop a craving for screens, especially with video games. There is something about the stimulation being delivered directly through the eyes to the brain and the instant reward of mastering levels that gives stimulus-hungry kids an intense desire for this experience. Parents of these kids often report that their typically cooperative child "becomes someone else" when it comes to electronics. Otherwise honest and cooperative kids will lie, cheat, and steal to get the screen experience they're craving. Turning the device off can also be a painful experience for both these kids and their parents. Few triggers set off a stimulus-hungry kid like separating him or her from a video game.

Although active and stimulus-hungry kids are most easily attracted to gaming, they are by no means the only type of kids who develop an intense relationship with screens. Kids who struggle with focus are also often attracted to video games. The screens provide their brains with enough direct stimulation to propel them away from a fuzzy and distracted mental state to a sharp, focused, and energized state, which is very rewarding. Anxious kids can be drawn to screens as well, but for different reasons. Anxiety is an out-of-control state with many negative mental and physical symptoms. Relief from this state can often be attained by controlling one's environment. The worlds in video games are highly structured and predictable, which soothe an anxious mind. In addition, in video games, the gamer is literally at the controls, which gives the gamer a sense of power and control not usually known in day-to-day life. We can see then that many types of nervous systems get pulled into the world of screens and gaming for various reasons and in a very strong way. With these kids, the fine line between entertainment and obsession can become hard for parents to distinguish. In fact, some kids get so addicted that they can't handle even small amounts of their favored activity and so do much better with minimal or no exposure to electronics.

So, does this mean that video games are bad and should be avoided? Well, anything is bad when we do it so much that it limits our access to other experiences that are good for us—such as socializing and achieving our goals. On the other hand, we all have things we love to do because they give us an experience that suits our individual temperament, and many of these activities are enjoyable but not necessarily productive. Many adults in particular see video games as a waste of a child's time, which is a matter of opinion. What is certainly true, though, is that we all have experiences that we find highly satisfying, and for many kids, video games carry that distinction.

There is a lot of emotional charge among parents who are still adapting to an electronics-filled world, and many of them take a moral position on the topic. This is understandable since this is an influence that was not present in their childhood, and so it elicits a protective response toward their kids. However, electronics are here to stay, so I find it more useful to understand how they interface with a child's particular temperament and whether balance is being preserved in the child's life. For example, are parents monitoring how much time their kids spend on screens, as well as the content of the shows or games? Games with graphic violent content, for instance, have been linked to reduced empathy in kids and so should be avoided. Also, are parents also keeping their kids' lives balanced with time for the outdoors, socializing, and family? The answer to these questions, along with an understanding of the child's temperament and likelihood of becoming addicted to screens, will reveal whether exposure to electronics remains a fun occasional treat or becomes a disruptive obsession.

How do you know if your kid has an addictive temperament or just loves video games? My theory is that the level of stimulus hunger in any kid is proportional to the level of reactivity you get when it's time to unplug. In other words, the harder it is for kids to stop the game, the more they must be craving the stimulus from the start. I have worked with some kids who have such explosive reactions when their parents try to get them to power down that the parents end up having to get rid of the games altogether. Some of these kids have difficulty with focus, some are highly active kids hungry for stimulus, and some have a combination of these traits. All these kids are much more vulnerable to becoming overly focused on these devices and of reaching the point of overstimulation, where their nervous system becomes flooded with stimulus and their rationality and self-control become compromised. This is true for such kids in all highly stimulating activities (sports, rough play, silliness, etc.), but especially with video games. In this situation, the child begins gaming and quickly moves past the point of satisfaction to a state of overstimulation in which the gaming is no longer satisfying but a source of intense craving—this is the state of video game addiction. For these kids, no matter how much time they have with the games, it's never enough to satisfy them.

It's hard to know when a child has crossed the line from intense interest to addiction. Every child has different tolerances. Certainly some kids who are less focused and highly active don't become addicted to screens, but then again many do. So, if you're wondering whether your child has crossed the line into addiction, you'll have to assess his or her temperamental vulnerability along with observing the reactivity, preoccupation, and other concerning behaviors the screens produce. This will give you enough information to decide whether the use of screens is enjoyable for them or creating a vortex of craving that produces stress and conflict for all involved.

Screens can provide parents with a powerful motivator to get kids to work on things like the core skills, homework, or family responsibilities. In addition, screens—especially games and phones—are an increasing part of the modern childhood experience, and they are a common connection among most kids. Kids who have no access to screens and games often feel alienated from their peers' conversations, which creates social stress for these kids who are left out of the loop. Screens can certainly become problematic for parents. But rather than take a rigid stance, I find it more useful to see screens as a way to better understand a child's temperament and to help them learn about the balance between playtime and responsibility. If you can allow some video game time and use it as a reward or a motivator, great—it can be a very powerful incentive. If it is not possible to use screens and maintain balance in your child's life, however, then you'll need to minimize your child's exposure to them—and that's okay too. Either way, if you've put some thought into how electronics interface with your child's individual temperament, then you are in the best position to make an informed decision about this modern phenomenon in your child's life.

Chapter Summary

Here is a recap of some of the highlights and tips presented in this chapter:

- Understand your child's basic temperament profile. Note the traits that are particularly high or low.
- Start to recognize how these traits contribute to his or her reactions and behaviors.
- Work with your child to develop strategies to help with pronounced temperament traits e.g. anxiety from high sensitivity, impulsivity, focus issues, difficulties with transitions.
- Teach your child to take responsibility for his or her temperament by explaining to relevant adults how his or her temperament creates dilemmas i.e. in the classroom, on the sports field, etc.
- Teach your child to joint problem solve with others about situations that trigger his or her strong temperament traits.
- Keep in mind that traits like sensitivity might be masked by more visible traits like activity level.
- Get to know your own temperament profile and see how it interfaces with your kids'.
- Watch out for overidentification.
- Learn to separate behaviors that come from temperament (that are largely out of your child's control), from his or her intentional choices.
- Understand how electronics interface with your child's particular temperament and make a plan for maintaining balance in this part of his or her life.

Chapter 6

∞

Dealing with Negative Behaviors

Punishment doesn't work. The reason behind this is very simple: it doesn't teach any new skills. Well, maybe it does, if you consider waiting for the punishment to be over a skill. But if you started reading this book at the beginning, you know that I'm talking about skills that can prevent negative behavior from happening again—the core skills. Without some new skills in the mix, kids' options are limited the next time they're in the same situation. Leaving them to figure out what new skills are needed, and how to apply them next time, is a tall order for kids to do alone. If they can't come up with new skills on their own, they are destined to repeat the same negative behaviors. Adding punishment doesn't teach the missing skills. In fact, expecting kids to change their behavior after punishment, without helping them build new skills for the next time around, is a set up for failure. It creates an unrealistic expectation on our part as parents and is a recipe for disaster for our kids.

Remember, kids' brains aren't done developing until they're in their early twenties. So it's a real mistake to expect them to analyze, understand, and evaluate their own behavior and then to problem solve solutions all by themselves, with only the motivation of avoiding punishment from their parents. Kids just don't yet have the developmental brainpower to pull this off by themselves. Without the guidance of grown-ups, their patterns of behavior simply won't change.

Why then has punishment remained the go-to method for teaching kids about their behaviors? First and foremost, because it provides the illusion that it works by getting the child's attention and interrupting the behavior for the moment. When you can stop negative behavior by yelling at a child, for instance, it sure seems to be effective. It's true that the yelling will likely stop the behavior, especially if you scream loud enough, but the real question is whether interrupting the behavior by overwhelming the child gives them any skills that will allow them to change their patterns of behavior? The answer is no. Punishment does communicate a parent's displeasure with behavior, so it does make a parent's values clear. But outside of that, it's pretty ineffective. Again, why has punishment remained so popular? I think it's mostly because of two things. First, it's easy to apply because most of us were taught how to do it during our own childhoods when we were on the receiving end of it. So it's something that we *can do* when our kids break the rules, and it's something we know well. Second, punishment is something of a cultural tradition. Punishment has long been the main parenting skill passed down from previous generations, and so it has inherited a value that it doesn't actually deserve. It has traveled down family lines for decades and become embedded in our ideas about child-rearing, thus remaining popular while holding an illusion of effectiveness—despite the fact that it's really not very effective at all.

So, punishment is old-school parenting, and we need to get rid of it altogether, right? Not so fast. Punishment doesn't work by itself, but it does have a small and important role in a more complete parenting response. Let me explain. Punishment, or "consequences" as it is called these days, is useful when it is combined with teaching the essential skills. When used in this way, punishment can do the things it's good at, like emphasizing the parents' values and alerting kids to a bad decision. Again, this is true only when punishment is applied as one part of a larger, more complete response that ensures a maximum learning of new skills. Applied in this way, punishment and consequences become part of the authority arm of parenting. When applied constructively and in combination with the empathy arm, punishment is converted from an ineffective and outdated intervention into one component of a complete and effective approach to teaching skills that helps kids change their behaviors. More on how exactly to do this in a moment—first, let's look at a couple forms of punishment that are old-school and don't work.

Guilt and Shame

Guilt and shame are two punitive methods for trying to control kids' behaviors that have a negative impact on the child. Guilt is when a parent tries to make a child feel bad about his or her behavior. Guilt-inducing comments like "How could you do that after all I do for you" or "If you loved me, you wouldn't act that way" are geared to activate a child's conscience, or sense of right and wrong, by making him or her feel bad about past behavior. Feeling bad about their behavior is then supposed to drive kids to control their behavior.

The problem with guilt is that its main focus is making a child feel bad as opposed to learning from mistakes. Making a child feel bad does not promote learning; instead, it damages the parent-child relationship and has a negative impact on a child's self-esteem. The fact is that most kids already feel bad after causing a problem (after they calm down), and they don't benefit in any way from being made to feel worse. Though it is true that a bit of natural remorse may help a child remember a mistake and could also help prevent the child from doing it again, this remorse should be the product of the child's self-evaluation, not the product of a parent's desire to make sure the child feels bad. In a parent-child conversation, a guilt-inducing statement like "You should feel bad because you hurt Sammy" would be better replaced with one such as "Now that we've talked about your behavior with Sammy, I wonder how you feel about what you did?" The revised conversation helps the child stop and focus on the fact that it feels bad to offend someone, and it also makes the remorse a part of the child's self-discovery, instead of something the parent imposes on the child. Attempts at making kids feel bad about their actions often backfire because eventually kids begin to lose respect for the guilt-inducing adult, which decreases their desire to take in that adult's advice. The natural response humans have toward those who try to create negative feelings within them is anger, resentment, and eventually a desire to disconnect.

Another problem with guilt is that it's an indirect form of communication on the parent's part. Instead of saying, "You did that, and I'm still upset with you about it and really want to know that you've learned from your behavior," which is honest and direct, saying something like, "I don't see how you can sleep at night after what you did," or worse yet, giving the child the silent treatment, promotes indirect expression of negative feelings, which is potentially confusing for a child.

Lastly, guilt replaces self-evaluation with too much focus on the adult's experience—in essence, the parent becomes the victim of the child. Isn't it better to have our kids strengthen their conscience by having them engage in self-evaluation instead of being focused on their parents' opinion? If a child feels bad after doing something, okay—maybe that experience will help the child not to do it again. We can then sit with our kids and help them figure out how not to do things that end up making them and others feel bad. But if we replace teaching self-evaluation with guilt, which instead requires negative feelings without self-evaluation, we are not actually helping our kids to build a conscience. Instead, we're simply trying to make our kids feel bad about things they've already done. Helping kids think about their actions, the impact on others, their own feelings afterward, and then helping them make decisions for themselves about future behavior is the best kind of teaching. Teaching by making the child feel bad is an old-school method of behavioral control that creates many more problems than it solves.

Shame is the cousin of guilt. The difference is that shame makes a child feel bad not about something they've already done but about themselves. "You should be ashamed of yourself," "You're bad," and "Why can't you act like (another child)" are slogans of this kind of teaching. As with guilt, these comments are supposed to steer kids toward good behavior by making them feel bad when held up to our adult ideal or the behavior of another child. Shame produces all the negative by-products guilt creates, with an even greater negative impact on self-esteem. It's bad enough that some kids are made to feel bad about something they've already done and can't undo because it's in the past (guilt), but worse is when a child's behavior is not separated from the child so that the only interpretation left is for the child to feel bad about himself or herself. This negative impact is magnified when parents use humiliation or shame the child in front of others, adding embarrassment to the child's experience. This kind of adult behavior does not encourage the child to learn about right and wrong; in fact, it does the exact opposite. It severely damages the adult-child relationship and creates emotional scars for the child that can take a lifetime to undo.

As with guilt, if an adult sits down with a child to help the child self-evaluate his or her behavior and they find that part of the child's experience is feeling ashamed about what's been done, then shame becomes a natural part of the learning process. But if the child experiences shame as a result of the adult's agenda to create that feeling in the child, then the child's self-evaluation is compromised, and the learning process is derailed. If you've used guilt and shame to pressure or to control your child to behave better, stop. Don't do this again. Instead, use the many techniques presented here, which are much more effective and will strengthen the parent-child bond.

Moving Beyond Punishment to Empathy and Authority

Okay, so it's clear that we need to move beyond guilt, shame, and punishment if we hope to help kids change behaviors in an effective and lasting way. How do we do this? Well, this is where the two arms of parenting kick into gear to help us help our kids develop the five core skills and ultimately get a handle on self-control. The first order of business is creating balance between the empathy and authority. Knowing when to move in with more empathy or authority is an important part of applying these two influences and is what I call *the art of parenting*. The art comes from getting a natural feel for each difficult situation and then figuring out whether more empathy or authority is needed. There's no formula for how much to move in with either arm because there are so many variables at play in each challenging situation. There are, however, some basic guidelines that can help you figure out which arm is most needed and when. For instance, the more challenging the behavior your child is presenting, the more you will need to set clear parameters to guide behavior, which is a product of the authority arm. On the other hand, moments when your child is overwhelmed but not presenting a behavioral challenge are the times you will need to move in primarily with empathy. Remember though that although empathy and authority are presented as separate influences here for clarity, in reality they almost always exist together to some degree. No matter how much authority we present to our kids, for instance, we always want them to feel on a deeper level that we still love them (empathy).

The graph below presents the relationship between the escalation of behaviors and the movement from responses of primarily empathy to increasing authority. You can see that when behaviors are milder, we retain a more empathic stance, and as behaviors escalate in severity, we move to more authority.

Behaviors and the Empathy-Authority Scale

Behaviors:

	Authority
Pushing or hitting	↑
Yelling or threatening	↑
Power Struggles	↑
Demanding	↑
Complaining	↑
Withdrawn or fearful	↑
	Empathy

Vulnerable states such as fear and worry require less authority because behaviors are not typically escalated. This makes it easier and more effective to stay in an empathic stance, tuning into the child's suffering. From there you can move to problem solving to see what solutions might be possible. An example of this might be when a child won't walk through the door of a new classroom because he or she is afraid. This is an intense feeling state, but it doesn't produce a disruptive behavior, so a parent can remain empathic. When we're aligned with our kids' feelings, they're more likely to work with us—in this case, to take a risk and to move closer and closer toward the classroom door. You might even throw in a special incentive to help your child be brave. Notice, though, that not much authority is needed in this type of situation. Emotional attunement and gentle guidance are most effective in these kinds of anxious moments.

The middle of the list presents mildly difficult behaviors (complaining, demanding, etc.), which often require empathy paired with some authority. Empathy and authority work well together for these types of situations because the child and the parent haven't been swept away by a rush of emotion and so are still able to think and make clear choices. The authority could be delivered in the form of holding basic limits and a warning about not "going there" with the behavior. An example of this might be when you're at the store with your child and he or she wants you to buy the neon green breakfast cereal with the toy at the bottom. The first three times they ask you, you stay empathic and respond, "That sure looks like fun cereal, and you even get a toy! I'm sorry honey. I know it's disappointing but we're not getting it. It's not very healthy for your body." On the fourth request, though, you're tired of broadcasting the same answer so you add a little more authority and say firmly, "Remember those cookies we were going to get for your play date when Thomas comes over? Well, we're not going to get them if you ask me again about the cereal. My answer is no." This amount of authority is meant to curb mildly disruptive behavior and warn the child that more authority will be applied in the form of consequences if the behavior continues.

At the top of the Empathy-Authority Scale are situations that contain escalated emotional and behavioral states, and may even include serious threats or physical aggression. Under these circumstances, the empathy arm is pulled back considerably in favor of the needed authority stance. An example of this might be when a child is chasing her sister through the house screaming that she is going to pull her hair out when she catches her. In this instance there isn't time or need for empathy. What's needed here is to get the situation back to safety and control. The parent might physically get between the kids, speak in raised and firm voice, and give directives and warnings about significant consequences for anyone who does not stop immediately. This level of authority is always needed when safety is an issue.

Developing the natural ability to move in and out with the arms of empathy and authority is the art of parenting and is not easy at first. I have found myself ineffective many times because I presented either too much empathy and not enough guidance or the reverse, which made the situation worse. Some parents effectively balance empathy and authority more naturally than others. The good news is that every parent can learn and eventually master the art of combining these two influences. And as you do, the confidence you will feel in your parenting will amaze you, because you will have an effective, balanced approach for dealing with all behavior situations.

A good example of combining both arms of parenting to achieve the best result is in the push for independence. The old saying rings true: *Don't do anything for your children that they can do for themselves.* This idea comes from the authority arm. It clearly sets the bar, or your expectations for your child's behavior. It is certainly true that we want our kids doing as much for themselves as they can. Doing things for our kids that they can easily do for themselves interferes with their self-confidence and creates dependence on the parent or parents. However, there are other important things to consider and that's where the empathy arm comes in. Since the empathy arm considers things such as the child's emotional state and temperament, it adds valuable information that balances the parent's decision on how high to set the bar when it comes to independence.

Parents who only use the authority arm become rigid and demanding about how their child will establish independence. They rarely stop to consider individual traits or circumstances. These parents fall back on delivering the same message regardless of the child's feelings or current situation. Their mantra is "Do it for yourself!" and doesn't ever change. This kind of influence can create resentment and actually lower a child's efforts for independence over time. Conversely, parents who think only about a child's difficulties or emotional state often end up helping too much. Indulgent parents create kids who feel entitled and dependent. Parents who give too much also experience burnout, becoming, in essence, a servant to the child. Neither of these parenting approaches is complete. Responses that combine empathy and authority—such as, "I need you to clean up your own mess, but since you told me you're super tired, I'll do part of it—but only if you do your part"—are much more complete and effective because they ask the child to exercise maximum responsibility and effort, while taking into consideration the child's feelings and circumstances. Over time, a child who feels considered while being guided will put more effort into cooperation and self-management—and thus become more independent.

Many households have parents that lean very far toward either empathy or authority in their parenting stance. Some of these parents don't add the other influence because it seems too difficult or they figure the other parent will bring the other influence. This is not complete parenting. Complete, effective parenting means not just defaulting to what is easiest or most comfortable, but doing what is best for the child. Each parent needs to have the ability to incorporate both empathy and authority. If you tend to default to one arm of parenting, work on balancing your skills by adding the other. Practice adding some firm, clear limits to your natural ability to tune into your child's feelings, or begin to put yourself in your child's shoes and consider how it feels to be on the other end of your authority and add empathy to your corrective messages. Practice adding this kind of balance to your parenting, and you will see how much more effective you become. You will also appreciate the improvement in your relationship with your child.

Now that you understand the relationship between empathy and authority, let's look at how you might deal with negative behaviors using more or less of either. When dealing with negative behaviors, I like to separate situations into two main types: *hot moments* and *reflective moments*. Each of these types of parenting moment requires different amounts of empathy or authority, depending on the difficulty of the behavior you are dealing with.

Hot Moments

Hot moments are the hardest to deal with because they are when kids are most upset. Hot moments are usually made worse by the added pressure of time constraints or circumstances like being in public where embarrassment for the parent becomes a factor. In hot moments, things are escalating, and you're dealing with heightened states of emotion and the difficult behaviors that result from them.

Because these moments tend to escalate quickly and contain heightened emotions, they are not the best time to help kids work on the skills they need for better behavior. Hot moments should instead be seen as the time to move in mostly with authority to calm things down and get the situation back under control. Hot moments are very difficult to resolve because as emotion increases, cognition decreases: (emotion ↑ cognition ↓). This means that the more upset a child becomes, the less able he or she will be to think, learn, and process information. Kids who are in the midst of a rage or a tantrum take in very little information because their nervous systems are flooded with the emotional experience. I say "kids" because that is the focus of this book, but obviously, these processes apply to adults too—after all, we all have the same basic wiring.

So kids and parents both become mentally challenged as emotions flare, making it much harder for both to think clearly, remain calm, and come up with viable solutions. These emotionally intense moments leave very few options for rational discussion and so are hard to use as teachable moments. What we focus on instead is containing the behaviors, and even success with containing behaviors can be limited because heightened emotion and decreased cognition make listening and compliance much harder for kids. Complicating things further is the fact that each child has his or her unique temperament, developmental abilities, and coping skills, which have a big influence on how well the child will handle emotionally charged moments. All these factors together make it very difficult for any one person to come up with a one-size-fits-all game plan that will work in every situation. Lots of people say they have the answers for what to do with escalated behaviors, but I have yet to read a book or hear a person present a method that works consistently across all situations. And this makes sense given the number of variables in play.

So what to do then? First, remain aware that any situation has many moving parts, so our response to a hot moment needs to consider the individual characteristics of both the current situation and our child. This means that what worked in one environment might be less effective in another. It also means that you, the parent, will remain the best guide for your child in these difficult situations. Not only do you know your child best but also you can figure out over time what seems to work to get things back under control and in which situations. This is why you can't rely solely on a book or someone else's experience. You have to combine what *you know* about your child (temperament, developmental level, coping skills, etc.) with methods that make sense to you, and then experiment to see what strategies are most effective for your child. In this way, you become the expert at dealing with your child's hot moments, and you develop strategies for helping your child de-escalate, based on suggestions from others (other parents, books, professionals, etc.) that prove over time to be effective for you and your child. There are many such suggestions in this book, which many parents have found effective. However, it remains your job to find the right fit between anyone's advice and what works for your individual child. Remember, you are the expert on *your child*.

Teaching Kids How to Calm Down

Before we move on to what helps in difficult behavior situations, there is one thing that can contribute significantly to preventing hot moments from getting too hot to handle, and that's teaching kids to cool down. Kids' nervous systems get overloaded easily. They are still developing the ability to regulate themselves and to stay calm. During moments of upset, a child's system revs up and gets ready to take on the stressor with either the fight, freeze or flight response. The child's bloodstream fills with the chemicals of the stress response, such as cortisol and adrenaline, and the mind stops taking in information to focus instead on the stressful event. This is the typical stress response for kids and adults, and it takes a lot of practice to learn to calm this process down once it has begun.

Helping kids learn to calm themselves is a worthwhile endeavor because it gives them the means to get their nervous systems back to a regulated state. Knowing how to calm one's self down gives a person a greater sense of control—something we lose as the swell of emotion takes over. Kids who are wired with a high level of either sensitivity or reactivity especially benefit from having some calming exercises to use. Here are a few techniques you can teach your child that will help re-regulate his or her system.

- **Personal Break.** Teach your child to take a few minutes away from the situation to gather his or her thoughts. This is not a disciplinary action but a coping strategy, so ask your child if he or she needs a break rather than telling your child to go.
- **Stop and Breathe.** Show your child how to keep his or her body from reacting by first saying a word such as "stop" or "freeze" out loud and then by taking five slow, deep breaths. Teach your child to count these breaths backwards, from five to zero.
- **Safe Place.** With your child, designate a special "chill-out space" to retreat to when he or she feels overwhelmed. Encourage your child to monitor when he or she is ready to come out. If your child is away from home and needs to chill out, teach him or her to imagine the safe place while taking a personal break wherever possible, away from the stressor.

- **Yoga.** Teach your child a few yoga poses to relax the body. Encourage him or her to practice the helpful poses when they feel tense or experience something negative.

- **Getting Outside.** Nature provides endless opportunities for exploring and unwinding—even in the backyard. Being in the natural elements is very soothing, so take your child on a walk and notice the sky, the trees, and any details of nature that you find together. This unwinds the upset mind and teaches kids to retreat to nature to calm down.

- **Progressive Muscle Relaxation.** Have your child tense and hold for three seconds, and then consciously relax each of the following muscle groups: the face, shoulders, arms and hands, stomach, and legs and feet. Have your child then notice how much calmer his or her body feels afterward.

If you have a child who gets tense or upset easily, help him or her learn two of the calming exercises. Offer a special reward whenever you ask your child to practice them, and he or she does. Start by having your child do a calming exercise during small upsets, when he or she is still thinking clearly and receptive to your input. As your child gets better at self-calming, ask him or her to follow through during bigger upsets. You can even give an extra special reward when your child remembers to do an exercise without being reminded.

The ability to self-regulate is an important skill that becomes more and more relevant as the pace and intensity of modern life continue to increase. Let's teach our kids how to reclaim the calm when life's events send their nervous systems into overload. This will help them get to the place where they can look at a problem rationally and then participate in finding a solution.

The Game Plan

Learning to use calming and coping mechanisms takes time and practice. So what do you do along the way if you reach a moment where you can't get your kid to calm down and problem solve with you? Well, then it's time to move to the next step, and for that you'll need a solid game plan. The components of an effective game plan are outlined in the sections that follow. They involve both understanding concepts, such as the emotional response cycle, and practicing parenting skills, such as using incentives and consequences. But before we move on to exploring those areas, we need to start by remembering this: the hot moments are emergency moments and are not the times to teach the core skills. Hot moments call for simple and direct communication that attempts to achieve two goals: to help the child feel understood and to get behavior back under control.

To help your child feel understood, remember to start with a simple statement of empathy, such as "I know that you're very disappointed" or "I can see that you're really mad about me saying no." This kind of communication soothes a child's frayed nerves and identifies the adult as someone who would like to help and not just frustrate the child. Even if it seems to have no impact on your child's behavior, start with an empathic statement. Over time it will increase the child's trust in your intentions and create a better relationship between the two of you, which means that the child will be more likely to take in your direction.

If the child seems too upset to take in your empathic statement, encourage the child to do a calming exercise before you discuss the issue any further. Remind the child that you want to be on his or her team and to listen to their ideas, but you can only do this when everyone is calm. If the child is uncooperative, you can either give the child some time without your input or offer an incentive for calming down and then talking with you.

Once the child is calm, invite the child to talk about his or her side of the issue, with a particular focus on feelings. This will allow the child to release the energy contained in the feelings and feel heard. If the child does share how he or she is feeling, make sure you stop and validate that you understand what their position is and how they feel. If the child is expressing his or her feelings with behaviors instead of words, share with the child what you think the intention of the current behavior is. Kids don't always consciously know why they are doing what they're doing, so it can help them organize their experience if you call it as you see it.

For example, to a child who is seeking your attention with negative behavior you can say, "It looks like you're trying to get my attention by spilling your water on the table, is that right?" To a child who is withdrawing and trying to make you feel guilty, you can say, "Maybe you want me to feel bad because I put you on time-out, which made you feel bad. Is that why you're not talking to me?" To the child trying to engage you in a power struggle, you might say, "It seems like you think that if you argue with me, at some point I'll change my mind. Is that right?" All of these responses help increase your child's awareness of the intent of his or her behavior, while also communicating your interest in understanding his or her upset.

When the child affirms your guess about the intent of his or her behavior, you can do two things. First, you can invite the child to tell you what they want you to know, and second, be clear about your response. For instance, if the child says "yes" he or she was trying to change your mind through a power struggle, first invite the child to tell you directly that he or she really wants to change your mind. You might say something like, "You know, instead of continuing to argue with me, you could just tell me that you really want me to change my mind." This encourages the child to use direct communication instead of honing skills at arguing and persuasion. And second, let the child know what your final answer is. For instance, you can say that you are disconnecting from the argument and that if the child continues to argue with you, there will be a consequence. The other option is to flex a little and let the child know that if he or she will stop the behavior and instead tell you directly, you will work with the child to find a solution. Either way, you're using the difficult moment to help the child work on clear, direct communication while being clear about your position. Encouraging this kind of communication when things are heating up creates clarity for each of you and helps move things away from reactive interaction.

Commenting to the child that you understand the intention of his or her behavior is similar to the empathic statement; both are geared to help the child understand that even though there is behavior that you don't like, you remain interested in understanding the child's experience and communicating constructively. The following example illustrates this process:

> **Parent:** I can see, James, that you're pretty upset [the empathic statement]. Can you tell me with your words what's going on? [The invitation to talk.]
>
> **James:** No! [James throws his backpack on the couch and storms out of the room.]

Parent: Looks like you're very upset. How about you do your five deep breaths to calm your body? Remember, you can earn fifteen minutes of video game time for practicing this now. [A reminder to use a calming exercise with an incentive for doing so.]

James: You're mean!

Parent: Looks like you're trying to show me how mad you are at me by throwing your backpack and calling me names. Is that right? [Sharing your understanding helps the child connect to the intention of his or her behavior.]

James: Yes I am!

Parent: Well, I can understand that you're mad at me because I did say no to the sleepover, but the way you're showing me is not okay and will lead to a consequence. I'm going to give you a few minutes to calm down, and then maybe you can tell me with your words why you're so mad about this. Then we can work together on a solution. [Here the adult provides more empathy, sets a limit on the behavior, suggests a calming break, encourages direct communication, and offers joint problem solving.]

This scenario uses all the elements discussed thus far: an empathic statement, a calming exercise, helping the child connect to the intention of his or her behavior, setting limits on the negative behavior, and encouraging communication through words for a constructive problem solving conversation. Of course, real-life situations won't always follow the exact order in which I presented these elements. The point is not to use these responses in exact order as a script but to apply them as needed when difficult behavior is emerging. Also, when dealing with older kids, around eight-years-old and up, teach them to call for a time-out (a break to calm down, not a punishment). It's good to teach kids to monitor their own level of upset once they're developmentally ready for this.

As you begin this process of speaking to your child's emotions and intentions in order to guide the interaction toward a positive outcome, you'll need to check in on your own frustration level too. Are you remaining calm enough to deal with the situation? In some situations you might, but in others, you might start to lose your cool. If you're feeling too frustrated, you won't be thinking clearly and will likely be more reactive, so it would be a good idea to call a time-out for yourself. It is certainly within your right as a parent to tell your child that you are too upset to talk at that time and that you will talk about the situation after you calm down. What you're looking for as a parent is effectiveness, and sometimes it's more effective to give the situation time to settle before you address the behavior.

Once you feel calm enough to proceed, you'll need to decide how things appear to be going at that point. If what you've done thus far has helped the child calm down and get into problem-solving mode, great. If you're still dealing with negative behavior, though, you have to decide whether to move in to control the behavior or to respond by ignoring the behavior, which I call planned or intentional ignoring.

Intentional Ignoring

So it all starts with an empathic statement or two to facilitate recovery and cooperation. If your empathy and invitation to talk about the issue in a cooperative way goes well, you're on your way to a constructive outcome. But if the child continues the difficult behavior, it's time to decide whether you're calm enough to be good in the situation. If not, you'll tell your child that you're too upset and you're taking a break. At this point, you might also hand the situation off to your partner, as long as your partner isn't too upset. If you're calm enough to deal with the behavior, then the next decision is how to engage the child.

First, decide whether to stay engaged or not. Many parents don't think of disengagement, or ignoring the child, as a form of intervention, but it is—and an effective one at that. Although most hot moments contain negative behaviors that you will want to address and get under control, sometimes you'll identify moving in to stop the behavior as less effective than staying out of the struggle. For instance, sometimes kids bait parents with provocative comments, even after they've been shown empathy and have been invited to talk about the issue. When kids bait, they are stuck in their anger and looking for a reaction from their parents, either to get their parents' attention or to punish them in some way. In these moments, it may be best to ignore the behavior entirely. The other course would be to ignore the first few comments and behavior, but if they don't stop, then set a clear limit, with the warning of a consequence.

Another situation in which it might be a good idea not to address escalating behavior is with children in the two- to five-year-old range who will provoke to see how much power they have. Kids in this age range are facing the developmental task of figuring out how much power and control they can have with others, so they will try on controlling and provocative behaviors. Many of these behaviors—such as telling you what to do or acting like they're in charge—can be addressed by adults simply clarifying the limits of the child's power and then disconnecting from the conversation. For example, you might say something like "I'm sorry, but you're not in charge of this," to which the child will likely say, "Yes I am!" You will then respond with silence, because there's nothing left to say. Any more conversation will give the child the impression that he or she does have the power to keep you engaged and negotiating, so you need to walk away from the conversation.

Kids in this developmental age-range tend also to become emotionally overwhelmed and can easily end up in tantrum states. For many of these kids, it's actually beneficial to let them experience the full course of their emotional cycle without much interruption because there are valuable lessons for them to learn from the process. Let's take a look at the typical emotional response cycle these kids go through, and then I'll explain some of the benefits when adults don't get further involved.

The cycle of emotional escalation follows a predictable course. It starts with a triggering event that elicits an emotional response. The emotional response then ramps up until it reaches its peak, at which point de-escalation starts. The de-escalation, or calming down process, eventually ends at baseline, or recovery, which is when the emotional cycle is done. An easy way to think about the emotional cycle is as a curve that extends upward and then goes back down.

The Emotional Response Cycle

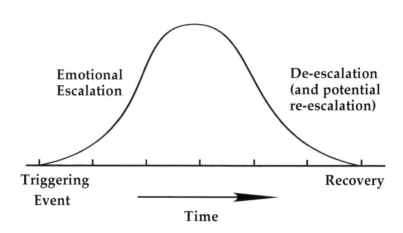

Emotional Peak

Emotional
Escalation

De-escalation
(and potential
re-escalation)

Triggering
Event

Recovery

Time

Understanding the emotional response cycle gives you several advantages. First, it allows you to identify and understand triggering events, the events that typically set your child off. Knowing your child's specific triggers allows you to predict which situations might upset them in the future, giving you the chance to work on preventative coping skills. Although triggers are different for each child, they often correlate with specific temperament traits—for example, having to wait for long periods challenges the naturally impatient active child. The other advantage of understanding the response cycle is that it offers an objective viewpoint during a distressing moment. When kids are in the midst of a tantrum, or an escalation, it can be very helpful to identify where they are in the process. Tracking the process keeps us from getting too pulled into their emotional turmoil and reminds us that there is an end in sight. In the throws of an embarrassing public tantrum, it can seem like it's never going to end.

The most important part of the emotional response is the recovery because as young children recover they learn that they can survive their emotional cycle and that things will be okay again. Again, two- to five-year-olds are very susceptible to tantrums, especially intense or reactive kids, and the experience is overwhelming for them. So it's important that they learn that when their world comes unglued, it will come back together again. An important note to add here is that when a child is approaching recovery, re-escalation can easily occur. Because the child's system is already on high alert, if he or she is stressed again, even just a little bit, the alarms go off again and the child returns to peak escalation in seconds. Some kids' nervous systems are more prone to quick re-escalation, so you'll have to observe whether your child is wired this way. It's important to be sure a child is fully recovered before you begin interacting with the child again.

If the response cycle is interrupted for some reason, then the child doesn't get to experience recovery and doesn't learn the important lessons gained from making it through the emotional event. There are a few problems that can occur if the natural response cycle is interrupted. First, there's the potential a young child will learn to fear his or her own emotions because they believe the emotions will go on forever. Of course, they won't, but the child needs to learn this by experiencing the flood of feelings and making it safely to the other side. Second, if the tantrum, or escalation, has a purpose—such as getting mommy to buy a toy at the store—then the child needs to see that the tantrum will not work as a means of coercion. Lastly, if a child perceives that his or her escalation scares, worries, or overwhelms the parent, the child can make the mistake of learning that strong feelings can be used to gain power or to punish others, which is not a healthy relationship to one's own emotions.

So how does the emotional response cycle get interrupted? There are many ways, and they usually come from the parents. Sometimes parents cut the cycle off just as the child begins escalating, other times when the cycle is right at its peak, and still other times interruption occurs just before recovery begins. The most common forms of interruption are diversions or distractions. Sometimes parents move in with humor to distract the child from his or her feelings. Other times parents will distract with interesting items or other things for the child to pay attention to. Sometimes parents become overwhelmed themselves during the process and sideline the child's emotions with a bigger explosion of their own feelings. At other times, parents may use threats or fear to stop kids from continuing through their emotional cycle. All of these circumstances interrupt the natural cycle and don't allow the child to experience the full process of their own feelings.

Why shouldn't we interrupt the cycle—after all we're talking about a tantrum? Well, that's a good question, and this is where it gets a bit complicated. You don't have to *never* interrupt an escalation, but because young kids especially need to learn about their natural emotional process, it's important to let their emotions run their course a good amount of the time. This is where planned ignoring becomes a useful tool because understanding the value of not getting involved in a child's emotional storm allows you to step out of the fight and let him or her have their experience without interruption. This might mean that you let them writhe and scream on the kitchen floor or at the park. If you need to go to another room, you'll step over the child and go about your business. What you have to monitor is the child's safety, but other than that, you'll stay out of the emotional moment.

Then there will be times when you're in public or in a rush to get somewhere, and you'll need to interrupt the cycle. That's fine, as long as it doesn't happen too often. You can use any distraction you like that doesn't elicit fear to keep the child from escalating or to get the child out of the cycle at such times. You might use friendly humor to help the child switch gears, or maybe you'll focus the child's attention on something exciting that's coming up. Again, there are many ways to interrupt the escalation cycle if you have to, just remember to do this infrequently because you run the risk of teaching your child that feelings are something to be avoided.

Whether you exercise planned ignoring or you interrupt your child, make sure you review the situation later (see the Review in Chapter 7) when your child has calmed down. This way you can help him or her understand the course of their feelings and why you stopped the cycle if you needed to stop it. So ignoring the behavior may be the answer, especially with the tantrums of younger children. Look carefully at a child's escalating behavior to assess the motivation behind the child's actions. If it feels like provocation, intimidation, or an old-fashioned power struggle, you may want to use planned ignoring. If you're dealing with an older child or behavior that violates the rights of others, you may decide instead to move in to control the child's behavior. When this is the case, it's time to address the negative behavior directly.

Keeping It Simple

Kids who are having a hard time controlling themselves need simple directives and clear choices. If you're dealing with a hot moment, you've followed the steps listed in the previous section (used an empathic statement, suggested a calming exercise, etc.), and you then decide that it's best not to ignore the child's behavior, it's time to move in and let the child know exactly what his or her choices are. Now you will be setting limits or giving a consequence, and when you do so, it will be important to keep your communication plain and clear. Keeping commands simple—as in "You need to stop that; this is your one warning"—is the best chance you have of penetrating the swirling clouds of emotion that upset kids become lost in. Part of keeping communication simple is being clear about the person you are talking to. I hear many parents address their kids using "we", as in, "Now, Rudy, we need to keep our hands off others' toys" or "Let's watch our tone, Ella, because we don't talk that way to others." The "we" really means "you" and should be avoided because it can be confusing to the child. Shifting from "we" to "you" is also symbolic of clear boundaries. When you are holding your authority with your child, you want to be clear that this is a moment when *you* are directing *him or her* because you are the parent, not the child's equal.

The same goes for asking vs. telling. Many parents make the mistake of asking their child to do something when they are really telling them. They may say, "Holly, would you like to have a seat and talk about what happened?" Then they're surprised when Holly says, "No!" That's when I would ask the parent, "Were you really asking her or telling her? You shouldn't give her the option of declining your invitation if you don't want her to." When the parent corrects, the statement becomes, "Holly, I would like you to come sit here and talk about what happened." It is important to be clear with our language as parents, especially when we are exercising authority with our child.

One thing that I remind myself of that is helpful with my own kids is that I don't have to make my point or teach the lesson in a hot moment. Part of keeping things simple in a hot moment is not loading up an already overloaded kid with too much information. When our kids are escalating and we're getting fed up, we tend to want to make them hear our opinion about their behavior. This makes sense, because their behavior is violating our standards in some way. But what we can remember that will take some of the pressure off of the heated situation is that we can teach the lesson at any time. In fact, addressing the problem with the child's behavior later may be more effective because the child's emotions will not be as intense, allowing him or her to process what we have to say. Another way to think about this is to skip the lecture when your child is misbehaving. Instead, focus on simple choices that get the behavior back under control. Later, discuss all the information you want your child to absorb about why you didn't like what he or she was doing. (In the next section, I'll present a good way to review difficult situations so that your child can learn the necessary lessons.)

In a hot moment, the communication that you're trying to keep simple and clear is going to be about choices. Whether you're trying to direct a child away from negative behaviors or just get the child to calm down, presenting the child's options in the form of simple choices gives him or her direction and a sense of control. Kids who are fighting with you, or each other, often want more control, but they're so upset that their emotions have taken over, making it hard for them to see the available options. So, giving them some options is a way to give them some control, while making the choices acceptable to you. Remember, the choices you give the child in a hot moment should be based on your assessment of what the child can realistically do and not on their emotional and irrational demands. You are in charge of the options, no matter how much your child tries to step into the role of decision maker. The goal in a hot moment is to get behavior under control. So make sure the choices you give your child are doable given the circumstances and the nature of your child's emotions. This may mean lowering your expectations at times to create an outcome that is both realistic and successful.

Since you are in control of the choices you will present, make sure that they help your child calm down and improve the situation for both of you. It's quite possible that your child might not like the options you deliver, but remember that this is not the time to escalate further by slipping into endless negotiation about the options. Instead, this is a time to stand firm and to use your authority to be clear about the choices. Also, try not to act overly invested in the outcome. You will likely prefer that your child make a certain choice, but try not to let your preference infuse the moment. Keep your child thinking about the choice *they* need to make instead of what *you* want them to do. If your child knows you want them to make a specific choice and he or she is mad at you, they will likely pick the choice that opposes you, even if it is not the best choice for them. So even though you do care about the choice your child will make, act as though you don't.

Let's look at an example with a boy named Lucas who just shoved his brother. Lucas's dad says, "Lucas, it looks like you're mad at Tyler. I just saw you shove him when he walked by. Your choices now are to control yourself and apologize to him or to go to your room." Lucas gives his dad an angry look, and his dad responds in an uninvested, even tone, "The choice is yours: you can spend your afternoon in your room or get back to what you were doing after you apologize to Tyler. I don't care which one you choose, but it's time to make a choice." Can you hear the tone of detachment? Lucas's dad would prefer to have Lucas decide to control himself and make amends with his brother, but he doesn't include his preference in his delivery of the choices. Lucas's dad knows that in an angered state Lucas will operate better if he can stay focused on himself and his choices (rather than his dad's wishes). He also knows that Lucas is now likely angry with him for calling him on his behavior, and so Lucas is more likely to choose against his dad's wishes. Lastly, with Lucas angry at his brother and now likely at his father too, his dad wants to give Lucas as much of a sense of control over the situation as possible. If Lucas can make a simple and less reactive choice, it will help him feel more control, exercise good judgment, and begin to de-escalate. In this scenario, Lucas's dad is exercising his authority to guide Lucas's behavior, and he is doing it in a clear and uninvested manner, which both guides the difficult behavior and keeps the interaction simple and easy for the escalated child to navigate.

Exercising authority by giving a child simple choices is an important part of dealing with difficult behavior, and it will often be enough to help a child get back on track. However, this is not always the case. At times, you will keep these steps in mind, but they won't be enough to keep the child from escalating further. When kids are upset, they are processing so little information that they are likely to get stuck in their anger, making them unable or unwilling to engage in decision making. For these reasons, parents need something to motivate kids to make a good choice. Before we move to talking about motivators, though, we should cover a few of the snags you can run into when communicating with your child about choices.

Diversions

When setting limits or giving choices, watch out for diversions. Diversions are kids' attempts to change the subject in order to avoid your limits or requirements. Not allowing the conversation to wander off onto another topic is an element of the consistency you want to present when dealing with difficult behaviors.

For example, kids learn very quickly whether they can make you feel guilty by playing the victim when you're in the middle of disciplining them. The situation might go something like this. Mom says, "Sarah, this is your one warning: stop using that tone with me or you will lose your TV show later." Sarah replies, "You hate me. I know you do because you went out with daddy and left me with a babysitter." This is Sarah's attempt to get her mom on another topic so that she doesn't have to deal with the limits mom just set. It is also likely a way for Sarah to let her mom know she's upset by mom's limit. Regardless, don't take the bait. The best response is to refocus the conversation on the original topic. So mom's reply might go like this, "I don't hate you, and I'm not talking any more about that right now. What I'm talking to you about is your tone with me, and I gave you a choice: change your tone or lose TV. It's your choice."

Another kind of diversion is the endless negotiation. This usually happens when you are saying no to a request. The purpose of the child's negotiation is to not have to deal with the final answer. Highly persistent kids are naturals at this technique and can pull parents in without their even noticing. The negotiator uses almost any means to keep the conversation alive because as long as you're still talking, your answer is not final. The child using negotiation as a diversion might ask you irrelevant questions or get you to argue about pointless details. If that doesn't work the child may try comments to provoke you into sympathy or anger. Either way the goal is the same, and that's to keep you on the dance floor. As long as the child has a partner, the dance isn't over.

Here is an example of a parent setting a limit and the child's diversions.

Parent's limit:
"I'm sorry, Mathew, but you can't go over to Reed's tonight. You have too much homework. That's my final answer."

Child's diversions:
1. "Technically, my homework isn't due until Friday, so I think I'm okay to go."
2. "Why do you hate Reed so much, mom?"
3. "I'll tell you what: I'll only stay for twenty minutes."
4. "How come you don't want me to have any fun in my life?"
5. "You're the meanest parent in the whole world!"

There are endless possibilities when it comes to diverting a conversation away from the answer a child doesn't want to hear. Kids and adults alike can become experts at this art. But this is not a skill you want to help your child practice, so guard against it by not participating in conversations about unnecessary details. Also, remember to hold firm with your limits—unless your child presents some information that is actually relevant to your decision.

What if the diversion has some truth to it? For instance, what if your child really does feel like you don't want them to have any fun in their life, and they're genuinely trying to tell you about it? Aren't we supposed to be good listeners and attune to our kids? How do we know when our kids are bringing up a diversion or a real issue that needs to be discussed? The answer is that we don't know for sure, but when we're disciplining our kids, we will not be discussing other topics. If they bring up something unrelated to the current discussion, we let them know that we will be happy to talk with them about that later but right now we're dealing only with the current situation. After our kids have accepted the limit we've set and that conversation is over, we can then ask them about a statement they made that might need more attention. If your child is still upset, however, wait until later when your child is calm again to inquire about a statement you want to learn more about. This way you keep your limit-setting moments free from diversions, while you show your child that you are always available for conversations about his or her concerns.

Will keeping language simple, making choices clear, and staying away from diversions lead children to make good choices? Well, that will do the trick much of the time and get you on the right path. But sometimes a child will be so stuck in a behavior that you will need a way to energize the child to make a good choice, and this is where motivators come into the picture.

Motivators—The Currency of Parenthood

Motivators are magnets that pull our kids in the direction of good choices. Motivators provide the energy that helps kids exercise self-control and self-management. They are essentially the things that we can add to or take away from our kids' lives to motivate them to make good choices. When giving our kids choices, we want to be seen as the messenger and not the warrior in battle. This is why we strive to present choices in a neutral tone and why we use motivators. It's easy to get pulled into a personal power struggle when trying to get an upset child to make a better decision. The way to avoid this is to let a motivator do the work. Using a motivator keeps you out of the struggle and instead makes the dilemma one between the child and what he or she wants. This is different from a scenario in which you try to convince your child to make a good choice, which keeps the upset child focused on you and the fact that you want to control them. Motivators don't replace authority; they are added to an authoritative stance to energize the child to move in the right direction.

Another reason to use motivators is that when kids are mad at their parents, anything parents ask them to do—"Please calm down" or "Stop screaming"—can be met with opposition. This is true for everyone. Imagine someone who's just made you angry immediately telling you how to act on top of that! None of us like to take direction from someone who is making us unhappy. Unfortunately, an essential part of parenting is saying no, and that creates a state of displeasure in our kids. So we can't get around the fact that we will upset our kids from time to time and that this is going to create anger and resistance to our ideas—at least until their feelings subside. So, after you make your child mad, don't invite him or her into a power struggle by also telling them what to do. Instead, help your child understand what his or her choices are, and let motivators do the work of steering them in the right direction.

An example of this might be you saying, "I'm sorry, but you can't have your friend over until you finish your homework." To this your child responds by getting angry and yelling at you. If you respond with "don't yell at me," you've provoked your child to yell again because your child sees that it's having an impact. However, if you say something like, "You know the consequence for yelling is no dessert. I'll leave it up to you to decide if you'll have dessert tonight," then you've used the motivator of dessert to help change the behavior. You've also stayed out of the power struggle. You've reminded your child of his or her choices and left the ball in their court, which gives them a sense of control.

Motivators can be incentives or consequences. Incentives are things that you can give to your child to help steer them toward good choices or reward them for doing something right. Some people call them bribes or carrots. I don't care what you call them—the fact is nobody goes to work without a paycheck. And it is work! When your mind is still developing and your coping mechanisms are limited, it is hard work to maintain control of yourself and make good choices. (It's hard for us grown-ups to do, and we have years of practice with fully developed brains!) So using incentives in certain situations can be helpful if they're presented in a thoughtful manner.

Identifying a few incentives and having them ready for hot moments is a lot easier than trying to come up with them on the fly, especially if you're getting upset. Of course, you can come up with incentives on the spot, such as stopping for ice cream when you're already out, but it's helpful to have a few incentives that you can use in a hurry.

You might worry that using incentives will give your child the wrong message. You may be concerned that it creates a dependence on external rewards and that it limits a child's ability to comply out of goodwill instead of coercion. My experience has shown me the opposite occurs. Most kids are experiential learners and largely concrete in their thinking. This means that they learn by being walked through a lesson rather than having someone explain it to them in abstract terms. In other words, kids learn best when adults help them have an experience of doing it right. When we support good behavior with external incentives, it gives kids something concrete, something they can touch, see, eat, or otherwise enjoy, something that is real for them. This experience generates the motivation to participate in good choices, which then allows them to experience the good feelings that come from cooperation. It also helps them build their identity around successful behavior and cooperation, which are self-reinforcing and over time make the external reward less and less significant.

A similar concern parents sometimes have about incentives is that a child will get so used to being paid-off that he or she will never do anything without the promise of some kind of reward.

This is a valid concern, and this can happen if we use incentives too often. But keep in mind that incentives are generally not used for minor incidents or for extended periods of time. Incentives are there to help a child develop new behavior or to get you and your child through a tough moment. I like to use incentives to help a child get through a situation I know in advance is going to be hard for him or her, such as participating in a boring adult activity or encountering a new challenge. I also like to use incentives to help kids practice the core skill of emotional communication. Getting a kid to open up and talk about a tough situation can be a challenge; greasing the wheels a bit with an incentive often makes it easier for the boy or the girl to get through such a conversation.

If you find yourself using incentives a lot, and your child is starting to ask you for something every time you want him or her to do something, then address this with your child. Help your child understand that rewards are only for times that are a real challenge and that you are the one who will decide when they will be given. Let your child know that you want to reward them for extra effort but that you also expect cooperative behavior even when rewards aren't being given because cooperation is an important part of the family system. Also let your child know that if he or she continues to bug you for extras, you will give fewer of them. Setting clear expectations about incentives is your responsibility as the parent as well as another way to help your child learn about limits and balance.

Incentives are great because they allow you to give to your child, which keeps a positive tone between the two of you. However, I have found that incentives are often less effective than consequences.

Consequences are the other way to motivate behavior change. When you either take something away or threaten to do so, you are using consequences in an effort to change a child's behavior. Some people also call this "losing privileges," which is a nice way to include the notion that the things kids get should not be taken for granted. As with incentives, having some go-to consequences in your back pocket will help during times of heightened emotion. Of course, you can also come up with consequences on the spot, which is especially useful if there is something coming up that your child really values. But, as with incentives, I have found that it's easier to have a few meaningful consequences that you usually use to help create behavior change, consequences such as going to bed early, loss of screen time (TV, computer, gaming), loss of desert, etc. Having these handy means that you don't have to scramble to think of a consequence when you're already frustrated and frazzled.

Some people talk about "natural consequences," and what they mean are consequences that are in some way tied to the current situation. So, threatening to take away an after-dinner treat because a child is misbehaving at a birthday party is not a natural consequence because there's no natural connection between the party behavior and the treat. Threatening to leave the birthday party because the child is misbehaving is a natural consequence because the punishment is clearly connected to the infraction. I try to use natural consequences whenever possible because they help kids make the connection between the situation they've created and the loss of privilege. However, sometimes the natural consequence is not as powerful as another one you might use, and in a really tough moment, you may need a more potent motivator.

For instance, let's say that your son is being too wild at the birthday party, so you threaten to leave if he doesn't settle down. Well, if he doesn't particularly care about being at the party, then the natural consequence may not work. If you want to stay at the party and need to get him under control, then you might decide to go with a stronger consequence that isn't natural, such as threatening to take away his video game time because you know that will stop his behavior. So, the decision to use a natural consequence or not will depend on the situation and how motivating the consequence you choose is.

No matter what kind of consequence you use, there is one thing you'll have to make sure you do—deliver. If you threaten to do something and don't, your child learns that you don't mean it, and they lose respect for your authority. This means that you don't want to threaten consequences that you're not prepared to execute, no matter how desperate you might feel.

Have you ever threatened your child with a monumental consequence in an act of desperation, only to realize as the words were leaving your lips that there was no way you could ever deliver the consequence? It's happened to most of us, and it creates a strange dilemma because you know you've issued an empty threat, which leaves you hoping your child doesn't call your bluff and continue the behavior. At the same time, you're trying to figure out how you might back out of the consequence without looking totally power-less. If you find yourself trapped in one of these unfortunate moments, not to worry—there is a way out! Totally frustrated, I once threatened to cancel my five-year-old's birthday party if her negative behavior continued. Of course, this was a totally empty threat, and I realized the ridiculousness of it as soon as I said it. Luckily, I knew of a way out that allowed me to change the consequence while preserving my authority. If you promise a consequence and for some reason can't or won't follow through, then simply tell your child that you've thought about it and changed your mind about the consequence. Your authority will be preserved if *you* are the one who changes the plan.

What we don't want is our authority eroded because our kids think that our threats are empty or that in some way they've overpowered or distracted us from following through on the consequence. In the incident with my daughter, I got lucky because the threat did stop her behavior, so I was not faced with the prospect of having to deliver on an unrealistic consequence. However, I was also racked with guilt about threatening to take away her much-anticipated princess party, so I had a talk with her later and apologized for the threat. I explained to her that I was frustrated and looking for a way to get her to stop doing what she was doing. We talked about how people sometimes say things that they don't mean when they get really mad, and I committed to using realistic consequences and she committed to practicing better listening in the future. In this way, I used my mistake to provide us with a good conversation about the impact of feelings on decision-making and a chance to practice repair.

Warnings are an important step before giving consequences and should be used. Before giving a consequence, you should always give a warning. This allows kids to see what's coming and prepare for the decision they need to make regarding their behavior. What you don't want is to add the feeling of surprise to an already emotionally overloaded child—that will always work against you. Warning kids of what's coming next is especially important if your child is low on the adaptability temperament trait. These kids already have a hard time switching gears. Kids who are high on the reactivity trait are also easily triggered and need time to process events, especially negative ones.

How many warnings do we give? Generally one. A child who

is capable of basic learning, which is most kids, can adapt to a one-warning system as easily as a six-warning system. Not only is it not necessary, giving a bunch of warnings erodes your authority and opens the window for diversions. If your child is low in adaptability or high in reactivity, you may decide to use two warnings—you don't need more than that. Just make sure your child has heard you. Eye contact is always important to have when you give a warning. It's the best way to know that our kids got the info. This is especially important for kids low on focus since they are distractible to begin with and often miss bits of information. For these kids, you'll probably want eye contact and an answer. If a kid is looking at you and able to form a verbal response, there's a good chance the kid got the information you're trying to give.

Just to clarify, we're talking about warnings for negative behaviors, which are different from warnings, or prompts, about upcoming transitions and other situations. The difference between warnings for negative behaviors and other situations is that with those for negative behavior your authority is activated and needs to be respected. In other situations, such as a child who is low focus and needs help getting ready for school, warnings or verbal reminders every five minutes may be part of your plan to help the child stay on track. In this case, the warnings are *prompts*, not a response to willful testing of your parental authority.

So, when you're dealing with negative behaviors, you'll move in mostly with the authority arm. You'll start with empathy to keep things constructive, and you'll invite your child to communicate and problem solve with you. If things don't improve, you'll remember to keep your communication simple and to create clear choices that will steer your child toward self-control. If needed, you'll use motivators to power their interest in making a good choice, or at the very least avoiding an unwanted consequence. You will do all these things to keep a hot moment from getting worse. Most of the time, this will work, and kids will get their behavior back on track. Sometimes, though, despite your best efforts, this won't work.

All parents from time to time have to deal with a child who has passed the point of no return. When this happens, our options are very limited and often we just have to ride it out. This might mean ignoring the behavior until the child enters the de-escalation phase or increasing your authority with a firmer voice and the threat of another, more serious consequence. You'll have to see what typically works best for your child. Kids who are struggling with self-control need to feel contained and safe, no matter how much they oppose us. Remember that it doesn't feel good for them to be out of control or engaged in negative behaviors, so we need to help contain them. Part of that means getting a feel for what a child can tolerate in the moment. In these most difficult moments, you'll have to see if what you're doing adds gas to the fire or calms the flames. Remember, you are the expert on what works best given your child's unique temperament and age. This is especially true as a child's behavior escalates. The higher the child is on the escalation curve, the fewer viable options there are for getting the behavior back under control. Having said that, there are some basic guidelines that can be followed for these situations, which I have outlined toward the end of this chapter.

When behaviors escalate, I always recommend a hands-off approach, if at all possible. This means that unless a child is unsafe, we keep our hands off of their bodies. Kids under five sometimes need to be held if they are hitting, biting, or acting in some way like this and won't stop. The older the child is, though, the more risk there is in putting your hands on them. There is no place in good parenting for hitting, spanking, pushing, or physically intimidating a child of any age. Although momentarily effective, these actions are wrong because they create fear in the child (not respect) and also other problems that will have to be cleaned up later. The bottom line is that corporal punishment teaches kids to solve problems with aggression, which causes long-term problems for your child. It also creates resentment and disrespect toward the parent, which decreases the parent's influence on the child. Parents who punish using aggression were often disciplined in this same way when they were children. These behaviors are deeply rooted in their parenting mind-set and define their understanding of how to teach kids. As parents, however, they have to find the strength and will to stop using ineffective and harmful parenting strategies. If you were taught to use such punishment in your childhood, don't do the same to your child. Preserve the parent-child relationship by using authoritative guidance to help your child learn about limits and consequences. There are other parents who end up using physical punishment and intimidation not because their parents did it to them but because of their own difficulty maintaining self-control.

Parents with reactive and intense temperaments can get easily triggered and are more prone to losing their temper and losing control. These parents especially need to try to stay neutral in the face of their kids' negative behaviors.

Staying Neutral

Staying neutral, or emotionally detached, during our kids' difficult moments is always a good idea because our emotionality clouds our thinking and makes it easier to for us to get pulled into power struggles. Staying in a neutral, non-reactive emotional state allows us to help our kids get through tough moments without getting triggered ourselves. We are much more helpful guides for our kids if we are not escalating along with them. That said, staying neutral is easier said than done. I'm a child therapist who works on this with parents daily and it's still hard for me to do with my own kids!

Why is this true? There are several factors at play. First, we love our kids so much and are personally invested in their success, so when they're failing in any way, we get upset because we want better for them. Another reason is that the job of parenting is so incredibly hard. Because we put so much into it, we want our efforts to turn out right. If our kids are the product of all this work and they're not turning out right, it's a failure for us too, which is frustrating and hard to take. Also, after experiencing our own childhood, where the grown-ups were in charge, we finally move into adulthood with the desire to create and control our worlds. But when our kids enter our lives, all of a sudden all that control is threatened. So we can find ourselves quickly overwhelmed by the feelings of chaos and helplessness that adding children to the picture can create. The last thing to consider is that kids these days act out in ways our parents may not have tolerated. I can't tell you how many parents have said to me, "My parents would never have tolerated that kind of behavior from me!" But the world is a very different place today than it was when we were kids. Child development is better understood, and kids have been given a voice for the first time in history. Kids these days have a sense of personal power and freedom that previous generations just didn't have. They are growing up in a world that has more respect for individual identity and less pressure to conform to the old norms. Advances in technology have further changed the lives of children, and dramatically so, giving them instant access to each other's worlds and the ability to connect, organize, and broadcast their views.

So many factors influence our kids' behaviors and challenge our parenting, and each of these challenges creates the potential for our confusion and frustration and threatens our ability to stay neutral. Not only is parenting emotionally evocative, modern life also adds factors that contribute to our reactivity. Kids occasionally break under the pressures of the world today, and parents do too. No one is immune from the stressors that accumulate in modern family life. So, it's important to remember that staying neutral when our kids are escalating is the goal, but it's not always easy to do. We know that it's best not to complicate our kids' upset moments with our own emotionality, but at the same time, we also remember to hold realistic expectations for ourselves because we are not without our own emotions, and we understand that many factors make it hard for us to stay non-reactive. So we try to keep a level head, and we just keep trying every time.

Staying Present

Another important aspect of responding to our kids in a hot moment is our ability to stay present. Staying in the present moment is very helpful when dealing with difficult situations. By staying present, I mean literally staying in your body, feeling your feet on the ground and the air coming in and out of your lungs. Being in touch with your physical state when you're stressed keeps you grounded and decreases the chance that you will escalate when your child is coming unglued. Staying present also keeps our field of vision broad. When we get angry with our kids, we tend to hyperfocus on the behavior we don't like, which causes us to miss potentially helpful or balancing details we might otherwise consider. The simple act of looking around and noticing the details in the room can provide a balancing effect and keep us from getting pulled too far into the struggle.

Another way to stay present is to be aware of the current moment. Our brains are association machines; like computers, they cross-link familiar ideas and experiences to efficiently process information. While this creates great efficiency in brainpower, it also means that when we're upset with our kids, our brains will likely connect the current situation to the past or the future. If a current struggle with your child transports you to a previous similar situation, then it is likely that all of the emotion from the past experience will come rushing forth. This can intensify the current moment and make us far more reactive to our kids than we would be if we stayed present and took it one situation at a time.

An example of this might be something along the lines of your child borrowing your phone to play a game on it and then forgetting where he or she left the phone. If this is the fourth time they've done that, then you'll likely link the current situation to all those past experiences and get really frustrated with them. In your frustrated state, you'll likely not be thinking clearly and may become unhelpful in the situation by yelling at your child. Since your brain has been hijacked by emotion, you'll likely also forget that children only learn through repetition and that it will take your seven-year-old many times before he or she learns to put things back where they were found. In this situation then, your primary focus becomes your emotionality (frustration) and not the skills your child needs to work on to prevent this situation from happening again. Your emotionality won't allow for resolution because both you and your child end up focusing on your anger. This kind of situation just leaves everyone feeling bad afterward and misses the opportunity to work on skills that might prevent the situation from happening again.

Things could go differently, though, if you can stay present in your thinking by reminding yourself: "Yes, this has happened before, and it is frustrating. But each day is a new day of learning for my kid. Let me teach my child once more about 're-tracing your steps,' which obviously still needs to be worked on." This type of present-centered thinking will keep reactivity in check and open the window for teaching your child about some important skills. After the phone is found, for example, you could talk with your child about how this frustrates you. No doubt, it's probably a frustrating situation for your child as well, and this could be a good chance for your child to practice talking about those feelings. The two of you could also engage in some problem solving of this situation. For instance, you might decide on a place that the phone is always returned to and set a consequence for not returning it there after each use. All this can take place when you stay in the present moment with the present dilemma and keep the past from amplifying a current situation.

Just as easily, and especially for highly sensitive parents, current behavior situations can quickly thrust us way down the road into the future, which creates its own set of problems. When our kids' behaviors upset us, our brains do the self-protective act of trying to anticipate this problem occurring again (future thinking). Future thinking has great survival value because it can help us avoid potentially dangerous situations based on past experience. But when this mechanism gets triggered in a current situation that is upsetting but not actually dangerous—such as when our kids are out of control—our departure from the current moment leaves us only partially present and only partially available to help our kids. As with being dragged into the emotional past, being catapulted into an anxious future limits our effectiveness as parents. I have worked with many families who have kids struggling with toileting issues that range from four-year-olds who are still not potty-trained to ten-year-olds who are having night accidents. Toileting problems seem to easily propel parents into anxious future scenarios, as they imagine their child being unable to be free from this unpleasant issue dominating their lives. When parents are sucked into a vortex of future worry, I remind them that all the energy consumed by the future-focused anxiety is energy that isn't being used to solve the problem in the present moment.

The more we can practice not getting pulled into the past or the future, the more available we will be to deal with the problem at hand, and so the more effective we will be. Whether you're dealing with a power struggle, a provocation, or an embarrassing tantrum, it's important to stay as present and as neutral as possible. If you notice that the stress of the moment is pulling you into the past or the future, stop, take a breath, feel your feet and the ground beneath them, and try to proceed with present-mindedness.

Of course, the benefits of staying present don't apply only to parenting. It's beneficial to be as *here and now* as possible in all our moments. Too much focus on the past leads to rumination, one of the ingredients in depression. Mulling over past experiences again and again does nothing to change what's already happened and robs us of our current life. Likewise, worrying about what will happen in the future keeps us in a state of perpetual anxiety, which has negative health risks and keeps us from solving our problems now. To keep rumination and worries from stealing our present moments, we can center ourselves in *the now* through meditation, exercise, walks in nature, or simply by practicing present-moment awareness.

More on Hot Moments

Staying neutral and present increases our effectiveness, especially in hot moments, when a child has escalated and is becoming partially or totally out of control. However, remaining present and neutral is not a guarantee that things will go well. They are simply elements to apply (like empathy) to try to get things going in the right direction. Even with these elements, a hot moment might continue to escalate. These hot moments are the most difficult times to feel effective as a parent. They are the hardest circumstances to control, and because of the heightened emotions involved, they are the most difficult to predict. This makes it hard to create an exact script that can be used in all behavior situations to produce an effective outcome. There just isn't one single way to deal with all the negative situations that might arise because there are too many variables. The best we can do is to understand our child's temperament and experiment with responses to his or her escalations to see what helps get our child back under control. Employing long-term solutions—such as working on the core skills, as well as a few others that I will discuss shortly—can help kids cope well enough to avoid many of these breakdowns. However, even kids with a solid set of skills will slip over the edge and fall apart from time to time. It happens to everyone.

Though the options become more limited the more a child escalates, there is a sequence of responses parents can practice that often steers the hot moment in the right direction. These steps begin when you find that the empathic, cooperative, problem-solving approach (which we always start with) isn't going anywhere. It is the turning point when you switch from an empathic stance to a more authoritative one and take control of the situation. *When* you make this shift in your stance will vary from situation to situation, so you have to rely on your judgment. When you do switch to a more authoritative stance, you'll want to take "the action steps" I share here, which will give you the best chance of creating a situation that allows all parties to feel more control.

The Action Steps

The moment you decide to shift to a more authoritative stance, change the tone of your voice to a calm but serious one, give your child eye contact, and deliver a strong and clear message about your expectations for his or her behavior and the choices to be made now. Start by setting a limit on the behavior you don't like, and deliver it in the form of a simple choice. Make sure to stay out of power struggles and diversions. Also, attempt to stay emotionally neutral by reminding yourself that this is your child's moment of struggle and learning, not yours. Give your child a warning and a chance to stop the behavior by communicating his or her needs or protest in a better way (in other words, "a do over"). For instance, you might say, "Stop! Let's try that again in a more respectful way." If that doesn't get your child's attention, mention motivators, whether an incentive or a consequence. If the behavior persists, deliver the consequence and detach from your child's response—your child is likely mad at you now for giving a consequence and may grumble or shoot you an angry look. Try not to let this get to you. Don't give more consequences for your child's grumbling or unhappiness. If your child's behavior continues to seriously escalate, disengage from arguing and encourage your child to take a personal break or go to his or her safe place to calm down (see the "Teaching Kids How to Calm Down" section). Remember the escalation cycle, and keep in mind that it will end. Also remember that the lesson you want to impart to your child about the behavior might not be learned in this moment, and that's okay. You may have to ride out the hot moment and have the rational discussion later when your child has calmed down.

When you notice the cooperative process breaking down, start these steps immediately. The quicker you can identify the behaviors you won't tolerate, the sooner you can take action and the better your chance of keeping things under control. Remember that once strong emotions begin to take over, the child is no longer available for rational thinking and decision-making. So to be maximally effective, don't sit and watch for too long; instead, decide if the behavior needs to be addressed, begin communicating, and if needed move in and take action.

I dealt with a hot moment of my own recently and tried my best to use some of these steps. It was time for my five-year-old daughter to be in bed. She had recently developed a habit of coming out of her bedroom after saying a final good night. Her reasons varied and always had an emotional urgency about them. Nevertheless, this was becoming a problem. It was keeping our other kids up, making her tired the next day, and cutting into the precious little time my wife and I could share without kids.

Here's what I did. Because I had an eye on her emotional life, I already knew that my daughter had been worried about going to kindergarten the next month. I kept this in mind on this occasion when she came out again after saying our final good night. I walked her back to her room and decided to talk to her about the feelings involved—confident that if I could help her with the emotional experience, that would solve the problem. I sat on her bed while we talked about getting bigger and going to kindergarten and both the exciting and the scary feelings all this brought up. If I do say so myself, I did a pretty good job attuning to her emotional life, validating her feelings, and helping her feel understood and supported. I then said a final good night and left the room feeling confident that I had solved the problem nicely. But it didn't work. My daughter came back out three minutes later. Again, I walked her back to her room and empathized with her feelings. I also invited her to problem solve the getting-out-of-bed situation, and we came up with a plan to talk about her feelings about kindergarten every night before going to bed. Again, I put her to bed, and again, she came out. The third time I walked her back, I was getting tired and frustrated, and I could feel myself losing my grip on the golden pillar of emotional neutrality.

I decided to take action by moving in with more authority. I could do this confidently because I had already done all I could using the empathic approach. To avoid a power struggle, I decided to try a motivator in the form of an incentive—candy at the snack bar at the little league game the next morning. I was sure she'd go for it, and we'd get on the right track. She rejected it immediately because she was too worked up. I was getting worked up too. After offering the candy incentive a couple times without success, I had to change my plan and use a consequence instead. My wife could see that I was about to lose it and raise my voice and reminded me that that wouldn't help. I put my feelings on the back burner and took her advice. I steadied myself, strengthened my authoritative tone, and took action. I told my daughter that if she came out one more time, I would take her favorite dolls and put them away for a day. This was a big threat because she loves these dolls and plays with them every day. I used my last bit of sanity to say in a calm but firm tone of voice, "I'm sorry you're so upset. I know you miss mommy and daddy at night. But if you get out of bed again, I will take the dolls." I knew she knew that I meant business. My authority, delivered in a clear and neutral way, cut through the emotions and fatigue and did the trick. Her crying began to quiet, and she stayed in her bed. I hugged her and walked out of her room. It had been forty-five minutes of an emotionally charged struggle. We had both been to the edge and almost gone over. I was beat but happy that it was over and that she was getting the rest she needed. I was also thankful that it didn't go horribly wrong. I could have easily gotten to the point of yelling or being so frustrated that I couldn't attune to her feelings. I didn't feel good about the threat to take her dolls, but it was the only motivator I could come up with that might work. I didn't want to spend yet another hour trying smaller incentives that might not work. I believe that the success of this hot moment came about because I was able to respond first by tuning into my daughter's feelings and only afterward moving to the action steps of increasing authority, communicating clear choices, and using a potent motivator.

Do you see how there's no one right way to do this? How it would be impossible to create one plan that would work in a multitude of circumstances? But there is a solid set of steps that give us the best shot at taking action in a way that is most likely to be effective. We may assemble these steps differently in each situation, but they are the right steps. Each time we practice applying these steps, we hone our parenting skills. We learn to apply the authority arm of parenting to control difficult behavior. We never stop learning how to be more effective.

The steps and interventions I am sharing work well for day to day behavior challenges, such as disrespect, power struggles, not listening, sibling rivalry, the testing of authority, and minor aggressions such as yelling, pushing, and tantrums. More serious behaviors, such as physical violence or serious threats of violence, stealing, sexual offenses, and the like often require professional counseling and guidance—at times even police intervention, especially for kids moving through the teen years. Addressing these more serious behaviors is beyond the scope of this book. If you are struggling with any of these behavior challenges, especially with a child in the teen years, get a consultation from a licensed child therapist.

Here's a recap of the basic steps to follow in a hot moment. I've also noted the main arm of parenting involved.

Hot Moments—The Basic Steps

- Start with an empathic statement, such as "I know you're really upset because I'm saying no to the sleepover." (Empathy)
- Monitor where your child is in the escalation process. If your child is too upset, ask him or her to take a few breaths or to take a calming break before you talk more. (Empathy and Authority)
- Invite your child to state what he or she is feeling. "Can you tell me how you're feeling?" Then validate those feelings, as in, "I hear that you're feeling it's unfair." (Empathy)
- State your understanding of the intent behind the behavior—for example, "You keep asking me about it. Are you hoping I'll eventually change my mind and say yes?" (Empathy and Authority)
- Monitor your own emotions and call a time-out for yourself if you're too upset. (Authority)
- If you're not too upset, decide whether to stay engaged or to detach and let the escalation run its course (planned ignoring). (Authority)
- If you stay engaged, invite cooperative conversation. Get your child into thinking and problem-solving mode by inviting him or her to create a compromise. "Let's think together about how we can work this one out. I'll hear about your side first, and then you hear about mine. Then we'll work on a solution, okay?" (Empathy and Authority)
- Or set a limit with simple and clear choices: "You're raising your voice. Your choice is to talk to me about the sleepover in a regular voice or I'm done with this conversation." (Authority)
- Don't allow diversions. "I'm not discussing what your brother got yesterday. We can talk about that later." (Authority)

- Stay emotionally neutral. Remind yourself that it's your child's emotional moment, not yours. (Authority)

- Stay present. Try not to magnify the current struggle with your frustrations from the past or worries about the future. (Authority and Empathy)

- Prompt for "a do-over," and use a motivator if needed. Give the child one chance to do the behavior over in a better way, and use an incentive or a consequence to motivate your child if you need to—for example, "I'm going to give you one chance to do this conversation over without the screaming. If you can't do that, you're going to lose your TV show tonight." (Authority)

- Notice whether the behavior escalates or de-escalates. (Authority)

- If the behavior escalates, stay neutral and hold your limit. Don't engage in an argument. Decrease eye contact and verbal exchanges. Give simple commands, such as, "We'll talk when you stop screaming." Keep yourself, your child, and others safe. Wait until the child's energy calms down, and then review the situation. (Authority) If your child becomes physically aggressive, keep everyone safe and consider consulting your pediatrician to help you determine whether you need to consult with a child therapist.

- Once your child's behavior de-escalates, allow your child time to cool down, and then review. (Empathy and Authority)

In this sequence we always start with attempts to get the child into a more cooperative state. The first few steps infuse the moment with understanding and emphasize the adult's desire to work with the child if the child can communicate his or her needs and stay calm. The empathic statement helps the child to feel heard. We empathize because we understand that in a hot moment kids' behaviors are their form of communication. They broadcast their needs and protests through the sounds and movements of their bodies, and if they don't feel heard, they will simply broadcast more loudly. So stopping to understand them and letting them know we understand can decrease the need for escalation in their communication with us.

Getting the child to start talking about his or her feelings shifts the interaction in a few other important ways. First, talking about feelings always helps to let the energy of an emotion out—energy that could be converted into negative behavior if not released. Second, adding language to a child's feelings helps to balance the child's brain-state by adding thinking, or cognitive activity, to the primarily emotional state. Emotions can easily hijack a child's system, and once a child is flooded with feelings, it can be very hard for the child to return to a rational mode. When a child is talking, he or she is thinking, and if a child is thinking, he or she is not totally submerged in emotion. So it is important to keep the language and logic-based half of the brain engaged during escalation. In addition, if the flood of emotion can be counterbalanced by rational conversation, you have the chance to move the interaction toward problem solving, rather than slipping further into a conflict.

So we respond to even an ugly provocation with an attempt to have the upset child communicate his or her feelings, stay rational, and work toward solutions. Sometimes this will work. You may even find that you can skip some of the basic steps. As a rule, however, don't skip the first three steps because this is where you help your child work on the core skills of understanding feelings and communication. If your child is not too upset, you might be able to resolve the matter with an empathic statement, a check-in on feelings, and a quick do over—with nothing more to do. This will become the case the more you apply these ideas because your child will get used to engaging in the process in this way and will be developing the five core skills (all of which work toward not getting to the point of no-return). For the times when the first few empathic steps don't work and your child continues to test, disobey, or provoke, you will need to move to the remaining action steps. They will get you through the difficult moments and heading toward recovery and eventual calm. Then it will be time to reflect on what happened and what can be done to create a different outcome the next time.

Chapter Summary

Here is a recap of some of the highlights and tips presented in this chapter:

- Remember that punishment (consequences) is only one part of a larger strategy for behavior change that also includes a focus on building new skills.
- Don't use guilt or shame to discipline kids.
- As the severity of behaviors escalates, move from an empathic stance to one that presents more authority.
- Remember that hot moments are not optimal for learning because emotion is high and cognition is low.
- The hotter the moment, the more you will direct the child with simple, clear communication and choices.
- When helping an escalated child, start with an empathic statement.
- Help your child learn two calming exercises and practice them with small upsets.
- Use planned ignoring when appropriate, to allow the emotional response cycle to run its course.
- Recognize diversions and don't let them get you off course.
- Use motivators (incentives and consequences) to move your child toward better choices.
- Try to stay neutral and present when behavior is escalating. It's your child's ride, not yours.
- If your empathy and invitation to problem solve is met with increased defiance, move in with the action steps quickly, calmly and with clear authority.

Chapter 7

∞

Reflective Moments

The hot moment is just that, a flash of emotion and behavior. Like lightening, it is bright, sometimes frightening, and hard to control. Hot moments are some of the hardest parenting moments, but these are not the only moments when we can provide our kids with guidance. A lot of learning and developing happens outside of the hot moment, for instance, when we're helping our kids work on the five core skills. We've talked about some ways to help build these essential skills in earlier sections. Now it's time to look at some other ways we can help our kids build these preventative skills, and one way to do this is to use hot moments to build what I call reflective moments of learning.

Unlike hot moments, reflective moments are calm. They are the moments when you and your child can work on a problem together. These moments are not filled with emotion for either of you, and so your ability to teach is maximized, while your child can be fully present for the learning that needs to take place. These are windows of opportunity to help build the core skills—skills that replace the need to impulsively act out feelings. Reflective moments are about looking at problems, understanding the feelings involved, and reflecting on options for better ways to express those feelings.

Any time you have behavior you don't want or a situation with your child that goes wrong, there is some learning that needs to take place. Sometimes the learning is for you—for example, figuring out how your child's temperament is playing into a situation or maybe learning to stop and listen to your child's feelings. Much of the time, however, the learning will be for your child—for example, increasing your child's ability to communicate feelings or to respect the limits you set. Either way, the fact that things went wrong or got out of control means that there are skills to work on and new ideas to be considered. The best time to work on these ideas and skills is during reflective moments.

When I think about how to help kids and parents get along better, I think about reflective moments. Hot moments are essentially damage control, and though they're important to plan for, they are certainly not the times when we can help kids mature, build skills, and reflect on options. If your parenting mostly consists of moving in to deal with hot moments, then you are essentially putting out fires that will reoccur. Similarly, from your child's perspective, if all that he or she is getting from you is reactivity and punishment when they're overwhelmed with emotion, then your child will likely repeat his or her patterns again and again. Many families that eventually come to see me are stuck in this pattern of dealing with the problem in the hot moment and then hoping that the problem won't return. If you think about it, you know you wouldn't approach most problems this way. As stubborn as I can be, if I try to fix something a few times without success, I eventually realize that I need a new plan. Reflective moments allow us to stop and create a new plan.

The work of changing behavior patterns and helping kids mature is largely preventative. This means that you will identify the core skills that your child needs to work on by observing his or her temperament and coping patterns, especially in hot moments, and then get to work developing those skills in calmer moments. Doing this kind of preventative work with your child will have a definite impact on the future course of your child's behavior. Unlike hot moments, when you're really just trying to get behavior under control, during reflective moments, you're building with your child a foundation of skills that will help your child to mature and cope.

I sometimes also call these skills "alternate skills" because they are skills that give a kid additional options for handling tough moments. Without alternate skills, a child is very likely to repeat previous behavior patterns because all the child knows is what he or she has been doing thus far. Reflective moments are the moments to teach and to practice the alternate, or core, skills. Reflective moments create the opportunity for a child to change his or her behavior patterns and to build a sense of self-control (which has a positive impact on self-esteem).

When to Reflect

Anytime you can get your child to stop with you and think about a situation that became difficult or infused with challenging emotion, you have a chance to help them learn to reflect. Again, intense emotional moments are not the best times to do this because thinking is clouded by the storm of feelings. When the storm has passed, use calmer moments to help your child think back on what happened and to reflect on the feelings and behaviors he or she experienced. We often have a window for these kinds of learning conversations during our one-on-one time with our kids. I have found that the time before bed, when my kids are winding down and distractions are minimized, is a great time to reflect on challenging moments from the day. Car rides and walks to the bus stop also provide a good time for discussion and reflection. Also, joining your child in an activity of his or her interest, like doing a puzzle together or playing catch, provides a non-threatening, relaxed atmosphere in which kids open up and think with you about their behaviors and feelings. Just make sure you're not joining your child in an activity that is distracting, like a video game, because they are likely to get annoyed by the interruption of your thoughts and questions.

A way to build in reflective moments is to create rituals that promote conversations about feelings. At my house, for example, we often have a short conversation during dinner about the "hard and easy" part of each of our kids' day at school. This quick check-in helps our kids work on the core skills of understanding their feelings and communicating, which often leads to practicing the skill of problem solving. Be creative and establish some openings for these kinds of conversations, which your kids can come to expect. This will normalize this type of family communication and create a forum for discussing more difficult events. And you're not limited to talking about your child's feelings. You can also use reflective moments to talk about situations in which other people had strong feelings or dealt with difficult situations— for example, you might reflect on the behavior of your child's friends or even characters on TV. All of these conversations will help your child get used to communicating and problem solving with you, which will make it much easier when you have to talk about your child's own difficult behaviors.

Preview and Review—Good Times to Reflect

Making reflective moments a part of your family culture is essential because these are the times when kids can learn how to work out problems and express themselves. If reflective moments are not part of your current family culture, then you need to make it so. It may feel awkward at first—for all of you—but like anything, the more you practice, the more natural it will feel, and the less resistance you'll get from your kids. I already noted some good times to work in reflective conversation, such as bedtime or during an activity together. I have found two other opportunities to reflect on difficult situations, which I call Preview and Review. If I had to pick the two most productive moments to reflect with kids, I would definitely say they're during the Preview and the Review.

Preview—Anticipating the Moment

Because kids' brains are not fully developed, they don't think very far past the present moment. This is a wonderful and innocent quality children have, but it also limits their ability to anticipate problems that lie just down the road. For this reason, previewing an upcoming situation is a golden opportunity for kids to stop and think about feelings that might come up and to anticipate situations that might get difficult.

Previewing upcoming situations helps kids expand their awareness beyond the present moment and add the extended perspectives of the past and the future. This skill is a key part of emotional maturity. It's a good one to help even younger kids practice. Preview also helps kids prepare emotionally for situations in which strong feelings might come up for them—and we all know that it's better to anticipate what might go wrong than to be surprised by it. Of course, it's probably more important to preview situations in which negative, as opposed to positive, feelings are likely to arise because negative feelings can turn into negative behaviors. So it's more useful to think about what might get difficult for a child at the upcoming birthday party than to help the child anticipate what might make him or her happy. There's nothing wrong with anticipating positive feelings; it's just that we're talking here about helping kids manage challenging behavior, which emanates mostly from negative feelings. Finally, doing a Preview facilitates problem solving, or making a plan for the difficult moments that might arise. Problem solving is a core skill, and problem solving before a situation gets emotionally charged can make the difference between things going well and things getting out of control. Remember that once feelings get to a critical level, rationality goes out the window, so we benefit when we have a plan worked out before the engines of emotion are revved up. Problem solving ahead of time also allows the child to enter the situation with a greater sense of control (and thus less anxiety) because the child has a disaster plan ready in case things go wrong.

Think about the difference in the following two scenarios, which both center on a planned play date for your son at the home of a new friend, Andy.

Scenario 1: You don't think much about it in advance and don't talk about it with your son. When you get there, you find out that that Andy has a little brother who is full of energy and always trying to get in on the older boys' play. This is particularly offensive to your child because it's what his little brother is always doing to him. You see your son getting agitated, but before you can move in to help, he pushes the little intruder and yells at him. The little brother wails, and his mother comes to his aide with a disapproving glance at your child. You're embarrassed and angry with your son and apologize to Andy's mom. She accepts your apology but never again invites your son over to play, which is too bad because your son really likes Andy.

Scenario 2: On your way to the play date, you start thinking about your son's temperament and how he can be reactive and somewhat impulsive, especially when he is excited or frustrated. You also think about situations that could get difficult at Andy's house. Instead of keeping this to yourself, you say to your son, "Let's think about what might get hard at Andy's house." Your son replies, "I don't want to talk about that." You then add a little authority by saying, "Well, if you want to go to Andy's house, we need to think about what might get hard and make a plan for it; otherwise, I will turn the car around and head back home." This motivates your child, who says, "I don't know what will get hard." So you say, "Okay, let's think together. There are a couple things that you really don't like when you're playing with friends. Can you remember what they are?" He answers, "Yeah, when other kids are bossy." And you add, "And also when little brothers or sisters get in the way." Your son says, "Yeah, that's right." And then you say, "And what I know about you is that when you get upset feelings, they happen big and fast." To which your child replies, "Yeah that's true too." Next you ask your son how he thinks he will feel if Andy gets bossy or if he has a little brother or sister who disrupts their play, and he says, "Mad!" You then make a plan with him: if either of those things happen, he will keep track of his feelings and come get you before he starts to get too annoyed. You also remind him that if he doesn't follow this plan, the consequence will be immediately leaving the play date.

When you get there and see the little brother, you look over at your son and quietly say, "Remember the plan." He looks back at you and gives you a thumbs up. A bit later, your child does start getting annoyed with the little brother, so he comes and tells you. You make a plan with Andy's mom to let the older boys have some time without interruption from the little one. The play date goes fairly well, and you and your son debrief on the ride home about how the plan went and what a great job you both did working together. The next week your son gets an invitation to Andy's awesome birthday party.

The difference in the two scenarios is not hard to see. The second situation included some preventative measures that kept the train from going off the tracks. Let's review what they were.

First, you trained yourself to think ahead about upcoming situations and how they might affect your son's temperament. This led you to the idea that a preview was a good idea for this play date with a new family. Your son didn't want to discuss it at first, so you flexed your authority arm and used a motivator (returning home) to help him agree to talk. You then reminded him of what you know about his temperament (reactive and impulsive were described in kid terms as "big and fast feelings"), which helped him increase his self-awareness. Then you helped your child anticipate his potential emotional response if a typically triggering situation actually happened. You also helped your son exercise his ability to problem solve by making a plan with you to address problems that might develop at the play date. And finally, you powered up more motivation on your son's part by flexing your authority one more time with a warning about the consequence of leaving if he didn't stick to the agreed-upon plan.

This kind of preview takes minutes of your time and energy

while saving you hours of regret and embarrassment. Think of it this way, you're going to have to put a certain amount of energy into such an event anyway. You can go in with no forethought, putting out fires as they start and crossing your fingers that disaster won't befall, or you can invest some time up front and give yourself an insurance policy, which doesn't guarantee something bad won't happen but does greatly increase the odds that it won't.

Keep in mind what you know about the kinds of situations and events that are emotionally evocative for your child. Then pair this with your understanding of your child's temperament to begin to anticipate situations that might get difficult. For instance, active, reactive, and impulsive kids do very well with a Preview because it allows them to stop, reflect, and plan—something they don't always do. A Preview helps highly sensitive kids anticipate and deal with their particular stressors, such as chaos, loud noises, and aggressive play—any of which can send them quickly into a silent and withdrawn mode. As you get to know the types of situations that create stress or reactivity in your child, you can talk with your child to try to anticipate how and when things might get difficult.

Typical situations that induce reactivity involve stress, energy, or emotions getting high. These situations create surges of emotional energy that come out as frustration, impulsive behavior, or social withdrawal. Creating plans to cope by taking a break, asserting one's needs, or getting help from an adult gives a child an additional outlet for the energy these situations create and helps the child stay on track. An additional factor is that emotions are amplified when the element of surprise is added to the mix. Preview helps to buffer the child from facing an unexpected situation by helping them think ahead and anticipate change or challenge.

It's not only frustrations and negative feelings that benefit from Preview. Many kids have a difficult time when positive energy gets too high. For these kids, a game of chase, chaotic fun in the jumpy house, and even structured sports activities can send their body's energy into the red zone. Once there, the chance of breaking down in some way increases dramatically. Preview can help these kids make thoughtful choices about which activities to participate in and how to monitor their body for energy overload.

You don't have to preview every single event or transition your child encounters. Every time you do use Preview, however, you'll be cementing important skills for your child. Using the Preview helps your child work on the core skills of communication, understanding feelings, respect, and problem solving, and so it contributes greatly to emotional maturity. As a general rule, the more you're worried that something could go wrong in a given situation, the more important it is to preview. Listen to that gut feeling you have when you're about to enter a situation and you think, "This could go wrong." With that realization, start the process. Although Preview mostly exercises the empathy arm of parenting, don't be afraid to flex your authority arm also, especially if you're getting resistance to the conversation. Use motivators to help your child develop the habit of anticipating problem situations and making plans for success. Also, feel free to balance a focus on what might go wrong with a focus on what might be fun. There's nothing wrong with anticipating good feelings. Just don't skip looking at the hard part because those are the situations that kids need the most help navigating.

Some parents are concerned that engaging a child in Preview plants the idea in the child's mind that something can go wrong and thereby increases the likelihood that it happens. This is not my experience. When previewing, we certainly do put the idea that a situation might get difficult on the table. But behaviors don't happen without emotional energy behind them. If I said to you, "Someone might offend you later when you go to the store," it's not going to make you get mad when you get there, unless something bad really does happen. So it's not the *idea* of feelings that makes them surge but the *experience* in a situation that either evokes strong emotion or not. If the child doesn't encounter the negative experience previewed, it is very unlikely that he or she will even stop to think much about the Preview you had. However, if the child does encounter the trouble, the conversation and the coping strategies you discussed will be remembered. So, we can clearly see that the benefits of looking at upcoming situations, exploring potential feelings, and planning for behavior choices far outweigh concerns that discussing potential challenges might somehow encourage a child to make them happen.

Parents of anxious kids sometimes find previewing potentially anxiety-provoking situations difficult. Anxiety creates so much suffering in children, and parents feel the emotional pain that their kids endure. They certainly don't want to do anything that might contribute to anxiety, including anticipated anxiety. However, parents need to keep in mind that avoidance is the silent companion of anxiety. Fear and worry rarely exist without it. So if your child is anxious, be sensitive about it, but don't collude with avoidance by not discussing potential anxiety-provoking situations with your child. Not talking about it gives fear more power and creates a spiral of fear and avoidance that become more and more paralyzing for the child. Instead of colluding with avoidance, normalize the anticipated fear by talking openly about it and planning for its potential arrival. Use Preview to think together about anxiety-provoking situations and to come up with some things your child can do to increase his or her sense of strength, control, and ability to cope with the uncomfortable feelings that might arise.

The Review—Reflecting after the Moment

Even if you know your child's temperament and triggers well, there will still be difficult moments that are impossible to predict. If the moment is not too hot, meaning that feelings and behaviors are not too big, you might still navigate the moment well by using empathy, choices, and some in-the-moment problem solving. However, if your child becomes very upset, then you may have to move to the action steps outlined earlier or simply hold steady and ride the situation out. In these cases, it will be important to review the incident later when your child has calmed down.

The Review includes a series of questions I developed to promote learning and to practice all the core skills. If a child misbehaves or doesn't handle a situation well, that is evidence that there are skills to be worked on. After the incident, if you punish the child or only make the child apologize, you will have missed the opportunity to help your child develop core skills. However, if you sit with your child for a few minutes and go through the Review, you will be helping your child practice the very skills needed to prevent the incident from happening again. The Review is the most important reflective moment I know. If you take only one new skill from this book, make it the commitment to start reviewing difficult moments.

Childhood is about making mistakes. It's about testing limits and trying on new behaviors. We don't want our kids to be perfect—that's an ideal that's impossible and unhealthy. What we want is for our kids to make mistakes, manage the disappointment that naturally follows, and then learn as much as they can from them so they can keep progressing and maturing as they grow.

Parenting is also about making mistakes, and a big and very common mistake that many parents make is that they expect their child to learn from their mistakes with little outside help. Or, as I discussed earlier, sometimes they mistakenly think that punishment will do the teaching for them. These are not ways to help kids learn from their mistakes. This would be akin to teaching your child to read by punishing him or her every time they didn't get a word right. Of course, that wouldn't work. Kids need help with letter recognition, word sounds, and understanding the rules of grammar in order to build a set of skills that eventually allow them to read on their own. So why would helping kids learn the components of self expression and behavioral control be any different? It isn't. Kids need our help with that too.

Emotional development is not covered in most school curriculums. It is not taught on the baseball field or in gymnastics class. A good teacher or coach will support moments of emotional learning, but they won't stop to teach the core skills needed to function well. This is our responsibility as parents—to tolerate the mistakes of childhood and help our kids develop a set of skills that allow them to feel good about themselves and get along with others. The Review is simple yet powerful because it covers all the core skills and promotes our kids' emotional maturity.

The Review is not a lecture but a conversation directed by thought-provoking questions geared to help stimulate learning. I find it so much more effective to help kids learn by asking them questions. Kids get so tired of the lectures adults love to give that they frequently tune us out when they sense one coming. If a child is answering a question, however, you can be sure you have that child's attention and that he or she is processing the information. Whenever possible teach your child by asking them questions. If your child doesn't have an answer, ask an easier question that leads to the answer. The goal is to help our kids find answers themselves, guided by our thoughtful, helpful questions. Finding their own answers builds kids' competence and self-esteem. In addition, answering questions provides a small amount of stress, which actually optimizes learning. A friendly question provides optimal stress, which is different from a boring lecture (no stress) or an interrogation (too much stress).

The Review is also not long. These conversations may take twenty or so minutes the first few times, but as you get better at coaching and your child gets better at participating, a helpful review can take as little as five minutes. The review is, at its core, a discussion about feelings because the child's emotions are what lie beneath the behaviors you're discussing. So, get your kids used to the fact that you will be talking about the hard times and figuring out the feelings, behaviors, and choices involved. As I've already said, making conversations about feelings and behaviors a part of your family culture is one of the best things parents can do for their family.

The Review

Spend a few minutes going over the following questions with your child after a behavior episode. Remember to ask questions rather than lecture your child.

1. **Remember when...?** Help your child recall the situation by asking a question or two that jogs the child's memory of the event. Give a few details, or recall the time when they had "big feelings" to help with remembering. Just be careful not to name the feelings for your child.

2. **What were you feeling?** Help your child verbalize the feeling(s) experienced in the situation, especially the feeling that occurred just before the difficult behavior. Younger kids and kids who are not so connected to their feelings will answer with "I don't know." You can help them think about the feelings involved by offering a few choices. For example, "Well, let's think about it. Do you think you liked what she did?" The child says, "No." Then you say, "So what would you call that feeling? Mad? Sad? Frustrated?" Having kids choose from a few options is helpful when they're stuck and decreases the chance that we're leading them with our ideas. Remember, this is their exploration.

3. **Validate your child's feeling.** Let your child know you get how he or she felt. Remember, you want your child to come to you with his or her feelings, so make sure you let your

child know you understand.

4. **What did you do with that feeling?** This is where we help our children separate their feelings from their behaviors. All feelings are okay, but what we *do* with them may or may not be. Did your child hit, scream, or run away? Ask questions to help your child become more aware of how his or her emotions got expressed through behavior.

5. **Do you think that's the best way to express that feeling?** This is an important moment of self-evaluation for your child. Most kids will say, "No, it wasn't," because the emotional storm has passed and they have regained the ability to think clearly by the time the Review comes around. If a child does answer, "Yes, I do," then he or she is either confused about what to do with their feelings or the child is testing you. If you think they're confused, respond with something like, "I'm not sure I agree with you. Let's think about it some more." Then have your child think about how the situation turned out because of his or her behavior (others got mad, your child got a consequence, etc.). If your child answered, "Yes, I do," as an act of defiance, then you need to flex your authority arm by reminding your child that the Review will take a *long* time without his or her real effort. You might also want to mention an incentive or a consequence to increase the child's motivation to participate.

6. **How could you express that feeling in a better way?** This is where we help our kids work on the alternate skill—the skill that could replace the impulse to act out feelings. Remember, it's not enough to tell kids what they can't do. Equally important is helping them figure out what the alternatives might be. When negative feelings lead to negative behaviors, the "better way" will almost always involve talking about those feelings. In addition, you can help your child think of other ways to cope, such as getting help from an adult, taking a break and counting to ten, walking away, asserting himself or herself with "I don't like that," etc. If your child's upset was with you, the alternate skill might be to tell you

about his or her feelings so that you could problem solve together or come up with a compromise (see Joint Problem Solving in Chapter 1).

7. **Replay the situation.** Sometimes I call this a do-over. This is your child's chance to practice the alternate skill you came up with in the last question. Having your child simply tell you what else they could do with their feelings does not necessarily mean that they will know how to apply the new skill in real-time. This is especially true with younger kids. Younger kids learn best through experience, so having them role-play the new skill will cement their understanding of how it works in practice. Have the child practice (with you) responding to the situation with words and good decisions. I usually say something like, "Okay, let's practice what you've figured out so I know you know how to do it. I'll pretend I'm Will, and you tell me that I scared you when I put the toy spider on your face." If your child's problematic behavior was with you, you might suggest something like, "Let's pretend we're back at that time before you yelled at me, only now you try letting me know what's wrong in the new way we just figured out—with respectful words."

8. **What will you do next time?** Planned behavior has a better chance of occurring, so have the child set an intention for the next time he or she is in this same kind of situation. I sometimes use this moment to help kids zoom out and see the two paths that are available. I might say, "Well, next time I guess you could do it the way you did this time, but then your teacher gets mad, you get in trouble, and then we have to do all this talking about it later. Or you could do what we figured out today, which is if you can stop and re-member to talk about your feelings and then get help, you won't end up in trouble and you could be playing right now instead of sitting here with me doing all this talking." Make sure you present the new behavior as *your child's* decision, because you want your child to really be invested in the course he or she will take next time. If your child decides to do it the "new way" the next time he or she is in a similar situation, congratulate your child for thinking this situation

through and coming up with a good plan for next time. This is the reason the Review can't be a lecture: to create confidence and a sense of self-control, the child needs to feel like *he or she* figured it out and set the course for future behavior choices.

9. **Apologize and make amends if necessary.** This step is about repairing relationships. Have the child apologize face to face and state what they're sorry for. If the person isn't there, the child can write a note, send an email, or make a plan for when they will apologize (your job is to monitor follow through on this plan). For highly sensitive kids who are easily embarrassed, do help them with this, but don't do the apology for them. If amends are needed, help your child figure out what to do to make the situation better for the offended party.

10. **Discuss consequences.** If you haven't already, discuss the consequence the child will get because of his or her behavior. If your child is cooperative during the Review, let your child know that since he or she sat with you to figure the situation out, you will be giving less of a consequence than you would have otherwise (or possibly none at all). For older kids, you can even have them help determine an appropriate penalty. This further emphasizes kids' sense of responsibility and can lessen their upset with you as the source of the punishment. Lastly, let your child know that the slate has been wiped clean, and you can all move on from the event. Kids that get into a lot of jams (those with impulsive, reactive, unfocused, intense, or rigid temperaments) can begin to feel bad about themselves after a while. It's important for them to feel that once the learning has been done, they can move on and start over. Help them do this with an encouraging and reassuring message.

(A copy of basic guidelines for the Review can be downloaded at www.betterbehaviorblog.com.)

Motivating Kids for the Review

Getting your child into the habit of stopping to reflect on their feelings and behaviors can be a challenge, especially at first. There are many reasons your child might resist this new routine, and this is okay. It can take time to get used to talking about feelings and problem solving behaviors.

It could happen that your kid is still upset with you because of a consequence you gave previously, or maybe your child just isn't in the mood to talk at the moment. This is often true for younger and more active kids—sitting still and talking about feelings and behaviors is often the last thing they want to do. So you're stuck with the dilemma of needing your child to review behavior incidents, while recognizing that the Review might feel somewhat torturous for him or her. With younger and more active kids, you can empathize with their not wanting to do a Review by letting them know that you understand it's not priority for them. It also often helps to reassure them that if they do cooperate and participate, you'll try to make it as quick as possible. The other thing you can try is including some movement with the conversation, like talking while you walk together. Just be careful that the activity you use doesn't become a distraction from the conversation.

It could also be that sitting and reviewing thoughts and feelings related to a difficult event creates an emotionally overwhelming experience for your child. Sensitive kids often re-experience intense feelings when they are asked to talk about situations that originally contained strong negative emotions such as anger or sadness. So asking them to sit and go over these types of situations is like asking them to relive them. For this reason, it's important to notice whether the Review is creating anxiety or extreme discomfort in a child. If your child is prone to anxiety, talk to them about the feelings that the Review brings up and empathize with his or her discomfort. Also, go slow and monitor their anxiety as you proceed and allow for short pauses if they're getting overwhelmed.

Also, make a plan for coping. Strong feelings need expression, but they also need containment. So make a plan that after the Review is done, you and your child will take all of the difficult feelings that were brought up and put them in a container and leave it closed for a while. For younger kids, this might be a pretend safe with a secret combination; for older kids, maybe a password-protected file they can visualize. The point is to require our kids to communicate about difficult events, while reassuring them that the feelings brought up can also be contained.

What happens if your child still refuses to do the Review? This is when you need a motivator. One motivator that I like to use is "a reduced sentence." When I tell my kids that we need to talk about what happened earlier and they protest or refuse, I empathize with their unhappiness and then remind them that the most important thing for me is that they've learned something from the event. I then let them know that if they can do a quick review, I will reduce the consequence I was going to give them, or for smaller infractions, eliminate the consequence altogether. This helps them see that my interest is in helping them learn from their mistakes and not in delivering punishment.

Another way to motivate participation in the Review is to simply wait for a motivator to show up. The great thing about kids is that all you have to do is wait and eventually they will ask you for something. "Can you make my favorite snack?" "Can I play on your phone?" "Can Claire come over to play?" It won't take long for your child to come up with a new request. So, if you have an incident that you want to review with your child, but he or she has been resisting talking about it with you, file it away until the next time your child wants something. Then you can do an if-then exchange, which goes something like this, "Sure, we can call Claire's mom to see if Claire can come over, just as soon as we talk about what happened earlier." If the motivator you chose is strong enough, it will get your child talking.

Time-Outs and the Review

Time-outs delivered as a form of punishment have limited impact on a child's behavior. This is because most of the intervention is focused on making a child sit and wait—which is not a skill that helps them function better. A time-out does provide a moment for the child to disengage and calm down; however, it is still missing the element of building alternate skills. For this reason, combining a time-out with a Review transforms a punishment into a true learning experience.

If you use time-outs, pair them with the Review to make them much more effective. Flex your authority arm when you get behavior you don't want by first giving the child a warning. If that doesn't work, send the child to a designated place to calm down and take a break (the time-out). When the child is calm again (and you too, if you were upset), make participation in a Review a condition for release from the time-out. Tell your child that the time-out will be over after you've talked a bit about what happened. Then use the guidelines for the Review to cover the necessary learning. Adding the Review to a time-out transforms it into something useful and in the long run will decrease the need for time-outs because you'll be building the skill set with your child that will improve behavior overall.

What and When to Review

Exactly which behavior incidents are worthy of a review? I hear this question a lot. Parents also make comments like, "If I stopped to review every little incident, we'd be doing Reviews all day long!" Well, you don't have to review every incident, but on the other hand, letting incidents go without review is a lost opportunity for learning. So, the rule of thumb is the bigger the behavior incident, the more important it is to review. The only other thing I would add is that even if an incident is not so big, if the behavior is part of a repeating pattern, then it's important behavior to review. The behavior of interrupting is a good example of this. If a child interrupts your adult conversation once, it would be a bit over the top to sit the child down and do a full review. However, if your child interrupts your conversation for the umpteenth time, it's time to sit down and review the behavior. So you'll decide what needs reviewing based on your child's patterns and the severity of behaviors. If I'm not sure whether an incident needs to be reviewed, I like to err on the side of caution and do at least a short review anyway. Engaging kids in emotional communication and critical thinking is never a wasted venture.

Similarly, there's no exact rule about when to do a review. If you're pairing it with a time-out, then you'll do it when the time-out is over. Otherwise, you'll have to factor in things like the child's age and temperament to figure out the best time to get it done. For instance, kids under five or kids who struggle with staying focused, do better when the Review is done the same day as the incident. If you wait any longer, it is likely that a young or a distractible child will have a much harder time remembering the details of the event.

Older kids can wait until the next day or even a day after that if you have to. Having all parties calm is essential to maximize learning, so you'll definitely need to wait until the storm has passed. Keep in mind though that the longer you wait, the less clear the incident will be in everyone's mind, making it harder to remember useful details. Obviously, you'll also have to factor in your own work and family schedule. If you're a working parent, you might want to develop a nightly routine that includes any needed reviews from the day. Also, as I said earlier, it's best to find a time to talk when your child is receptive. I call these your child's "emotional access points." Since the Review involves talking about feelings, it's important to consider your child's mood and receptivity before embarking on a Review. Find a time when your child is most open and calm so that you can maximize the learning that takes place during a Review.

Here's a good question: what if you're worried that your child isn't giving you the whole story or, worse yet, is lying during a Review? This could happen if you're reviewing an incident that happened when the child was under someone else's care, such as with a babysitter or at school. What you do then is focus on the behavior that you have observed or that you learned about. Remember that the Review isn't a fact-finding mission with the goal of discovering the ultimate truth. Of course, you want your child to know that it's important to be honest, but at first, as your child is getting used to Reviews, it's important to build trust in the process. So encourage honesty during Reviews. If you catch your child lying at any point, talk with him or her about trust and invite your child to be straight with you about his or her mistakes. Reassure your child that there's no need to hide them. You can then decide whether a consequence is warranted for the lying or whether you'll forgo a consequence this time if your child will commit to honesty in future reviews.

For kids, the first reviews often feel like another version of being in trouble or getting a lecture. This will be true until the child learns to trust that this is not the case. So don't let your first reviews become interrogations or debates about who was at fault for the incident. Instead, use the series of questions in the Review to focus on building trusting communication with your child, while encouraging accountability for everyone's part in the event.

Doing reviews is a great way to increase learning and family communication for both kids and parents. There are many benefits that come from Reviews, such as increased parent-child communi-cation, increased responsibility and accountability for the child, im-proved emotional expression, and more frequent joint problem solv-ing. One last benefit worth mentioning is that talking to others about events and problems helps us integrate mentally and emo-tionally. Emotionally charged events often go by in a blur and are hard to make sense of afterword. This is especially true for kids, whose brains aren't developed enough yet to process and organize all that transpired. Because of these developmental limitations, kids often have a hard time organizing the details of challenging mo-ments, including understanding the order of events and the causal relationships between them. It's hard for a child to problem solve and take responsibility for an event that is remembered as an emo-tional blur—or put another way, not yet fully integrated.

So sitting and talking with a parent about the sequence of events, the feelings and behaviors involved, and the impact of the event on everyone involved provides a child with an organized and integrated map of an otherwise confusing and difficult experience. Organizing the event in this way greatly increases the learning that can come from the experience because it helps the child create a coherent story of the event—a timeline with decision points. It also helps a child understand and then release the charged feelings that get stored up during a difficult moment. Think of it this way: after an episode of difficult behavior, what we want is for our kids to understand the moral of the story, the lesson we want them to learn about their behavior. If the story doesn't make sense to them, then it's much harder to get the moral.

Taking Responsibility

Many parents want to know how to help their kids take more re-sponsibility for their actions, and many kids do struggle with this skill. Sitting with your child and doing Reviews is a great place to start because many of the skills necessary for personal accountabil-ity are developed there. But there are also many situations, such as in school, in which we don't have the time to sit and talk it out—and adults frankly just want to see the kid own the mistake and move on. What do we do then? How do we help our kids start tak-ing responsibility with others? I have developed some steps to help kids practice taking responsibility with others, but first let's think about why this is such a pervasive issue in the first place.

Why is it so hard for kids to take responsibility for what they've done? The answer seems simple at first but gets more complex when we factor in temperament. The first reason is that children don't want to get in trouble. That makes sense. Nobody likes to face the music when they've made a mistake, especially if it's upset others. If your child is having a hard time dealing with occasional mistakes, then the remedy is pretty straightforward: do Reviews and use a motivator to help your child participate and problem solve with you. Remember to empathize with the child's reasons (such as, it's embarrassing, they're afraid they'll get in trouble, etc.) for not wanting to talk about these kinds of situations. If the mistake occurred with others, use the steps I'll be sharing here, which should be helpful.

For many kids, however, taking responsibility is a deeper issue than simply avoiding punishment, and the solution requires a more complete understanding of the underlying dynamics. Kids with reactive or impulsive temperaments often fall into a pattern of avoiding responsibility because they struggle so much with self-control and so frequently find themselves in the midst of difficult situations. Each of theses moments has the potential to be defined by the child as a personal failure, which over time erodes their good feelings about themselves. People can only endure so many failures before they begin to develop defensive coping mechanisms to try to salvage their self-esteem. And one of the easiest ways people can cope with repeated failure is to deny their part in the problem. Many kids (and some adults too) end up in this position, vehemently denying their role in a situation even when the facts speak otherwise. This can be puzzling for parents and teachers who don't fully understand the dilemma the child is in.

In this kind of situation, the child is asked simply to admit his or her part in the event, but there's more going on for the child than that. Admission would mean acknowledgement of another failure, and some kids' sense of themselves can be so fragile that to admit another failure would be to give up on feeling good about themselves. So when adults ask these kids to simply admit their mistake—it's not that easy. This request puts enormous pressure on them by forcing them to choose between the preservation of self-worth and an admission of guilt. This creates a double bind, a no-win situation for the kids. Whatever they choose to do, they suffer. When push comes to shove and a child with fragile self-esteem is forced to choose between surviving emotionally (deny another failure) and giving the adult what he or she wants (admission), the child will prioritize survival. This choice reflects a healthy desire for self-esteem, but it also impedes a child's ability to unlock from a defensive posture and admit mistakes.

Now this might all sound very dramatic, and may seem like it applies only to kids who are totally out of control and failing all the time, but that's not the case. I know many kids who either are very sensitive (and hard on themselves) or have mild but chronic struggles with self-control, and these kids also develop this mechanism of self-preservation through denial. So if your child is "a denier," take a careful look at why he or she is locked into this pattern of coping. You may discover a struggle to feel positive about themselves concealed beneath the defenses.

From the adult's perspective, on the other hand, taking responsibility for mistakes is seen as a simple solution and the ultimate measure of maturity for kids. Many adults approach it as something to keep pushing for in the child, until the child's ability to defend his or her story crumbles and the truth is finally discovered—not unlike an interrogation. Finding the truth and having children take responsibility is important, but seeing it as purely a battle of the wills is not only oversimplified but also can contribute to the problem by confirming the child's suspicion that it is not safe to come out with the truth. So, accountability is a process that we need to help kids develop while understanding the reasons behind their denial.

As usual, after putting some effort into understanding the underlying cause of a problem, we are now at the "Well, what to do about it?" question. If your child is in a chronic pattern of denying his or her part in events, begin trying to understand why this is happening. Look for patterns of struggle as well as temperament traits prone to affect self-esteem, such as high sensitivity, impulsivity, and reactivity. Then talk to your child about why it's so hard to admit things. Empathize with the challenge of taking responsibility for our actions while still trying to feel good about ourselves. This process will help both of you move forward toward your objective of getting to the truth while preserving self-worth. You can also use the Review and the four steps that follow to help your child move toward more accountability.

If you're talking with your child about taking responsibility with people outside the family, who might not have the time or inclination to sit and do a Review, then help your child work on the following four steps. These steps give kids a few simple skills to help them show friends and other adults that they are taking responsibility for themselves. When discussing difficult events with others, remind your child to use these steps.

1. Start with a good attitude. Tell your child that passing the attitude test may just be the most important part of the interaction. Let your child know that if adults or friends perceive even a hint of defensiveness or negativity, they'll be much less likely to want to hear your child's part of the story. It can be hard for kids to keep a good attitude in situations where they feel the other person has falsely accused them or assumes that it's all their fault. Nevertheless, they need to try to start the interaction with a respectful tone.

2. Admit your mistake. When adults or your child's friends are frustrated with your child, this is what they want to hear. Even though your child may want to begin the interaction by explaining why he or she did what they did, that's not the way to begin. Adults, especially frustrated ones, will mistake explanations for talking back, and they won't listen. So teach your child to start by admitting his or her part in a situation, and let your child know that full admission is the fastest way to get through it.

It's when talking with kids about this step that I remind them that mistakes are an essential part of learning, and I empathize with the difficulty of admitting our mistakes—especially if we're worried about getting into trouble as a result. I also offer empathy for how bad we can start to feel about ourselves if we keep creating problems we don't mean to. I reassure kids that adults will be much less upset and their consequence will often be reduced when they can participate in a conversation that shows they can admit mistakes and learn from them. In addition, I sometimes encourage parents to offer incentives to help a child who is struggling with accountability practice admitting mistakes to others.

Occasionally kids are falsely accused and asked to admit mistakes for which they are not actually responsible. If this occurs, the child should still keep a respectful attitude and admit to adults that it does appear he or she is the cause of the problem. The child could then say something like: "I know that this situation has caused a problem for you, and you think it's my fault. I'm sorry for that. I want a chance to tell you my side of the story, and I am telling the truth." Just remind your child to use this response only when he or she is truly innocent; otherwise, trust will be eroded with the adults in their lives.

3. Apologize (and make restitution if needed). This step usually gets tagged onto the end of step two. Most kids admit their part in things and then apologize right after. But if your child isn't in the habit of adding the apology, talk to your child about its importance. Help your child understand that apologizing is an important part of the process of taking responsibility for mistakes and that it also repairs relationships. Also explain that apologizing helps clean the slate so all parties can move on from the event and put it in the past. Apologizing can feel embarrassing and even humiliating for some kids, so I also offer empathy for how difficult it can be. For infractions that also call for restitution, if there is a way for the child to repair or make up for what was done, then that's a good idea too. Restitution can take many forms, from doing a favor or repairing a broken item to paying for the damage caused. Problem solve with your child about what he or she can do to repair the damage that was caused.

4. Share your intention. Most of the time, it's only after adults have heard a child admit his or her mistake and apologize—all with a good attitude—that they are ready to hear more about the child's side. Now is when the child can share and clarify his or her intention and explain why he or she did what they did. All kids need to be able to share information about what they were trying to do (intention), especially when it comes to dealing with mistakes. The fact is that most of the time kids don't mean to cause problems. Problems arise when kids' judgment or self-control is not developed enough to prevent poor choices or when their temperament makes self-control difficult. So being clear with others about their intention is important for all kids because it reminds adults that the goal of the behavior was not to cause a problem, even if it did. I also try to help kids understand that stating their intention helps keep them from being seen as a troublemaker—which they're not. Stating their intention is a way to help others understand them better and preserves their reputation.

If your child is in the habit of denying responsibility for his or her actions, orient them to these four steps. Talk with them about the importance of practicing these steps with teachers and others, which will show them that they are acquiring this skill. You might want to make a list of these steps and post them somewhere so that your child can see them and return to them with you when a mistake is made. Don't forget to empathize with how hard it is to do all this, especially at first, and add some incentives to help your child shift from habits of defense and denial to habits of self-accountability and responsibility.

Chapter Summary

Here is a recap of some of the highlights and tips presented in this chapter:

- Don't use hot moments to teach skills. Instead wait until things have calmed down and use reflective moments.
- Create family rituals that promote reflective conversation, such as during dinnertime or just before bed.
- Know your child's temperament and look for emotional access points. Use these times to reflect.
- Teach your child to reflect by asking questions. Skip the lecture.
- Use Preview to anticipate difficult situations or strong feelings that might arise.
- Follow the steps of the Review to help your child learn from mistakes or moments where his or her behavior escalated.
- Use a motivator if you get resistance to the Review.
- Pair Reviews with time-outs to create learning moments for younger kids.
- If your child has a hard time taking responsibility for mistakes, help him or her practice the 4 steps outlined in the "Taking Responsibility" section.

Chapter 8

∞

Adding Structure

In addition to building skills, there are some other areas we parents can focus on to help our kids develop good behavior patterns. One of these areas is structure. Providing structure in our kids' lives goes a long way to helping them develop more self-control and accountability. Kids' behaviors often improve when we find ways to increase the amount of structure in their daily lives. Structure can take many forms. In this chapter, we will discuss some of the forms I have found most effective. When I talk about structure, I mean the limits, rules, predictable schedules and routines that help kids stay organized and in control.

In my experience, some of the kids who benefit most from a high amount of structure are those who will fight us the hardest about it. They are the willful, active, and impulsive kids, who love adventure and novelty and are naturally driven to test adult limits. These kids don't know it, but a clear set of rules and some regular routines are often what stand between them and a train wreck of disorganization. If you let a kid with this type of temperament set the level of structure in the house, it will be super fun for a short period of time and then turn into a disorganized mess. Of course, persistent and active kids do need room to have their own ideas and learn through hands-on experience, but because they are children, their brains haven't yet developed the judgmental capacity to know how much structure to keep in the mix so that things don't get too chaotic. So it's up to us parents to help strike the balance between the freedom kids want and the structure that's good for them.

Another group of kids that benefits from structure are the sensitive ones. Structure not only reigns in the wild, it also soothes the overwhelmed. Sensitive kids are prone to anxiety and over-whelm. The predictability that structure adds is comforting to them. When sensitive kids know what's coming at them, they can mentally prepare and get used to it before they actually have to deal with it. Also, sensitive kids are rule followers who like to know that other kids are following the rules too. Having predictable routines and clear rules for everyone decreases the amount of energy sensitive kids have to spend trying to anticipate the next moment or what other kids might do.

Similarly, kids who are low in adaptability depend on structure to get through the day's many transitions. Because change and transition are a particular challenge for these kids, their parents need to keep a fairly consistent routine with lots of structure and advanced notice about upcoming changes. Kids who struggle with maintaining focus also need high structure. Distractible kids have a hard time organizing themselves and their tasks and belongings. Because their brains jump from focus to distraction so easily and often, their experience becomes fragmented. These kids benefit when parents provide the guardrail of structure that keeps them from veering off the road of organization and focus.

When a child is struggling with self-control, one of the first things I look at is how to help the parents increase structure. Increasing structure is a solution that can be kick-started easily and doesn't depend on the child developing many new skills. Adding more structure is often more of a challenge for the parents than the kids, while it is equally beneficial for both.

What does increased structure look like? For some families, it's a matter of establishing routines for the morning, bedtime, homework, mealtime, and other daily routines. For other families, more structure comes from developing a family calendar that tracks everyone's events and appointments. Still other families find structure by sitting down for a family meeting and creating a set of rules (with clear consequences) that everybody in the house will live by. Here is a short list of ways to increase structure in your house:

- Make a list of morning and evening tasks for your child, and post it for them to see. For pre-readers, draw or cut out pictures. Reward the child for doing the routine without too much help.
- Make a plan for homework and other potentially "boring"

or low-stimulus activities. Include an agreed-upon routine, breaks for movement, and rewards for following the plan.

- Start having regular family meetings (which are covered in the next section of this chapter).
- Brainstorm family rules with your kids. Write them down, and post them.
- Make a short job list for your child (or each child if you have more than one) and designate a time on the weekend to complete the assigned jobs.
- Get your child a calendar (paper or electronic) and have the child write and track their schedules.
- Eat a family meal together daily.
- On weekend days, go over the plan for the day with everyone during breakfast.
- Use a reward chart (also covered in this chapter) to help your child work on changing specific behaviors.

Family Meetings

Family meetings are a great way to add structure to family life. They also have the important benefit of keeping the channels of family communication open, which contributes to good functioning for everyone. Family meetings are the place where each person is allowed a voice to discuss his or her experience of family life and to address specific problems. This is especially important for kids who need more opportunities to practice self-direction and the responsibility of being part of a group. Family meetings are also a great time for parents to give feedback to their kids about what's working and what needs attention. Lastly, family meetings are a place to have some fun and build family cohesion.

Family meetings don't need to be overly formal but should include a routine everyone can count on. For instance, you can schedule the family meeting before a weekly movie or dinner night out. Another way is to have family meetings less frequently but still follow a regular pattern, such as placing a sign on the refrigerator announcing that a family meeting will be held on a specific upcoming date. Regardless of how you build family meetings into the family routine, here are some basic elements that should be included in the meeting itself:

- Have a set of ground rules for the meetings that create a safe atmosphere for everyone. Some of these will be just like school rules, such as no interrupting others, respecting others, raising your hand to speak, etc.
- Designate an object as "the speaker's totem," which means that the person holding that object has the floor while others listen or raise their hand to comment.
- Give each family member a chance to have the floor and allow everyone the freedom to talk about any aspect of family life that they want.
- Have everyone use "I statements," meaning each person focuses on his or her feelings and perceptions, not on blaming or accusing others.
- Allow the venting of frustrations—even about parents.
- Parents validate that they understand a child's complaints even if they disagree.
- For every complaint a person shares, that person must also suggest a solution.
- Use voting when appropriate to make family decisions.
- Follow up on previously addressed issues to track progress.
- Discuss not only behaviors and problems but also plans and suggestions for upcoming vacations, holidays, and outings.
- Celebrate the family's teamwork with something fun, such as a game, a song, or some other special treat at the end.

Reward Charts

Reward systems are a great way to add structure to a child's life. This is especially true when there are specific behaviors you want to help your child change. A reward system is really just a way to both help your child focus on the behaviors or skills you want them to work on and to also keep track of their progress. There are many benefits to using a reward system.

First, a reward system helps with structure because it identifies a behavior or behaviors that need addressing and keeps both the parents and the child focused on them. This is often much easier than trying to focus on changing a behavior only in the moment when it comes up, because those moments are usually emotional moments or hot moments, when learning is limited. Similarly, a reward system helps kids practice more accountability for their behaviors because they have to think about the targeted behavior goals and review their progress with you daily. As accountability increases, so does personal responsibility, as the child becomes a partner with you in tracking progress and adjusting goals as necessary.

A good reward system also keeps a child motivated to want to work on behaviors. This is key, because personal change is hard. We all need help staying focused and energized to work hard on our personal goals. Using a good motivator makes a child want to work on his or her goals while it also gives them a chance to access the things they desire. In addition, a good reward system helps kids internalize the idea that access to their favorite things is directly tied to managing their behaviors.

Another benefit is that a reward system decreases the need for parents to come up with consequences on the fly. When we get behavior we don't want and need to move in with the authority arm of parenting, it can be hard to think of ways to motivate our kids to change their behavior in that moment. If you have a system in place, then you don't have to think of a consequence in that moment. You simply remind the child of the reward system and the impact their behavior will have on it. If the system is clear and the reward is important, the child will be motivated to get back on track.

Lastly, a reward system facilitates Reviews. Going over your child's goals daily gives you the chance to discuss any difficulties your child had with a specific goal, and to create a plan for better coping. If you require a short review for poor performance on specific goals before your child can get his or her daily reward, you have a strong, built-in motivator for getting your child to participate in Reviews.

There are many ways to set up a reward system for your child and many opinions on which is best. You can find lots of examples of reward systems online, as well as interactive websites that are sometimes motivating and fun for kids. My theory is that the system that works and is consistently doable for parents is the best one to use. I usually use a reward chart (also called a behavior chart) such as the one that follows. It is easy to use, targets specific behaviors, provides a visual account of progress, and leads directly to a strong motivator.

Noah's Reward Chart

Goals	Mon.	Tues.	Wed.	Thurs.	Fri.	Sat.	Sun.
No Hitting							
Respectful Words							
Get Ready for Bed							
Talk about Feelings							

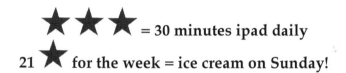 = 30 minutes ipad daily

21  for the week = ice cream on Sunday!

Go Noah!

Download & customize your own home reward chart at betterbehaviorblog.com

Reward Chart Tips

Use the following tips to help set up an effective reward chart for your child.

- Limit the number of goals to a maximum of five. For kids under five, have no more than four goals.
- Be as specific as possible about the behavior or behaviors you want your child to work on—for example, "Stop hitting," not "Be good."
- Make one of the goals fairly easy to attain. This will give your child a sense that goals are doable.
- Have one goal be "Talk about feelings." This goal will help motivate your child to work on this core skill, as well as helping your child with Reviews, since a review counts as

"talking about feelings."

- Don't aim for 100 percent success in order to give a reward—that is, something like four out of four stars. Instead, give the daily reward for progress on three out of four stars.

- After you create the chart, sit with your child and explain to him or her the system you're creating and how it will work.

- Go for success in the first week. Make sure your child gets the reward most days that first week. After your child gets a taste of being rewarded and is feeling confident and invested in the system, begin to raise your expectations. In other words, lower the bar at first. It's okay to reward efforts in the right direction at the beginning in order to get your child invested in the system.

- Adjust rewards if they're not motivating behavior change after a few weeks. For kids who crave novelty, you'll need to change the reward every few weeks or at least whenever you see motivation drop.

- Don't allow access to the reward item at other times. Keep your child hungry for the reward.

- Review the chart daily with both parents present, if possible. Have your child self-evaluate—that is, something like, "Tell us how you think you did on goal number one?" Then parents weigh in to say whether a star or a sticker was earned and why.

- Praise your child for meeting a goal. Acknowledge your child's efforts, even if a star or a sticker wasn't awarded that day.

- After the daily chart review, discuss which goal or goals need more effort, and discuss ideas for how your child might do better. The point is to praise success and keep raising the bar as your child progresses.

- After your child has achieved consistent success with a goal, keep that goal for at least a few more weeks. Then switch to another behavior that needs work. Discuss what the next goal should be with your child, and put past goals on "a success chart" that is placed next to the reward chart. This way your child has a visual representation of all the progress he or she has made.

The Treasure Box

Many of the kids who struggle with self-control are the same kids who crave a lot of stimulus in action and new experiences. Novelty is a great source stimulus for kids who are wired like this. You'll want to consider this when establishing rewards with them. Keeping novelty in play can have a significant impact on whether a reward remains motivating. So if your child is a stimulus-seeker, build a fair amount of novelty into his or her reward system to keep them focused and interested.

One reward that I've seen a lot of parents have success with is the treasure box. Get an old shoebox with a lid and decorate the outside so that it's particularly enticing to your child. Use bright colors and things on the outside that pique your child's interest. Then fill the box with an assortment of small items. Some people mix treats with small toys or coupons for free activities, for example. Just make sure that there's enough variety in the box to keep it interesting. When it's time to get a reward, have your child reach into the box without looking. Not being able to see inside keeps novelty high and holds the child's interest. Once in a while, add a new item to the assortment to keep your child guessing about what he or she might find next. This is a great way to give out rewards and maintain a fairly high level of novelty and motivation.

School Charts

Sometimes a child's most difficult behaviors happen at school. Maybe adapting to the rules or structure is what's hard for them. Maybe it's staying focused on the schoolwork or dealing effectively with peer issues. Regardless of the specific challenge, a reward chart can be used in the classroom to help a child stay focused on the specific behaviors or skills he or she needs to work on. Most teachers welcome helpful suggestions from parents, such as instituting a behavior chart, especially if the teacher feels the parents will reinforce success on the chart at home.

I like to structure a school chart around class study periods so that the child can get feedback on how they're doing in different study topics and work environments—for example, quiet time, group activities, reading, math, PE, recess, etc. This way a child (and parents and teachers) gets feedback about the kinds of topics or class situations that are particularly hard or easy for the child. At the end of this section, you'll find a sample classroom chart, which can be kept either inside the child's desk or in a notebook on the teacher's desk.

Many of the tips for starting a reward chart at home also apply to a school chart—such as being specific about targeted behaviors. In addition, though, you'll need a plan for how the teacher will get the daily chart information to you. Can you trust your child to bring it home? Some teachers prefer to email parents a daily summary. You'll have to decide with your child's teacher what will work best—just make sure that the plan includes a way for you to get the stats on your child's chart daily.

This leads us to another important point: make sure you reinforce progress on the school chart at home. This means an after-school reward for doing well on about 75 percent of the goals on the school chart. It also means doing Reviews as needed for times when the child doesn't do well on a goal. You can even make success on the school chart a goal on the home chart, for instance the first goal on your child's home chart might read "Get at least 3 stickers on your school chart."

Sometimes teachers want to try out their own ideas for dealing with classroom behaviors first—which is fine. If this is the case, don't push the chart idea. Simply offer it to the teacher as one idea you're willing to support if the teacher wants to try it. Often just having parents who are interested and who offer helpful ideas is enough to fuel a teacher's patience and goodwill toward a challenging child. Teachers who feel supported by parents (rather than criticized by them) are less likely to burn out and are more likely to stay positive with a child, which is extremely helpful.

There is also the dilemma of a reward chart in the classroom putting an unnecessary or an embarrassing focus on a child who is already struggling. Some teachers are very aware of this and reluctant to further single out a child by putting them on a chart system. This is certainly a downside of using a reward chart at school. If the teacher or parents are overly concerned about these issues, then a chart at school may not work. Sometimes though, it's simply a matter of parents discussing the potential benefits and challenges of using a reward chart with the child and teacher and then problem solving any concerns together. For instance, you may decide to keep the chart in a discrete binder on the teacher's desk or in the child's notebook. Following is a sample school chart, which can be modified to fit your child's individual goals and class periods.

Noah's School Goals

Class Period Goals	8-9:15	9:15-10	Recess	10:20-12	Lunch	12:30-2
Ask for help when you need it.						
Best effort on work.						
Respectful Language.						
Do not interrupt.						

Teacher's Coments:_____

_____

You can download and customize a copy of the school reward chart at www.betterbehaviorblog.com

    With this type of chart, the teacher would put either a sticker or the teacher's initials in each box to mark successful behavior for that class period. An in-class reward might also be given, such as free time, a homework pass, or getting to be the teacher's helper. In addition, a home reward is given by the parents for getting a predetermined number of stars or teacher initials each day.

Chapter Summary

Here is a recap of some of the highlights and tips presented in this chapter:

- Think about the amount of structure in your family's daily life. Is there enough? Are rules, routines and responsibilities presented and enforced clearly?
- Imagine in what ways adding some structure might improve your child's behavior.
- Choose a few of the suggestions for increasing structure from the list at the chapter beginning and put them into practice.
- Plan a family meeting. Think together about ways to make family life better, and give each member a job to do to contribute to success.
- Consider using a reward chart for behaviors you want to change. Follow the guidelines for setup, and make sure you have a potent motivator.
- If your child is struggling in school, suggest a school reward chart to his or her teacher.
- Download a customizable home or school reward chart at *betterbehaviorblog.com*
- Review chart progress daily and make sure to give your child positive feedback for effort and even small amounts of success.
- Remember that structure controls behaviors and soothes anxiety, so create more structure in your family's life if you're looking to create change.

Chapter 9

∞

Feeling Good, Strong, and Happy

Self-esteem is one of the most important things you can focus on with your child. Self-esteem is similar to self-worth, or the value you place on yourself as a person; it's essentially how good you feel about yourself. People with high self-esteem feel valuable, worthwhile, and important. They like themselves and trust that others like them as well. People with high self-esteem feel their ideas are important and are not afraid of failure. They are generally happy and feel a sense of security in the world. This experience stands in stark contrast with the experience of people who struggle with low self-esteem. Kids and adults with low self-esteem often feel unworthy, powerless, unlovable, and broken. They don't feel a sense of security in the world and often have a hard time trusting others. Kids with low self-esteem don't believe in themselves and don't feel like others believe in them either. They often walk through their days lonely and with a sense of hopelessness about the future.

Like most other traits, self-esteem is not fixed at high or low but a gradient on which our feelings about ourselves fall somewhere. Most people talk about high or low self-esteem as if those were the only choices when they're not. They are certainly important markers on the scale because everybody agrees that it's better for people to be at the high self-esteem end. But self-esteem is also not static. Some days I really like myself, and some days I'm really sick of my limitations. Some days I feel I'm doing great, while on others I feel I've failed somehow. Like everything, self-esteem fluctuates naturally, and that is to be expected. So it's not as though we're going for "feeling great about yourself all the time" with our kids. What we want is to gauge their overall sense of their own value and then to help them feel generally good about themselves most of the time. Plotting our kids' day-to-day self-esteem rating is not necessary, but knowing in general how they feel about themselves is very important.

If we can help kids feel more worthwhile and positive about themselves, then everything else we try to do with them will go better. Everything is built on self-esteem, so its importance cannot be understated. It truly is the foundation for all other functioning. How can we help our kids develop a high level of self-esteem? It all starts with the messages we give them. Kids need messages that show them that we value them, that they are important—not because of what they do, but because of who they are. Practice some of the esteem-building suggestions that follow to help your child feel good about him or herself:

- Tune in and witness your child for who they are (vs. what they do). Comment on positive character traits you see in them, like kindness, honesty, thoughtfulness, humor, perseverance and humility.
- Spend time enjoying your child. Whether it's watching them sing a song or just cuddling on the couch, create feel-good moments.
- Appreciate what your child brings to the family. Whether it's hard work, fair-mindedness or simply a unique perspective, appreciate his or her contribution.
- Slow down and listen to your child. It's the best way to show them that their thoughts and feelings matter.
- Acknowledge your child's skills and accomplishments. Celebrate his or her mastery and success.
- Play with your kids. Play is their profession, so follow their lead and notice how competent they are at this important skill.
- Model positive self-esteem. Your child forms his or her self-concept in part by mirroring yours. So be kind to yourself and set realistic expectations.

We also need to keep self-esteem in mind when we discipline our kids. We don't want to engage in parenting that controls behavior but also chips away at self-worth. Harsh punishment, criticizing, and humiliating a child do this, which is the reason, of course, not to use these methods. Instead, we use the strategies outlined in the previous chapters and try to help our kids remember that *they* are inherently good although some of their behaviors may not be. This approach helps young, developing minds preserve a positive sense of themselves, even while they learn to acknowledge and take responsibility for their negative behaviors and poor choices.

Protecting our kids' self-esteem while disciplining them is accomplished when we help kids separate their feelings from their behaviors (as we do in step four of the Review). Separating feelings from behaviors validates a child's emotional life, which preserves self-esteem, while it also helps them look at their behavior choices. This is a critical distinction because the goal of discipline is not to make kids reject themselves but to have them reject certain behaviors. So we take care to present this distinction clearly when we discipline. Self-esteem is preserved when we tell kids, "Your anger is valid, but your behavior is not okay."

Kids' brains are extremely pliable as they grow. They adapt quickly to incoming messages, which is what optimizes them for learning. If the messages they get when they make a mistake feel like criticism of their personal self (that is, their feelings, intentions, or bodies), then they begin to feel that a part of them is bad or defective. This is where the impact on self-esteem happens. If there are too many negative messages directed personally at a child, such as "You're so clumsy" or "That was dumb," the child will start to believe the message is an accurate evaluation of them, and they will begin to form their identity around such messages. If this happens, the child will then begin to live up to this identity and produce the behavior that fits the negative label. This usually produces more negative comments from adults, which, of course, propels more negative behavior from the child. Thus, the cycle begins.

Many parents unwittingly address their child as "naughty" or "bad." They don't understand the impact this has on the child's self-concept. They actually mean to address the child's behavior, but the words they choose label the child as the problem. There is, of course, a big difference between rejecting a child's behavior and rejecting the child, and it hinges on how personal the message is. Rejecting a child's behavior has much less impact on self-esteem because the behavior is not an internal part of the child. The behavior is a product—or an action—separate from the internal self. This is an important difference to recognize because the internal self can't be changed, so rejecting it equates to rejecting the child's worth. And kids who don't feel worthy are destined to struggle.

In addition, kids who are personally criticized for their behaviors (as opposed to having their behaviors criticized) are put in a precarious situation. If they agree with a parent's critical evaluation of them (for example, "You're naughty"), then they are agreeing that *they* are something negative. They are accepting an internal flaw that the parent has assigned to them. If, on the other hand, they reject the parent's critical evaluation of them, then they have to reject information from their primary source of learning and trust (the parent), and this leaves them psychologically alone. Kids are not programmed to be alone in this way, so they often accept a parent's inappropriate criticism as fact—even when it injures their self-worth. This happens because it's psychologically safer for kids to question themselves than it is to reject information coming from their primary source of security. This process highlights the powerful impact parents have on their kids' self-esteem. And at no time is a parent's feedback presented in a more penetrating and emotionally charged manner than when a parent is frustrated and disciplining their child. Disciplining our children can be an opportunity for learning and guidance or a process that dismantles our kids' self-worth one criticism at a time.

Separating the child from the behavior is especially important for kids whose temperaments lean toward the extreme. For example, very sensitive kids are frequently already hard on themselves when they make mistakes, so they are much quicker to label themselves negatively. In addition, kids who have challenging temperaments get a lot of "correction" from adults, which can be experienced as moments of failure. Because of the number of disciplinary moments they encounter, these kids' self-esteem can easily be chipped away. For both of these temperament types, it's important to monitor the impact of our guidance on the kids' feelings about themselves. Without self-esteem, children are lost. It doesn't matter how smart, rich, or connected they are, if kids don't feel good about themselves then they won't even try to fulfill their ultimate potential. Help your child unlock all his or her potential by staying conscious of how you speak to your child about behavior challenges. Weed out messages that criticize your child in a personal way, and replace them with communication that focuses on the behavior instead.

Here are some suggestions that transform messages about the child into comments about the child's behavior:

- Instead of saying, "Don't be mad," say, "You might be mad, but I don't like your behavior."
- Instead of saying, "You're naughty (or bad)," say, "You've been making bad choices."
- Instead of saying, "Don't be a baby," say, "This might be scary for you. Can you try to be brave?"
- Instead of saying, "You're lazy," say, "I feel like you can try harder."
- Instead of saying, "What's wrong with you!" say, "I'm not sure why you're acting this way, but it's frustrating me."
- Instead of saying, "Don't be rude. Say hello when someone speaks to you," say, "It seems like you're feeling shy. Can you still try to say hi?"

The way we say things has a big effect on kids. In the examples above, you'll notice that the focus shifts from labeling the child to commenting on the behavior. Also notice that it's okay for parents to say that we're getting frustrated or mad because of the behavior. This is honest and certainly happens to all of us. We just want to take care to help kids distinguish their behavior from their self (their feelings, intentions, and identity). It's critical to help even very young kids understand that although their behavior does come from them and they are responsible for their behavior, their behavior is not them, but instead a product of them. Learning this allows kids to own and respect their feelings, while learning to separate and evaluate the behavior they display as a result of their feelings—a process that promotes personal responsibility while preserving self-esteem.

Self-Confidence

Closely related to self-esteem is self-confidence. Self-confidence differs from self-esteem in that self-esteem is a child's assessment of his or her intrinsic self-worth, while self-confidence is a product of a child's belief in his or her abilities. Kids with self-confidence have an inner sense that tasks—even ones they have never tried before—will go well. They trust in their abilities and have the stamina to tolerate the moments of failure that are part of the learning process. This allows them to try new things and to take risks, even in situations where the chance of success is uncertain.

In contrast, kids who lack self-confidence have a hard time believing they can do things well. They approach new tasks with trepidation and have a pessimistic or negative view of how they will do. Taking risks is hard for these kids. They're often anxious before they have to perform in front of others. They quickly learn to avoid taking risks and typically stick with the few activities they know they can do well. Getting these kids to move out of the protective cocoon of avoidance can be very difficult.

Confidence and self-esteem impact each other and can pair up in complex ways, some of which create difficulties for kids. For instance, some kids have high self-confidence but low self-esteem, which might sound confusing at first. This kind of child feels very confident in his or her ability to perform certain tasks but does not feel like a worthwhile or a valuable person on the inside. Kids with a lot of natural talent in a certain area can fool observers into thinking that they also feel good about themselves. Why wouldn't they? They do so well when they're performing. The natural athlete, the math wiz, the funny kid—exceptional performance can take many forms. These kids often get center stage for the things they do well—but they may well feel invisible when it comes to the negative feelings they harbor about themselves.

Many high achievers do indeed feel good about themselves, but some don't. The hard part is that it can be difficult to distinguish between the two. Because appearances can be deceiving and so much attention is given to these kids' wins and successes, people often miss the suffering that lies just under the surface. It's very important for us to understand how high achievers feel not only about their successes but also about themselves.

High achievers can also fall into the trap of perfectionism and addiction to praise. Celebrity status can be enjoyable but also limiting. When everybody expects a child to do very well at certain things, that child can lose interest in trying new activities because they carry the risk of failure. Addiction to praise follows a similar process. High-achieving kids can begin to depend on the approval and adulation of others to feel good—essentially turning over their esteem to others. Childhood is a time for experimentation and self-discovery, for success and failure, and being trapped in a perfectionistic or praise-dependent mind-set seriously limits these kids' ability to develop through the natural process of trial and error.

Not all high-achieving kids are silently falling apart behind the scenes. This profile is less common than the high achiever who actually feels good about himself or herself. But there are also many kids who are struggling with the dilemma of success and low self-esteem, and because these kids usually don't cause problems for their parents and teachers, their suffering often goes unnoticed. These kids often feel alone and misunderstood and are at risk for anxiety and other stress-related issues. Parents of confident high achievers should keep an eye on their kids' self-esteem. If your child is a high achiever, get a clear read on whether your child's achievement is a product of your child feeling good about him or herself, or whether such achievement is hiding an insecure and vulnerable person. Look for signs of low self-esteem i.e. negative comments about him or herself, perfectionism, refusal to take risks, or a negative outlook. And talk to your child—about how he or she feels about him or herself. Take a look beyond the achievements.

Another type of confidence profile to consider is when confidence is present in a child only under certain conditions. These kids usually have a fair amount of self-esteem, which is what differentiates them from the group I just discussed. The difference, though, is that these kids have high self-confidence in certain areas, but low self-confidence in other areas. This is not a product of not feeling good about oneself as much as it is the result of an overemphasis or development of some skills and not others. For example, gifted kids can fall into this trap because they're often naturally very good at certain things. Parents sometimes add to this uneven profile by overemphasizing these talents. If parents place too much value on specific skills, such as in sports or certain academics, it can overfocus the child on these areas. This can lead to high levels of development in certain areas, but underdevelopment in others.

Kids in this situation may have solid self-esteem, but their self-confidence is overly tied to their specific talents. So they end up with self-confidence that is either high or low, depending on the specific task. This can be thought of as situation-specific confidence. Of course, everyone has certain skills that we feel better about than others, but for kids with this confidence profile, the difficulty comes from the large gap they feel between what they are good at and what they aren't good at. This kind of child can be doing math problems two grade levels ahead of the class and have no problem getting up in front of the class to show everyone how to do a difficult equation, but be paralyzed with fear by social relationships, which the child finds challenging. A confidence profile with high peaks and low valleys makes for a rough ride for these kids. We need to make sure our kids have a well-rounded skill set that highlights their natural talents but also helps them develop in areas that are challenging for them.

Self-confidence is about trusting in your ability to manage the different areas of your life well. It's a knowledge that comes from an internal place and doesn't require external sources of validation. The different life areas for kids include schoolwork, social relationships, and recreational activities. Once established, self-confidence doesn't depend on the approval of others. However, it does need certain conditions to grow. Kids are dependent on adults to supply the right soil for their self-confidence to take root. Some of the key materials for building kids' self-confidence include being allowed to persist until success is achieved, having one's efforts and abilities acknowledged by significant others, and feeling that parents and other significant adults trust the child's abilities. This last item, trust, is a very important component because the trust that confident kids feel in themselves begins with the messages of trust they get from their parents. When kids have the experience of adults trusting in their abilities, their judgment, and their moral compass, kids internalize that trust, and learn to trust in themselves.

Here are some suggestions for helping your child build a solid foundation of self-confidence.

- Encourage your child to learn new skills. If your child doesn't easily succeed, help your child learn to keep on trying.
- Acknowledge the skills your child has already mastered, and guide your child to feel proud of his or her hard work.
- Help your child develop a positive outlook.
- Teach your child to use positive self-messages when he or she takes on new tasks, such as, "I can do this."
- Help your child tolerate failure as part of the learning process.

- Don't make goals too hard or too easy for your child.
- Acknowledge your child's good ideas, even when they're not practical.
- Teach your child to ask for help when he or she gets stuck.
- Acknowledge that fear and worry do show up when learning new skills, but encourage your child to move past them and to try anyway.
- Tell your child that you trust him or her, and show this by giving your child increased responsibility for himself or herself as they grow.
- Ask your child for his or her opinion about problems and show trust in their judgment to create solutions.

Self-confidence establishes an internal compass that kids take wherever they go. It becomes a source of inner guidance and makes them feel they can trust their own skills and decisions. Help your child build this solid inner compass. As our kids grow and move out into the world, we will feel confident too, knowing they can navigate challenges and make good choices even when we are not with them.

Resilience

Self-esteem and self-confidence contribute greatly to another important character trait—resilience. Otherwise known as gumption, fortitude, toughness, or psychological strength, resilience is the ability to tolerate and bounce back from adversity. This is a trait we wish for all children because all kids face challenges, large and small, and need the ability to recover and grow from them. Like esteem and confidence, resilience is not something that children are born with. Instead, it is a part of their personality that develops over time as they face challenges. Resilience moves beyond esteem and confidence in that it is not only feeling good about oneself or one's abilities but also knowing that one has the ability to problem solve and deal with difficult situations. In addition, resilience signifies emotional strength. By emotional strength, I mean the ability to handle and withstand emotional stress and suffering, which all kids will face many times in the course of childhood. Lastly, resilience is the ability to tolerate failure. It's the ability to take on tasks that are daunting and face the prospect of failure without losing interest and motivation. This is not easy to do. The strength kids need to work hard at challenging tasks (vs. avoiding them) comes from their resilience.

How is resilience developed? As is true with most character traits, many influences are involved, and some of them are beyond a child's control, such as social and cultural factors. However, as is also true for most skills and traits, by far the biggest contributing factor is family relationships. Since early relationships (particularly parent-child) are the arenas for building life skills, they are also the place to develop resilience. When we help our kids, for instance, work on the five core skills, we are contributing greatly to their resilience. The core skills combine to develop a strong foundation of aptitudes and character traits that support a child's integrated sense of self, emotional strength, and ability to problem solve difficult situations. Together these foster the ability to face adversity and bounce back from disappointments and failures.

In addition to supporting our kids' development of the core skills, here are a few tips for helping them develop resilience:

- Help your child develop a plan for getting through tough situations.
- Help your child take action. Help him or her take that first step.
- Help your child connect to others when facing adversity vs. going it alone. These others could be parents, relatives, friends, role models, and community support (church, community centers, etc.).
- Help your child keep challenges in perspective by helping them to see other areas of life that are going well for him or her.
- When your child faces a challenge, remind him or her of other adversities they've overcome.
- Help your child set realistic goals.
- Help your child learn to ask for help.
- Have your child help others get through tough situations.
- Help your child express the feelings involved, and then validate those feelings for your child.
- Help your child identify his or her character strengths.
- Help your child develop a hopeful, optimistic disposition.

- Help your child accept adversity by staying present and focused on coping, instead of avoiding stressors or just complaining.

Perfectionism and Happiness

Self-esteem and self-confidence are the structures that allow for resilience, and resilience is the foundation for good coping. A child who has developed these traits is in good shape to function well and to deal with challenges in constructive ways. But what happens when these skills are not fully developed? Well, then kids develop other ways of coping that are not as healthy. Perfectionism is one of these ways.

Perfectionism happens when children hold impossibly high standards for themselves as a result of either perceiving or actually experiencing pressure to do so from their parents or others. Perfectionism is an issue that is closely related to self-esteem because at its core perfectionism is a means to compensate for feelings of inadequacy. The basic idea is that if you're feeling good enough about yourself, then a good enough performance will satisfy you. But anyone starting with feelings of insecurity may compensate for those feelings by setting extremely high personal standards. This is an attempt to create a strong buffer against failure, which is the insecure person's ultimate fear. The paradox of perfectionism is that although it is an attempt to increase feelings of self-worth and control by doing things "just right," it ends up ultimately damaging self-esteem by making the person feel more and more out of control.

For people who have not dealt with perfectionism, it might not seem like such a big deal. In fact, it might seem like the right kind of problem to have. It makes your child work extra hard and do well, right? It makes for an extra "good" kid who stays out of trouble, right? Well, these statements are partially true, and these partial truths are probably why more parents don't see the signs of perfectionism as being as serious as they are. Certainly most parents want their children putting in as much effort as they possibly can, especially when it comes to schoolwork. It's also true that kids should try as hard as they can and develop a good work ethic toward their schoolwork or their chosen extra-curricular activities. Some kids do underperform and need their parents to set clear expectations about how much effort they want the child putting into their tasks.

However, there is also increasing pressure on kids, both in family and school life, to perform at their highest abilities all of the time. This pressure to succeed has turned into what seems to be a national anxiety around success and school performance. Such pressure particularly affects more sensitive kids, who already have high expectations of themselves and are prone to taking on too much work and responsibility. The notion that a child will be successful in life if he or she just keeps a high enough GPA and goes to a school with one of the best reputations is a dangerous trap. The GPA and prestigious school can open certain doors, but a fatigued, frazzled and anxious child will walk through those golden doors without noticing their shimmer. This is because it's impossible to actualize full potential when the self is out of balance. Again, it's not that our children shouldn't be focused on academic success but that this focus has to be balanced with other life skills, as well as enough downtime to enjoy all the other types of learning kids need to experience during childhood.

I sometimes think of childhood as a salad bar. Kids are supposed to nibble on this, take a bite of that, toss what they don't like in the trash, and come back for seconds of whatever tastes terrific. How else are they going to truly find themselves? It certainly won't come from homework only. Kids need opportunities to learn and study, but they also need time to dream, to play, to be bored, and to cure their boredom.

Playtime is an especially important component of childhood learning because so many skills are developed and sharpened during play. By play, I'm not just talking about a four-year-old with dolls. Humans of all ages need to play, though of course it looks quite different at different developmental levels. Play at any age represents freedom, the freedom to explore one's interests and develop one's skills and the freedom from the pressures and structures imposed by living this modern life. The benefits of play are numerous. For kids they include the development of creativity and imagination, social skills, the abilities to organize and to plan, and decision-making—many of the skills necessary for success in adult life. So leave time in your child's busy life for unstructured play, and play with them yourself. With younger kids, let them be in charge and direct the play, they will take you into their wonderful world if you will simply follow.

The overscheduled and pressured world our kids live in leaves many of them in a chronic state of fatigue and stress. Despite the allure of the idea that the right college or the right amount of money will produce happiness, the truth is that this is an illusion. Happiness, like security, is an internal state, and it is the product of being in the present moment and being true to one's self—one's internal compass. The happiness our kids get from success on a test is fleeting because it's based on a performance, which is a temporary state. True lasting happiness comes not from performance, but from developing aspects of our character that make life better for us, such as integrity, purpose and the ability to maintain good relationships. It's the product of living in alignment with our values and emotional health, which can only be defined personally by each of us. Happiness is not based on what someone else says will feel good or is right for us. When our kids are too oriented to other people's notions of happiness, they don't develop their own ability to find and create personal satisfaction. This is how they lose touch with their inner compass and ultimately become dependent on others (adults, friends, media figures) to define happiness and satisfaction for them.

Many highly-scheduled, fast-track kids get a lot of experiences, but because so many of these experiences are orchestrated by their parents, many of these kids don't develop the ability to produce their own satisfying moments. And if you can't produce your own happiness, you'll always be chasing someone else's idea of what might satisfy you. This is the concerning by-product of the overscheduled, high-achiever lifestyle because there is an endless stream of marketing media telling kids and adults what exactly we need to buy, watch, listen to, and look like in order to finally reach fulfillment. Kids are especially vulnerable to advertising and the media and are often lured into a false sense of thinking they understand what creates happiness. The marketing blitz aimed at kids prioritizes consumerism over personal growth and so does little to support children's long-term health and happiness.

The problems created by overworking and overscheduling our kids are related to the problem of perfectionism. Perfectionism is a form of anxiety that is developed in response to situations that put too much pressure on kids. Too much homework, too many activities, and too much expectation to compete and win—all begin to take their toll on a child. After some time under the weight of this kind of pressure, many kids begin to put pressure on themselves.

This is when perfectionism begins to get its teeth into our kids. Soon a hardworking attitude turns into a self-imposed impossible ideal that only reinforces the need for a child to work harder. And since kids' brains don't yet hold things in perspective well, it's easy for them to slip into the trap of perfectionism without even seeing it happen.

Perfectionism provides a child with a certain amount of relief from the pressures of performance by giving the child a momentary sense of control. But the control it provides, like the performance itself, is fleeting, so it leaves the child immediately looking for the next fix—something else to provide a sense of control and relief. The obvious problem is that the child gets pulled into a cycle that keeps him or her focused on gaining relief by performing better and better, which only puts more pressure on the child—pressure that needs relief. With the demands of adult life, including college and work, looming in the foreground, teens are especially at risk for perfectionism or it's antithesis, relief. Relief from anxiety can be found in productive and unproductive activities. Many teens choose to numb themselves with drinking, drugs, or risky behaviors to take their minds off the pressures they're under. Obviously, these are not the solution to feeling pressure, for they ultimately create many more problems than they solve.

Many parents unintentionally contribute to this pressure by repeatedly encouraging their kids to "win" or "succeed." Even the old "do your best" can add a burden of pressure for a sensitive child. The problem is not in putting forth good effort, but that the focus remains on the end result and not the process. This is like focusing on getting rich to become happy instead of enjoying life and working hard at whatever is really rewarding. One way focuses on the illusionary goal, while the other makes the best of now and finds satisfaction in the process.

Anxious, perfectionistic kids are looking for a sense of control. One way parents can help them find it is to adjust how we praise our kids. When we want our children to know that we are proud of them, we can focus on their effort and the skills they are developing rather than their intelligence or talent. The reason for this is that kids don't have much control over how smart or talented they are, but they can control how hard they try and their commitment to building skills. When a parent says, "I know you'll do well on your math test because you're so smart," the child may like the vote of confidence but may also feel pressure to stay "so smart" on all math tests. Another way to praise a child in this kind of situation is to say something like, "I have a feeling you'll do well on your math test because you've been studying so hard." This statement still gives the child the vote of confidence, but it is tied to the child's efforts toward studying, which the child does have control over. The statement is also specific. Smart and talented are general terms in and of themselves, so they have less meaning for a child. In contrast, mentioning the specific skills a child is working on makes it clear to the child exactly what we're noticing. A specific compliment is also likely to be felt as more genuine than a generic pep talk. Shifting how praise and encouragement are delivered can have a big effect on how pressured and anxious a child feels.

We clearly don't want to pressure our kids, but we also want them to work as hard as they can. So the big question remains: how do we get our kids to develop a good work ethic but not fall into the pressurized trap of perfectionism? Here are some things we can do:

- Keep an eye on the sensitive child. If your child is very sensitive, know that he or she is programmed to please—and to be hard on themselves. These kids are also prone to anxiety, which easily leads to perfectionism.

- Model imperfection. Get control of your own perfectionism because your child will do what you do. Give your child permission to make mistakes by acknowledging your own.

- Teach both the value of mistakes and how they're a necessary part of learning.

- Teach your child about self-forgiveness. After a mistake or a bad performance, help your child remain nice to himself or herself.

- Emphasize the process, not the outcome. Help your child focus on making the road to the destination enjoyable. Take the focus off the grade, the score, or the final product.

- Encourage independent thinking, even when it doesn't provide the best answer. Use everyday problems to encourage your child to practice solving problems. And don't help too much.

- Value courage and perseverance over competition.

- Help your child find happiness and satisfaction by having him or her evaluate what makes him or her feel good.
- Give your child downtime, and don't micromanage his or her free time.
- Slow the family pace down, and notice life's wonderful details.
- Discourage materialism. Don't emphasize getting things to be happy.
- Teach your child to use positive self-statements when faced with a challenge—such as, "I will try my best and enjoy the ride."
- Talk with your child about the pressures he or she is under. Encourage your child to release stress by talking with you and participating in activities that he or she finds rejuvenating.
- Praise effort instead of intelligence or talent.

I recently worked with a fourteen-year-old boy who could have been a poster child for the sensitive, perfectionistic, goal-driven, and very unhappy child. This boy's parents brought him to see me because he was lonely and unhappy. When I asked him about friends, he admitted that he wanted friends but also that he didn't have time for them. He explained that he couldn't make any extra time in his schedule for friends because they would get in the way of his $3-million dollar house. Confused, I asked him to explain, and this is what he told me.

Getting his $3-million dollar house meant that he needed a very high-paying job. A very high-paying job would come from going to one of the top colleges in the country. Going to one of the top colleges in the country depended on him both going to one of the best private high schools in the country and getting perfect SAT scores. Getting into one of those prestigious high schools and getting top SAT scores depended on the boy keeping his grades perfect this year (eighth grade) and doing lots of extracurricular and leadership activities, which would look good on his high school and college applications. All of this left no time for friends or anything else.

I told him that all made sense, and then I asked him, "Who are you going to have over to your $3-million dollar house?" This was a smart kid, who answered, "Probably no one because I won't have any friends. High-paying jobs take all your time." I then asked him if he thought he would at least finally be happy in his big house. This was the most tragic part of this boy's story. He replied, "No, I won't." "Then why do it this way?" I asked him. The boy replied, "Because it's what I'm supposed to do."

This bright kid knew that the road he was on, with its laser focus on achieving goals for materialism, would leave him unhappy and lonely, but he couldn't stop himself. He literally couldn't see any other way. The strange thing was that I knew his parents well. They were very successful people (so they had modeled success), but they were also down to earth people who did not pressure their son about grades or overemphasize material gain. The boy's orientation was something he had come up with outside of his parents' influence, and it was precisely the thing that was keeping happiness out of his life. I did not get to see the transformation I had hoped for in him because soon thereafter he was accepted into a private high school some distance away, so we lost touch. I was fortunate enough to have some sessions with him before he left, though. I tried to help him include an orientation to his own happiness in his picture of life. Also, knowing his thoughtful parents, I believe they will continue to help their child unravel his tangle of misconceptions in order to eventually help him become a happier person. It still makes me sad, though, when I think about how lost this great kid was and how far he was living from his own happiness.

A growing body of research has identified some common contributors to happiness that hold true across cultures and age. I have summarized several of them below. As you read through the list, try to identify what you are emphasizing in your family and what needs to be added.

- **Have internal, rather than external, goals.** Happy people tend not to have goals based on external measures such as status, image, wealth, or social position. Instead, they tend to have goals that are internally based, such as personal growth, integrity, honesty, and creating positive relationships.

- **Gratitude.** People who are grateful experience more happiness. A focus on gratitude helps us think beyond the self and appreciate what we have instead of endlessly wanting more. Gratitude also helps us show appreciation in our relationships, which improves them and thereby leads to more happiness.

- **Community.** Happy people have a sense of connection to those around them. Creating ties to others in our community provides a sense of belonging and security that promotes happiness.

- **Close and supportive relationships.** People with close relationships that allow for emotional expression gain a sense of support, emotional connection, and bonding with others that increases the quality of their lives.

- **Generosity.** People who share and give to others are happier. Sharing fosters cooperation, which creates better relationships. Giving also creates a positive sense of self, which improves self-esteem.

- **Inclusion.** Happy people don't exclude others; instead, they practice inclusion and social connection.

- **Find meaning.** Those who are happy don't do things only out of obligation or to meet a goal. They engage in things that give them a sense of meaning and purpose. Happy people often also have a spiritual connection to something bigger than just themselves.

- **Express feelings.** People who can express both positive and negative feelings are happier. Communicating our feelings releases them and creates mutual understanding and connection in relationships.

Notice that making money and buying stuff didn't make the list. Countries that have increased their wealth and consumerism, in some cases by as much as 50 percent, haven't shown any correlation with an increase in happiness. This is important information because it dispels the popular belief that money buys happiness. Knowing this allows us to focus our parenting on the things that actually do increase happiness in our kids' lives. Many parents share with me a strong desire to have their family life be happier, so it's helpful to know which keys actually unlock that door. If you want to increase the happiness in your kids' lives and your life, look over the preceding list and start practicing some of the recommendations. They will open the door to real happiness.

Chapter Summary

Here is a recap of some of the highlights and tips presented in this chapter:

- Keep an eye on your children's self esteem and talk with them about how they are feeling about themselves.
- Look for signs of low self-esteem, such as: negative comments about oneself, being extra harsh or unforgiving of oneself, feeling stuck in a powerless or 'victim' position, etc.
- Practice some of the esteem-building suggestions from the bulleted list.
- Be careful to preserve esteem when disciplining your child. Avoid comments that criticize the child and instead make your guidance about the behavior.
- Remember that not all high-achieving kids feel good about themselves. If you have a high-achiever, look beyond the accomplishments to find out how they're feeling inside.
- Put into practice three of the confidence-building exercises from the list.
- Help your child build resilience by facing adversity, problem-solving with others and not giving up.
- Practice optimism. Your kids will follow.
- Keep an eye out for perfectionism, especially if you have a sensitive kid.
- Instead of focusing on goals and achievement, focus on hard work and enjoying the ride.
- Give your child plenty of down time (mostly non-electronic) to play and relax.
- Discourage materialism/consumerism in your home.
- Follow the suggestions on the happiness list yourself. This will model for your kids what to focus on to capture the state of satisfaction in their lives.

Chapter 10

∞

Family and Social Relationships

If one of your kids struggles with his or her behavior at home, then it's likely that this is having a significant impact on everyone else in the house. Kids who struggle with self-control occupy a lot of the family's energy and airspace. Their needs for support, encouragement, or discipline often get prioritized before the needs of others, simply because these kids have such a big impact on the unit as a whole. Siblings can end up resentful and discouraged, either from having to endure the child's behaviors directly or from constantly losing their parents' attention to the struggling child. Likewise, this type of situation can be very stressful for parents, who end up frantically trying to give everyone what they need, while trying to preserve a bit of themselves in the process.

Maintaining a sense of balance and fairness can be difficult for parents in this type of situation, and they often feel at a loss for what to do. Parents who know that one of their children needs extra attention usually try to give it to the child, but then they worry (rightly so) about the cost to the others in the house. When parents come to me exhausted from daily battles with a struggling child and worried about the impact on their other kid(s), I start by helping them do two things: process feelings and restore balance.

Having to live in the same house with a brother or a sister who struggles with behavior can create a lot of stress for the child's sibling(s). Parents naturally want to remove stressors from their kids' lives, but this is not always possible, as is the case when the source of stress is another one of their children. What to do then? Begin by processing feelings with the other kids in the house. A lot of benefit can come from simply helping siblings express the feelings that their brother or sister evoke in them and then having their parents validate those feelings.

Kids are extremely resilient, and one factor that seems to support their resilience more than any other is emotional support. When children know they have trusted adults who can help them release their stress and validate their experience, it can make the difference between being able to tolerate chronic stress and breaking down from it. So, opening the channel of emotional communication with our kids is the first order of business. Help your kid(s) tell you about the effect their sibling has on them, and try to understand and validate their unique experience. This conversation helps them release all the negative emotions and energy they've stored up during difficult times. It also does the important job of decreasing feelings of emotional isolation, of feeling alone in their experience. Decreasing isolation for people who are suffering is important because the isolation amplifies negative feelings, which increases the suffering the person has to endure. Emotional communication can also lead to problem solving, particularly of difficult situations, and so it contributes to a greater sense of control for the sibling(s). Parents don't want any of their children to suffer any more than they already do, so helping siblings process the stress of living with a brother or sister who struggles can provide a lot of relief.

I want to be clear about something: processing feelings with siblings is in no way about bad-mouthing the struggling child. Parents should maintain a neutral tone about the struggling child as they listen and validate the feelings shared by the sibling(s). You can even educate the sibling(s) about why their brother or sister has such a hard time with behavior (whether it's temperament, social challenges, etc.). Helping siblings understand (in age-appropriate terms) their struggling brother or sister's difficulties can help the sibling(s) not take the challenging behavior personally, which can preserve the kids' relationship with each other.

The other thing that you can do to help the situation is find ways to restore balance. You can't, and wouldn't want to (except in the most extreme cases), remove the struggling child from the home, but you do need to show the sibling(s) that you care about fairness and balance by making an extra effort to give the sibling individual attention. Some "special time" with mom or dad goes a long way to achieve this. One-on-one time with a parent (or both parents) gives the sibling(s) time to soak up the parents without the usual diversion of the struggling child. Daddy or mommy dates, special outings, playtime, or simply joining the sibling(s) in their favorite activity can be satisfying ways to catch up and connect for both the child and the parent. These are the moments when you can find out what's going on in your other kid(s) lives and get details on their thoughts and interests. These moments of personal connection do a lot to help the other kid(s) in the house feel really seen by you—an experience they may not get a lot of when the struggling brother or sister is around.

Sibling Roles

You'll also want to keep an eye on sibling roles when you have a child that takes a lot of your time. In the face of family stress, siblings can easily slip into specific roles in an attempt to get their needs met or to help restore balance. Although some of these roles are appropriate for a sibling, others are not. For example, an older brother or sister can become "the good child" or the little parent because he or she sees that their parents are stretched thin by the struggling child's needs. These kids will focus their energies on being overly helpful with their parents and come to see themselves as an extension of the parental unit. They sense that things are out of control or not safe, so they begin to prioritize supporting their parents over the interests and activities of their own childhood. Of course, there's nothing wrong with a helpful child, but there is a problem if that child's focus on family responsibilities robs him or her of the innocence and freedom of their own childhood. It's fine to give older siblings extra responsibilities around the house, but be on the lookout for the sibling who is too helpful or adult-like. That child could be out of balance.

Another common role kids take on is becoming "the invisible child." The invisible child wants to recede into the background because he or she can't tolerate the stress and conflict in the house. These kids are often sensitive and may not have the skills to deal with the struggling sibling, so they take on the job of not making waves. The main problem with this role is that this child's needs also become invisible. While parents are distracted by the struggling child, the invisible child becomes isolated in his or her experience of family life.

More reactive kids will do the opposite of becoming invisible. They will begin to make waves, becoming more disruptive than the struggling child. Reactive kids may engage the struggling child in fights or turn their frustrations on their parents or younger siblings—making things even harder for everyone. This family role, like the others, is a signal to the parents that things are out of balance and the sibling needs help. Keep in mind that disruptive behavior can take many forms. It's possible that the sibling of a challenging child may become overly silly or humorous in an attempt to distract family members from the difficulties at home and to secure some personal attention. The key term here is *disruptive*. If the sibling's behavior seems too pronounced, whether positive or negative, it's likely the sibling is trying to communicate that there is something wrong.

If you have a child in the house who is struggling with his or her behavior, you will have to keep an eye out for this child's impact on his or her sibling(s). You will also need to understand the signals each child's temperament sends to indicate that things are not going well for that child. Talk with your child and find out what is going on emotionally with him or her. Then you can think together about what can be done to make your child feel better and to restore balance. And I'm not just talking about homes with a child who is totally out of control. Mildly difficult kids or kids going through a difficult period can create high stress too, especially for sensitive parents and siblings. If there is tension in the house because of one child, keep an eye out for the sibling(s) as well. Although the roles siblings take on can help them feel a sense of control, when they are developed as coping mechanisms for family stress, those roles can also stifle kids' range of experience and emotional growth.

Sibling Conflict

Sibling relationships are unique in that they are likely the longest relationships our children will have—relationships that will outlast the parent-child relationship. These connections can be a great source of support for kids during and beyond childhood because they have qualities that other relationships don't, such as shared genetics, common experiences, and similar values. However, these relationships can also produce conflict, especially during childhood, as kids vie for parents' attention, individual power, and family resources.

Sibling conflict can be very disruptive to family life, and if left unchecked, it can take a toll on the children's relationships with each other. Of course, there is going to be a certain amount of conflict that naturally arises between siblings as they grow and learn. In fact, sibling relationships are where brothers and sisters first develop and test their social skills. This process will produce a fair amount of low-level conflict that is necessary because it helps these kids develop the ability to assert themselves, problem solve, and manage the ins and outs of long-term relationships. However, too much conflict in sibling relationships is not healthy and can create dynamics between kids that prevent them from having good relations not only in childhood but also into adulthood. So, the stage is set early on for how relationships develop among siblings. Parents need to stay aware of the level of conflict present among their kids to ensure that these relationships get off to a good start.

Parents should start by understanding the difference between sibling conflict that is natural and productive and conflict that is damaging. The main way to differentiate is by looking at two factors: the frequency and the intensity of the conflict. If the fighting is happening too often or the conflicts are getting so big that they feel out of control, then they are likely producing suffering for the kids. Parents also need to consider each child's temperament, because different temperaments have different tolerances for conflict. Sensitive kids are easily overwhelmed by conflict, while less sensitive or active and stimulus-hungry kids may actually enjoy it. Keep an eye on sibling conflict and tune into the impact it's having on each child in the family. The easiest way to do this is by talking to your kids about how they feel their sibling relationships are going. Such conversations, along with your observations, will help you decide whether you need to step in or let the kids figure it out for themselves.

If you decide that you need to help mediate sibling conflict, there are some steps you can take that will go a long way to creating more peace in the house. When I say mediate, I don't mean referee. Your job is not to jump in and solve your kids' relational problems but instead to help them build the skills to do this themselves. This way, you stay out of the referee role and remain the parent who helps kids manage their own relationships in a constructive way.

The first step in helping kids decrease conflict is to increase communication. Set aside some time to get the kids talking to each other about feelings and solutions. This can be done during a family meeting or through a one-on-one meeting that you arrange for the kids to begin to work things out. Either way, the steps are similar and not too complicated. First, agree on some ground rules—such as no interrupting, no name calling, sharing feelings, and suggesting a solution for every complaint that is voiced. As in the Review, the siblings need to be calm before you attempt this. You want them to be able to access all their faculties.

Follow these steps to help the kids work out their conflict through discussion:

- Get the kids together during a calm moment, in a place with minimal distractions.
- Go over the ground rules.
- One child is the speaker, and the other is the listener. Switch back and forth as necessary.
- Have the speaker state specifically what he or she doesn't like, including the feelings it creates.
- The parent validates the speaker's feelings—"Well, I could see how that would make you mad."
- Then ask the listening sibling to state his or her understanding of what upset the child who is speaking—for example, "What is she saying she doesn't like?"
- Switch and have the other child become the speaker. Repeat the previous steps with this child—that is, stating the problem, parent validation, and the listening sibling stating his or her understanding of the speaker's upset.
- Next, have the kids take turns thinking of solutions to the problem e.g. take turns, share, respect personal space or property, etc. Encourage flexibility and compromise.
- Make a plan to use the solution(s) for future conflicts. Have each child commit, or promise, to do it the new way next time.
- Have the kids apologize and if needed make amends. Also have them decide that the current conflict is *over* and that they are moving on.
- Praise or reward the kids for working it out with words and practicing flexibility and compromise.

The Two-Step Plan

One strategy I use a lot with kids who are having conflict with siblings (works with peers too) is what I call the two-step plan. The two-step plan is a way to help kids think about what steps to take when someone is doing something they don't like. The simplicity of the two-step plan makes it easy for kids as young as three to understand and use. It's not just for the young though; twelve-year-olds use it with great success too because they know that when they're upset it helps to have a basic plan that's easy to remember and use.

The two-step plan goes like this: whenever someone is doing something you don't like, use the first step, which is to tell the person to stop. (For older kids this can be revised to "Tell the person what upsets you and ask the person to stop.") This step orients kids to stick up for, or assert, themselves first, which is an essential skill. It also saves parents from being the continual referee, which can happen when kids develop the habit of running to mom or dad first with every little problem.

A question I often get from kids is "How many times should I tell them to stop?" That's a great question, and my answer is twice. What we don't want is for a kid who is being treated badly to have to endure mistreatment too long. We also know that each time the child has to tell a brother, sister, or friend to stop, the child gets more frustrated. If the child has to repeatedly ask for the behavior to stop, by the fourth or fifth request, the upset child will be at a breaking point and much more likely to resort to lashing out with negative behavior. So I tell kids that it's okay to tell their brother, sister or friend to stop two times, because it's possible they didn't hear them the first time. After that, though, it's better to move to the next step before getting too upset, making a mistake, and getting in trouble for something they didn't even start.

Moving on to step two, which is also straightforward: if the other kid doesn't stop, get help. The purpose of this step is to give the child an action to take that will help resolve the problem. Kids run out of ideas quickly when they're involved in conflict, so getting help from an adult can bring a multitude of solutions to the table. This will happen, of course, if the adult wants to be helpful. Some adults have the notion that kids need to work things out for themselves. Although this is generally a good idea, it isn't when a child is genuinely stuck. If a child has tried to work it out without success, then the next best option is *not* to stay in the situation doing the same thing over and over until things fall apart, but to get help. Without help, it is possible that the child might end up either giving in to a more dominant sibling (or peer) or becoming so frustrated that a physical fight develops. Both of these outcomes are far worse than getting help from an adult.

Kids and adults ask me, "Isn't that just teaching a kid to be a tattletale?" The answer is no. A tattletale is someone who runs to adults every time there's a problem, which is not what the two-step plan suggests. There's a difference between tattling and getting help, and it's whether the child has tried to be assertive and solve the problem first. If so, and the problem didn't get resolved, then the child needs help and asking for it is appropriate. This is not tattling; it's being smart.

The two-step plan helps kids focus more on managing themselves versus focusing on what the other child is doing, and it also gives them a strategy that's simple enough to remember in the most upsetting situations. Teach your kids how to use the two-step plan. Also, feel free to be creative and modify the plan to suit your child's age and abilities. I know some older kids who turn it into the three- or four-step plan, adding steps like "decide to ignore" before getting help. Talk with your child about how to apply the two-step plan to his or her specific situation, and reward your child for working the plan and doing his or her part—even if it doesn't change the other child's behavior immediately.

Tips for Parents

Earlier I shared suggestions to help siblings resolve conflict. Here are some additional tips for improving family relationships in general. Read through these and see which ones you're currently using and which ones you might try:

- Encourage your kids to express to you the feelings their siblings help create, both positive and negative.
- Help your kids express their feelings to each other verbally.
- Accept and validate all feelings, especially negative ones (jealousy, anger, etc.). Releasing bad feelings makes room for good ones.
- Encourage your kids to try to work it out between themselves

before getting help. Acknowledge their problem-solving abilities.

- Teach your kids the two-step plan, and reward them when they use it.
- Praise flexibility, generosity, and compromise in their problem solving.
- Focus on cooperation instead of competition. Teach win-win compromises.
- Give siblings jobs to do together.
- Acknowledge each child for his or her individual traits and contribution. Don't compare kids.
- Help your kids understand "fair but not equal," which means you will always try to make things fair, but they won't always be exactly the same. Instead, you will base your expectations on individual ability, temperament, and circumstance.
- Don't lock family members into roles, such as "the good kid." Help everyone experience many roles in the family.
- Have consistent rules for emotional and physical safety for all family members. Enforce those rules.
- Balance attention and "special time" for each child.
- Notice and praise effort as well as the positive things each child does to contribute to good family life and relations.
- Focus on siblings' similarities, and help them take pride in being related, and part of your great family.
- Have regular family meetings to increase family communication and problem solving.
- Get family counseling if there's too much sibling conflict—which will damage their adult relationship as well. Such conflict may also signal imbalance in other areas of family life.

Peer Relationships

Kids struggle with peer relationships in much the same way they struggle with siblings, and many of the same factors apply. Although the situations and roles differ, the basic skills needed to successfully manage relationships are the same—whether we're talking about the family, social, school, or later the work environment. What does differ among these areas are the types of relationships, developmental factors, and settings in which the relationships occur. Peer relationships contain special challenges for kids because they are ever evolving as they continue to grow and change. This means that kids have to constantly update their relational skill-set and incorporate the new developmental abilities they are acquiring. At the same time, kids need to discard old social habits as they become unnecessary or inappropriate for their current age. This is a complex developmental process that creates a unique set of challenges for the social child.

Here is an example from my practice. A ten-year-old boy named Grant was sitting on my couch and very unhappy. He described his life at recess as very frustrating and confusing because of the way his two best friends were playing. As we talked, he shared with me that the two boys, both also ten, played mostly silly and obnoxious pretend-play ideas, which bothered him. When I reminded him that this was the way he had always described playing with them in the past and that he always described it as fun, he replied that it used to be fun but now he didn't feel like playing that way anymore. This kind of play was starting to feel too young for him.

We talked about what could be done about this, and he shared that he had come up with a solution, which was to tell his friends they were being too immature and to stop playing that way. I thought for a moment and then asked him to think about how he thought they would feel if he told them how they should play. Grant then realized that it wouldn't go over well. We talked about whether there were other kids to play with who weren't acting so silly, and he said that he did like how some of the other boys in his class were focused on developing sports skills. But he was also quick to say that the kids who were still playing in a silly way were his best buddies and that he didn't really want to play with anyone else. He was stuck.

I told Grant that it seemed to me that he was standing on the fifty-yard line (he loves football). On one side of the field was a younger team goofing around like he used to, while at the opposite end zone was another team, more serious but still enjoying each other as they worked hard at improving their skills. And then I told Grant I imagined him standing on the fifty-yard line looking at his friends on the younger team, longing for the freedom of that camaraderie but also feeling that that kind of play was not really *him* anymore. I told Grant I also saw him turning the other way, toward the more mature players, and wanting to be more serious and focused like them but feeling intimidated by a new way of being with friends. What a lonely and confusing place that was, standing out there in the middle of the field and not feeling at home on either team. How much easier it was when he belonged to one team and the pull of the next level (maturity) didn't have its grip on him. As I described his situation using this analogy, I could tell by the welling in Grant's eyes that he knew I understood how it felt to be in this unique place. This understanding then allowed us to move forward and begin to work on some solutions for his dilemma.

This scenario illustrates the ongoing interplay among social, emotional, and developmental factors that are continually shifting during childhood. Grant was in one of those awkward places. Kids face these kinds of dilemmas throughout childhood. Whether it's making friends, asserting one's self, resolving conflict, or sorting out other developmental changes that are ever emerging, kids social lives can be a great source of satisfaction as well as overwhelm. So we come to the important question, what can we as parents do to help? The good news is that if we're helping our kids develop the five core skills, we're already working on the answer. Although the situations and details shift, the skills needed to resolve social problems and function well are all contained in the five core skills.

Let me give another example. Six-year-old Shanti comes home from school looking upset and complains that some girls are leaving her out of their "special club." With the two arms of parenting, we can begin to help her practice the core skills. The authority arm would have us clarify and set any needed limits. In this case, Shanti isn't behaving in a way that needs to be stopped, so we don't need to present much authority. The empathy arm would have us encourage Shanti to express her feelings about the situation (understanding feelings). Doing this, we've opened the door to a conversation about the situation (communication), which helps Shanti release the emotional tension she's been holding. After we validate her feelings, we look at what Shanti can do about the girls' behavior toward her (problem solving). The solutions we would be looking at would likely include Shanti practicing flexibility, good communication, and the assertion of her needs. We would encourage her to remain respectful even though the girls are not being nice to her (respect and flexibility), and then together we would come up with a plan, like talking to the girls, as well as a back-up plan, like getting a teacher's help (the two-step plan). This example illustrates how we use the two arms of parenting to help our kids develop core skills that not only improve family life but also support social development.

Like sibling and family conflict, social difficulties can get complicated, but the process we use to help our children does not need to be. You can use the two arms of parenting to help your child work on the five core skills, which will help your child effectively tackle any social situation. Not only will you be helping your child solve a current dilemma, you will also be helping your child to strengthen core abilities that can be used again in the next social dilemma, which is undoubtedly just around the corner.

Boundaries

You know that uncomfortable feeling you get when someone is talking to you and stands too close? What about when someone you don't know well begins to pry into your business, asking questions that feel too personal? There is an invisible protective shield around each of us that delineates our personal territory. We can't see it, but we can certainly feel it, like a sixth sense, and it has a powerful influence on all our relationships. We call these territory markers our boundaries. Boundaries exist both around individuals and between people in relationships. They serve as natural barriers that insulate and protect close relationships and that also help individuals maintain a comfortable sense of separation. We need to make sure we're promoting good boundaries with our children. Let's take a closer look at what this means.

The easiest way to define boundaries is as natural barriers between people that keep us physically, mentally, and emotionally safe. Good boundaries are essential for healthy relationships of all types, and we parents are in charge of teaching our kids how to establish, maintain, and respect them. Good boundaries also help kids respect themselves. A child who can set appropriate boundaries with others is a child who can protect himself or herself from the negative influences others might present.

Kids need to learn that each person in the family has his or her own physical boundary, a personal space that includes the person's body and the area an arm's length beyond the body. Family members also have their own physical space, which includes their room or the part of the room where they sleep, and their personal belongings. Knowing that they have their own protected personal and physical space gives kids (and adults too) a sense of security and control. It also teaches them to respect others' physical boundaries, which is an important part of maintaining good relationships.

Physical boundary violations happen all the time for kids, in both family and peer relations. They give kids lots of chances to practice understanding how boundaries work. "She pushed me." "He won't get out of my room." "She told my secret." "He took my turn." These are common complaints and indicators that a child's natural boundary alarm has been set off by others. Kids aren't the only ones who violate boundaries though. Parents can unwittingly cross the line with kids too, making kids feel uncomfortable. Even typically positive interactions, such as showing affection, or tickling, or physical play, can feel like an invasion when children get to the point where they no longer want to participate and the parent doesn't stop. Most kids will let you know if you've gone too far with physical play or closeness, but some won't because they don't want to disappoint adults. Younger kids are at risk because they don't yet have the vocabulary to defend their personal space. So it's the parents' job to monitor physical boundaries and help their kids learn to say when they've had enough or don't like how something feels. Helping kids identify and protect their physical boundaries is a part of creating physical safety.

Mental and emotional boundaries are as important to maintain as physical boundaries. These boundaries have less to do with physical space and more to do with the recognition that each person in the family is entitled to his or her own perspective and emotional security. Each person's viewpoint and ideas should be seen as equally valid and important, regardless of age or developmental differences. This means, for instance, that when your three-year-old adds an idea to the family conversation and your seven-year-old says that idea is "wrong," you stop your older child and help him or her understand everyone's right to add their input. The easiest way to say this is, "In this family, everyone's opinion counts."

The same ideas about safety and respect apply to everyone's emotional lives. Behaviors like threats, belittling, teasing, or constant correcting have a big emotional impact on the person subjected to this behavior, especially over time. Even silliness and excessive joking can feel like a violation when it impedes a child's ability to communicate and be heard. I've worked with families in which one parent tries to keep the mood light by turning almost every moment into a humorous occasion. This is great if everyone else is in that kind of mood, but if a child is talking about something serious, the parent's joking can feel dismissive to the child. Siblings can do this to each other too, especially if they are always trying to outsmart each other. Sarcasm, funny comments, and one-upping can be offensive to the child who is trying to be heard and to be taken seriously. All of these forms of emotional stress, whether they are of a critical or humorous nature, disrupt family relationships and degrade the self-esteem of the child on the receiving end. No household is completely free from some conflict and relational stress, but no one should have to endure ongoing emotional violations, either.

Too much sibling conflict can be a sign of poor boundaries. It might seem like kids who fight frequently are too disconnected and need to get closer, but that is not always the case. In fact, it is more common that kids who fight a lot are actually too close. This might seem counter-intuitive, but it's true. Much of the sibling rivalry that I see in families occurs because a child is spending too much time thinking about what the other child is doing or getting, rather than focusing on what is going on with himself or herself. It is this overfocus on the sibling that creates the emotional charge between kids as well as an overfocus on things like fairness. Fairness can be an especially tricky issue for parents because the more the kids complain about it, the harder parents often try to create fairness, which is very difficult to do. This is a common issue in families and often becomes an exercise in frustration for everyone involved.

What to do about fairness then? Well, the first order of business is to let your kids know that you understand how important fairness is to them. And fairness is a big deal for most kids because it not only reflects their developing ability to measure and compare things but also symbolizes their parents' love for them—often displayed in concrete terms through the things that they get. It's helpful for kids to know that their parents understand this. However, after you acknowledge your kids' interest in fairness, the next step in resolving fairness issues is to let them know that you're not going to play the trying-to-make-everything-totally-equal game. Kids, especially the younger ones, are concrete thinkers who measure fairness by sameness, which means it's easiest to feel things are fair if they look the same to them. The obvious problem is that it's impossible to make everything that they get look exactly the same. So, the hard part is that you have to stick with the principle of things being fair but not necessarily *equal*, even though the younger kids in the house may not totally get the concept. Over time, though, your kids will understand and come to appreciate that you have done your best to create a household where there is an overall sense of fairness and balance.

Another thing you can do to strengthen the boundary between siblings is to encourage each of them to focus less on what the other has and more on their own responsibilities and experiences. This means that you don't allow yourself to repeatedly be the audience for the "it's-not-fair" conversation. When one of your kids begins to compare and complain, you can briefly empathize that it's upsetting to feel like things are not fair, but then tell the child: "I don't want to talk about what (sibling) has. Tell me instead about what you want, and use your own ideas, not theirs." This way you're directing your child's attention to focus on his or her own experience and needs without constant reference to another.

In the same way that you want to decrease your kids' focus on fairness, you'll want to discourage them from running to tell you what the other child is doing or not doing. I find myself asking siblings, "Is that your business?" I do this to help them understand the boundary between what involves them and what doesn't. Siblings who are overfocused on monitoring their brother or sister are usually either trying to be the little parent or to get the sibling in trouble—and both are inappropriate roles for them. Instead of allowing them to focus so much of their energy on their brother or sister, encourage them to discuss their needs and feelings with you and remind them not to take on the role of family detective. Strengthening boundaries in this way will help keep the kids in your family from crossing into their sibling's territory, which will then reduce frustration, resentment, and sibling conflict.

Another boundary issue that takes an emotional toll on kids is when adult issues burden them. This can be more subtle than sibling conflict, but it's just as damaging. Childhood should be about learning and exploring, not the weight of adult problems. This means that adults should not bring kids into their fights or ask them to take sides. This also means that adults need to be careful about what kinds of topics they discuss with their kids and in front of their kids. Because kids' brains have difficulty grasping complex or global issues, information that is too far beyond their daily experience can be confusing and produce anxiety. This is, of course, more relevant for the younger child but still applicable into the teen years. Specifics about parents' personal problems, financial stressors, or intimate relationships should not be discussed with kids. Clear boundaries are critical for ensuring that children stay focused on the tasks of childhood, so parents should not use their kids for emotional support. If you are struggling with a personal issue, seek support from adult relationships and avoid putting your child in the role of personal confidant.

Keeping an eye on good family boundaries creates an atmosphere of respect and safety for everyone and provides a good foundation for healthy functioning. If you model a good balance between being close and respecting boundaries, you teach your children how to be both connected and respectful in their relationships. A good sense of boundaries will do a lot to help our kids manage their social relationships and pave the way for them to create healthy family relationships of their own someday.

Family Tone

Family tone is another important element that helps create an environment that promotes kids' healthy functioning. By family tone I mean the overall feeling that family members get from their experiences within the family. Another way to describe tone is the emotional atmosphere that exists within a family. For example, do words like stressful, chaotic, or angry describe your family's tone? Or are descriptors like loving, connected, and fun more accurate? One good test of family tone is to ask members to pick the first word that comes to their mind when you ask, "What's the atmosphere like in your family?" Another good indicator of family tone is the feeling members have when they're away from the family. Family tone reverberates in us, and we carry it with us out into the world. When we're away from the source of the tone (the family), we can often hear it more clearly. A negative tone will produce feelings of relief when a person is away from his or her family, while a positive family tone will obviously create feelings of longing or nostalgia when a person is separated from the rest of his or her family.

Of course, each family member could describe family tone somewhat differently, but most family members will agree on whether their family tone is generally positive or negative. As parents we need to have a good read on the tone we are promoting in our families because we are the ones responsible for setting and maintaining our family's emotional atmosphere. Our general attitude and outlook have a big impact on the tone our kids experience. In addition, various circumstances contribute to family tone. Challenges such as financial difficulties, marital problems, illness, or developmental issues create family stress, and stress certainly impacts a family's emotional tone.

There are several ways to improve family tone, which also improves the relationships among family members. Most of these ideas are common sense, but it's often helpful to have a short list for those times when you notice the tone in your family becoming more negative. Foremost, how we communicate within the family contributes greatly to overall family tone. Negative words, criticism, teasing (even playful teasing when it's excessive), pessimism, and competition, all create a tone of negativity and rivalry. On the other hand, communication that emphasizes a positive outlook, hope, generosity, and cooperation will create a positive tone.

In addition to communication, respect among family members also contributes to a healthy family tone. Respect includes regard for others' personal space, belongings, and bodies. A family in which all its members, from the youngest to the oldest, feel respected is a family that will maintain a positive tone. Just spending time together also contributes to a family's positive tone as well as connection. Make sure your family slows down from its busy pace enough to share face-to-face moments such as meals, fun activities, and downtime. As the old saying goes, *the family that plays together, stays together!*

As parents, we need to be careful to create and maintain a constructive tone in our families, even during hard times. For instance, when you are disciplining your child for the worst infraction, your child should still be able to feel your love and respect. Tone should also be restored after you lose your cool and yell or do something else you later regret. The way to do this is to admit to your child that you lost control, apologize, and remind your child that you do love him or her even when you're very upset with them. In doing this you will be modeling taking responsibility for one's self and making amends, which will help restore a constructive tone.

Families with kids who struggle with self-control are especially prone to an erosion of positive tone. If you have a hard-to-parent child, try to spend more time noticing the child's strengths and successes. Notice and comment on these frequently, and stay in touch with the things you like about your child. Keeping this positive tone will work for you because you will be helping your child feel more positive, which will then make your child want to try harder to show good behavior. If you've fallen into a negative tone with your child, begin to invest more positive energy into your child and your relationship, and you'll soon see the tone improve. This isn't always easy, especially if you've struggled for some time with your child and a negative tone has taken over. But do it anyway, persist, and you will see and feel the difference it makes.

Family Identity

Building a cohesive family identity is important because it provides a sense of physical and psychological protection for all family members. It's essential for kids to feel they are part of something important—and something they helped create. When kids feel they are part of a clearly defined family, they also feel safe. They understand that there is a boundary between their family and the outside world, which creates a family safety-zone where they can retreat and escape the pressures of the world. A strong family identity also gives kids a sense of power and belonging. Additionally, a healthy family identity creates a template for successfully participating in social groups outside the family. This in turn strengthens a child's identity as an individual who can move in and out of different social groups with ease.

Family identity is important in another way also. It preserves the family legacy. By this I mean that it allows family members to retain the memories, traditions, and customs—even the recipes—of those who have passed. The identities and influences of those no longer present continue on through the rituals and customs preserved as part of a family's shared identity.

It's clear that family identity is important. In fact, it's so critical for us humans to feel we're a part of a group with a shared identity that when kids don't get it from their families, they look for it elsewhere. Some kids will find it through sports or other constructive groups, but others will turn to gangs and similarly destructive groups to try to capture that essential sense of protection and belonging they need. It's important that our kids have a strong family identity to ensure they get a sense of pride and belonging from their family life at home. How do we build and support this identity? There are many things we can do, and it all starts with spending time together. Here are some suggestions for building a strong family identity:

- Develop family rituals, special things your family does together. This could be anything from Sunday pancakes to a silly song you sing together before bedtime.
- Talk to your kids about what makes your family special or unique.
- Preserve cultural traditions and connections.
- Work together. Clean up, fix things, wash the car, or volunteer somewhere. Working together creates bonds.
- Re-tell the stories of past times and of family members no longer living. Family history is part of identity.
- Do your own spin on holidays. Create a new holiday ritual that your kids will always remember.
- Have unscheduled family hang-out time. This allows for spontaneous fun moments to arise.
- Talk together about spiritual or religious beliefs.
- Get away together. Have vacations and adventures with only your family.
- Create family identity statements that emphasize something positive about your family, such as, "We're the Garners, and we take care of our planet," or "We're the Campos family, and we help others."

I still remember something my father said when I was about ten years old that relates to family identity statements. I saw someone smoking a cigarette on the street and asked my dad about smoking. He replied, "We're Kemplers. Kemplers aren't smokers." I didn't think it registered at the time, but when I became a teenager, that statement became a powerful influence. Many times throughout high school and years later I was offered cigarettes, and when that happened, I always remembered my father's statement: "Kemplers aren't smokers." Something in that family proclamation gave me a sense of pride in not being a smoker, and it helped me resist the social pressure to try on that behavior. Again, family identity can be a strong protective mechanism.

The Value of Affection

Another aspect of parent-child relationships that has a powerful impact on security and connection is affection. Massage therapists and other bodywork professionals know about the power of touch and the physical healing it can produce. Touch and affection also contribute to psychological and emotional health. In the first year of life, we are soothed and given a message of fondness and protection by the touch and sounds of our caregivers. This affection welcomes us into the world and tells us over and over again that everything will be okay. These early experiences of affection not only provide a sense of security they also forge the bonds of attachment that will last with us the rest of our lives.

Our brains are wired with many neurons, including a type called mirror neurons. Mirror neurons help us reflect upon and understand the actions and experiences of others. This experience of naturally tuning into those close to us helps us develop our connection with them and creates emotional ties. In addition, research suggests that these specialized brain cells help us develop the ability to have empathy for others. The discovery of these brain cells is important because it shows that we are literally wired to stay connected with other humans, not only for survival but also for our well-being and happiness.

Showing affection through touch and words is a powerful way to fill our needs for connection and security with others. This is especially true for children, because as they grow and develop they need reassurance that the bond they share with their parents is still strong and present. This connective lifeline gives children a strong attachment to their parents and a secure and confident outlook toward the world. It also becomes one of the main ingredients in a child's self-esteem. So, showing our children affection goes a long way toward helping provide them with a lifelong sense of well-being and security.

Show your kids that you love them and are present for them. Hug them, squeeze them, hold their hand, and tell them the feelings you have for them. Don't let your household be the kind I hear described too often by parents who say, "Growing up in my house no one ever hugged or said I love you. We just assumed our parents loved us." Guessing that your parents care about you is very different from your parents showing you directly. Children who are left guessing about their parents' feelings toward them are in a difficult position. With their limited awareness and insight, they may guess wrong. Lack of emotional communication is often perceived as a lack of love. And we don't want our kids making this mistake.

Kids' experience of affection and connection has far-reaching implications later in life also. Adults who did not receive much affection from their parents can still have positive relationships with them later, but these parent-child relationships are missing the depth of connection that affection creates. Many adults complain of a disconnectedness from their parents as a result. In addition, adults who were not taught how to connect to others in this way when they were young often have difficulty showing affection for others in their adult relationships. This can, for instance, create a disconnectedness in marital relations that can threaten the long-term stability of the marriage.

Men are more prone to overlooking the value of affection. This is because boys and men regularly receive messages from the media and social culture that affection and emotion are synonymous with weakness. This is cause for concern because it's not true. In fact, the opposite is true. Boys and men who are in touch with their feelings and can express affection are the males who actually experience the most personal freedom. They are not relegated to a narrow set of feelings and behaviors that deny them the full range of natural expression.

Males who have access to the full range of their emotions also have access to the full range of their power. This is true because emotion is the driving energy that propels behavior, and so the broader the source of emotional drive, the greater the potential for personal power. With emotion providing maximum freedom and power, it remains a mystery why so many cultures believe that boys and men who express emotion (other than aggression) and affection are in some way weak. This outdated belief is not only not true, it continues to damage the lives of boys and men today. Let's work to change this by encouraging boys and men to value all aspects of themselves, including their more vulnerable feelings.

There's something special about a parent who feels free to

be goofy, loving and vulnerable with his or her kids. Watch the faces of kids who experience a mom or dad like this and you'll be looking into the eyes of happiness. This is the most compelling evidence of all; kids need their parents to show them what it means to be emotionally complete, which, of course, includes the ability to show affection and love. If you're a parent who wasn't taught how to be open with affection toward your kids, start practicing now. And watch their faces as you do. The look of love reflecting back in their eyes will let you know that it's the right thing to do.

Chapter Summary

Here is a recap of some of the highlights and tips presented in this chapter:

- If you have a child who struggles with his or her behavior, check in with siblings. Find out how stressful family life is for them and help them share their feelings (especially negative ones).
- Maintain balance for siblings by having one-on-one or special time with them.
- Don't let the kids in your family get locked into narrow family roles e.g. "the good child," "the trouble maker" or "the invisible child."
- If there is moderate to high levels of sibling conflict in your house, take steps to help. Follow the bulleted suggestions to help your kids begin to discuss and work out conflict.
- Teach your kids the two-step plan. Have them use it for sibling and peer conflict.
- Teach your kids to value cooperation more than competition.
- Encourage your kids to come to you for help with friendship issues. Help them engage the five core skills to handle social dilemmas with maturity and skill.
- Take steps to create strong physical and emotional boundaries for all family members.
- Help your kids understand the concept of "fair but not equal."
- Work to create positive tone in your family, especially if you have a child who struggles.
- Use the list of suggestions to build a strong and unique family identity.
- Show your kids lots of affection through words and gestures. If you came from a "low affection" family, work on getting comfortable with outward displays of emotion and vulnerability.

∞
Epilogue

Helping to create better behavior in our children requires us as parents to understand the underlying influences at play. Once we do, we can go to work to create the change we want by helping our children build the necessary skills that allow them to do well. In this book, we've covered the main influences, such as temperament, developmental level, and family dynamics. We've also discussed the five core skills our children need to develop that contribute to their emotional and social and maturity. Likewise, we've addressed areas we need to develop as parents that promote effective, connected, and balanced parenting—including the two arms of parenting, united parenting, self/couple care, emotional attunement, problem solving with our kids, the Review, dealing with negative behaviors, self-esteem, and healthy family dynamics. What a list!

My sincere hope is that whether you are trying to create behavior change for your child or just fine-tuning your parenting skills you will find the topics in this book as helpful and effective as I have in both my personal and professional life. The ideas presented here are the areas that child and family therapists focus on when helping parents and kids. You should have access to them too. I have compiled them here to help you do what we do, support the growth and well-being of both kids and parents. Absorb the topics in this book. Practice the bulleted suggestions. And continue to hone your parenting skills. And most of all, remember that you are a good parent—and getting better all the time.

Visit www.betterbehaviorblog.com to access helpful parenting articles and materials. If you find this book valuable, give it a positive review on Amazon, like it on social media, and tell other parents about it. Help spread the word!

My very best to you and your family,

Noah

Additional Good Books

First Feelings: Milestones in the Emotional Development of Your Baby and Child, by Stanley Greenspan and Nancy Thorndike Greenspan

How to Talk So Kids Will Listen and Listen So Kids Will Talk, by Adele Faber and Elaine Mazlish

Raising Cain: Protecting the Emotional Life of Boys, by Dan Kindlon and Michael Thompson

Raising Happiness: 10 Simple Steps for More Joyful Kids and Happier Parents, by Christine Carter

Raising Your Spirited Child: A Guide for Parents Whose Child Is More Intense, Sensitive, Perceptive, Persistent, and Energetic, by Mary Sheedy Kurcinka

The Challenging Child: Understanding, Raising, and Enjoying the Five "Difficult" Types of Children, by Stanley I. Greenspan

The Explosive Child, by Ross Greene

The Highly Sensitive Child, by Elaine N. Aron

The Highly Sensitive Person, by Elaine N. Aron

The Out-of-Sync Child: Recognizing and Coping with Sensory Integration Dysfunction, by Carol Stock Kranowitz

The Whole-Brain Child: Twelve Revolutionary Strategies to Nurture Your Child's Developing Mind, by Daniel Siegel and Tina Payne Bryson

Transforming the Difficult Child: The Nurtured Heart Approach, by Howard N. Glasser

Additional Online Resources

ADHD information and support: www.chadd.org

Parenting: www.empoweringparents.com and www.parenting.org

Temperament information: www.preventiveoz.org

USA.gov parenting website: www.usa.gov/Topics/Parents.shtml

PBS parenting website: www.pbs.org/parents

Tufts University child and family web guide: www.cfw.tufts.edu

Early childhood information: www.zerotothree.org

CDC child development website:
www.cdc.gov/ncbddd/childdevelopment

Social and communication skills: www.socialthinking.com

Autism information and support: www.autismspeaks.org

About the Author

Noah Kempler is a licensed Marriage and Family Therapist, an author, and parent educator who specializes in helping kids and their parents develop the skills to get along better. Noah helps kids with a variety of emotional, behavioral, developmental, and social challenges and focuses on emotional communication within the family. In addition to family therapy, Noah runs social skills groups with his wife, Stacey, who is also a therapist. Noah and Stacey have three awesome kids and live in the San Francisco Bay Area.

Visit Noah's website and blog at www.noahkempler.com

Made in the USA
San Bernardino, CA
22 June 2016